Boccaccio's "Novelle" in the Theater of Lope de Vega

José Porrúa Turanzas, S.A.
EDICIONES

stuðia humanitatis

Directed by
Bruno M. Damiani
The Catholic University of America

ADVISORY BOARD

Boccaccio's "Novelle" in the Theater of Lope de Vega

Nancy L. D'Antuono

studia humanitatis

Publisher and distributor
  José Porrúa Turanzas, S.A.
  Cea Bermúdez, 10 - Madrid-3
  España

Distributor for U.S.A.
  Studia Humanitatis
  1383 Kersey Lane
  Potomac, Maryland 20854

Printed in the United States of America
Impreso en Los Estados Unidos

Cea Bermúdez, 10 - Madrid-3
Ediciones José Porrúa Turanzas, S.A.

To Anthony S. D'Antuono
and to the memory of
Linda Crisci D'Antuono

Contents

Abbreviations

AION-SR	Annali Istituto Universitario Orientale, Napoli, Sezione Romanza
Archiv	Archiv für das Studium der Neueren Sprachen und Literaturen
BAE	Biblioteca de autores españoles
BCOM	Bulletin of the Comediantes
BH	Bulletin Hispanique
BHS	Bulletin of Hispanic Studies
BRAE	Boletín de la Real Academia Española
GSLI	Giornale Storico della Letteratura Italiana
HR	Hispanic Review
I and L	Ideologies and Literature
JHI	Journal of the History of Ideas
JWI	Journal of the Warburg Institute
MLJ	Modern Language Journal
MLN	Modern Language Notes
MLR	Modern Language Review
NRPH	Nueva Revista de Filología Hispánica
PMLA	Publications of the Modern Language Association
RABM	Revista de Archivos, Bibliotecas y Museos

Preface

This book treats of eight plays by Lope Félix de Vega Carpio,[1] the plots for which are taken from Giovanni Boccaccio's *Decameron*.[2] The study turns on the hypothesis that a more accurate understanding of Lope de Vega's artistry as a

---

[1] The eight plays are, according to the date of composition: *La boda entre dos maridos (Dec.* X, 8) 1595–1601; *El halcón de Federico (Dec.* V, 9) 1601–1605; *El ejemplo de casadas y prueba de la paciencia (Dec.* X, 10) 1599–1603; *El anzuelo de Fenisa (Dec.* VIII, 10) 1604–1606; *El servir con mala estrella (Dec.* X, 1) 1604–1606; *El llegar en ocasión (Dec.* II, 2) 1605–1608; *La discreta enamorada (Dec.* III, 3) 1606; *El ruiseñor de Sevilla (Dec.* V, 4) 1603–1608. The dates for these plays have been taken from S. Griswold Morley and Courtney Bruerton, *Cronología de las comedias de Lope de Vega*, ed. rev. (Madrid: Gredos, 1968). Citations from these plays, unless otherwise indicated, are taken from the Academy edition of Lope's plays: *Obras de Lope de Vega*, ed. Marcelino Menédez y Pelayo, 15 vols. (Madrid: Real Academia Española, 1890–1913). There are, to my knowledge, no authoritative editions of these plays.

[2] See Giovanni Boccaccio, *Decameron*, ed. Vittore Branca (Firenze: Le Monnier, 1965). All citations from the *Decameron*, unless otherwise noted, are taken from this edition. In the preparation of this study I have also examined the authoritative Italian edition 1527; the expurgated Italian editions of 1573 and 1582; the Catalan translation of 1429 (first edited and published in 1910) and the Spanish translation of Medina del Campo, 1543. Full details regarding these editions will be provided in Chapter I.

playwright can be gained from the close analysis of these Italian-based plays. Lope's Boccaccian comedies, perhaps less significant than some of the plays for which he has been acclaimed, are often passed over or, at best, evaluated superficially. Credit for any skill in adapting them is only hesitantly given. This reluctance may be predicated on the belief that a borrowed plot is not worthy of serious consideration beyond the establishment of source. It is my intent to dispel this misconception.

To date, no full-length work has taken into account Lope's particular talent for bringing to the Spanish stage some of the finest of Boccaccio's tales. Partial analyses of individual plays have failed either to suggest or to illustrate an overall mode or technique of adaptation. No effort has been made to approach Lope's adaptations on the basis of the unique set of dramatic principles according to which his art was conceived and must be judged. Nor have the major themes and motifs of these plays been examined within their socio-historic context. To ignore this broader construct is to present only a partial view of Lope's creation.

To acknowledge these omissions is not to discredit previous scholarship on the subject. The contributions in the nineteenth century of Schack, Schaeffer and Wurzbach to the establishment of Italian novellistic sources are invaluable. Menéndez y Pelayo's discussion of the *novelle* and their relationship to the origin of prose fiction on the Iberian peninsula is a rich mine of information. Certainly, the most comprehensive study of the *Decameron* in Iberian letters remains that of Caroline B. Bourland. In more recent years, the works of Eugene Kohler, J. C. J. Metford and Cesare Segre have done much to sustain interest in these plays. More, however, remains to be said. The present work, while acknowledging the valuable groundwork of previous scholars, hopes to take the investigation further along.

There are undoubtedly numerous ways of approaching this study. One scholar may prefer to examine the plays on the basis of the order of the *Decameron* tales; another, by the degree of indebtedness to each source; and a third, by the chronology of Lope's plays. All of these methods, however, tend to focus attention on segments of the corpus rather than on the whole. I have chosen a method which I believe to be more encompassing in that it discusses all eight plays in the light of several aspects: the multiplicity of sources (Chapter I); the thematic reshaping necessary for the works to have greater relevance for Lope's audience (Chapters II, III and IV); and, lastly, the stylistic innovations, those deriving from the *Commedia dell'Arte* as well as those that are uniquely Lopean (Chapter V).

While I do not wish to exaggerate the significance or findings of this endeavor, I believe that the facts it reveals may help us to understand more fully Lope's working habits. A knowledge of what he added or subtracted from the source and the stimuli which provoked his reshaping will illuminate not only what he brought to the borrowed material but also what we might expect to find in the rest of his theater. In this light, the Boccaccian plays are important not only for what they reveal about the totality of Lope's art but also for what they tell us about Lope de Vega's dramaturgy during his early, formative years.

In classifying the Boccaccian plays as belonging to Lope's early period I am encouraged in my denomination by Morley and Bruerton's *Cronología*. The authors maintain that Lope's dramatic output can indeed be divided into three major periods, within loosely defined limits, on the basis of internal evidence consistent with biographical and historical data as well as with metric patterns. It is generally accepted that "early plays" refers to those written before 1600; that the middle period spans the years 1600 to 1620; and that the plays of the final period were written after 1620. The Boccaccian plays encompass the years 1595 to 1608. The absence of autograph manuscripts results in the broad dating of each play within a two to three-year span. I believe, therefore, that we may safely define this particular group of *comedias* as belonging to Lope's early period.

It is hoped that this study will be of special interest to those professionals and students who have some familiarity with Spanish literature in general and the Golden Age theater in particular, as well as to comparatists in the area of Italo-Hispanic literary relations. For the hispanist who is not familiar with the Italian material, I have included plot summaries of each source story.

I acknowledge with appreciation the assistance provided by the College of Arts and Letters of the University of Notre Dame which enabled me to consult several rare editions of the *Decameron*. I am grateful for the courtesies extended to me by the libraries of the University of Michigan; the University of Notre Dame; the Lilly Library, Indiana University; the University of California, Berkeley; and, the Huntington Library, San Marino, California, for making available to me a large number of primary sources.

To the editors of the *Bulletin of the Comediantes, Hispano-Italic Studies, Kentucky Romance Quarterly*, and *Romance Notes*, I express my thanks for permission to adapt for use here portions of my articles appearing in their respective journals.

Warmest and most heartfelt thanks go to my husband and fellow scholar, Gerald L. Gingras, for his intellectual support and unfailing good will; and to my friends Joel Leftoff and Sr. Elaine DesRosiers, O. P.; to Bruno M. Damiani, fellow hispanist and friend, for his editorial counsel; to Catherine M. Flanagan for her patient editorial revisions; and, to the staff of Porrúa Turanzas, s. a. for their kind cooperation.

Vale.

Introduction

The influence of Boccaccio's *Decameron* on Spanish letters was far-reaching and of long duration. Widely read both in the original and in translation, the *novelle* were a wellspring at which Spanish men of letters satisfied their thirst for over one hundred years. To writers and literary theorists of Spain's Golden Age, Boccaccio was the master of the storyteller's craft. Tirso de Molina, for example, finds no words more eloquent to honor Cervantes' prose than to label him "Nuestro español Boccaccio."[1] In *El curial del Parnaso*, I,..Fol. 68v, Matías de los Reyes would wish for "la Rethórica de Demósthenes, los conceptos de Petrarca y la dulçura de Boccaccio . . . ."[2] Francisco de Lugo y Dávila counsels his readers, "y si quisiereis perfeccionar con más arte estos preceptos, leed todo el segundo libro de la retórica de Aristóteles . . . y para la práctica harto os dará

---

[1] Tirso de Molina, *Cigarrales de Toledo*, Edición transcrita y revisada por Victor Said Armesto (Madrid: Imprenta "Renacimiento", 1913), p. 10.

[2] Matías de los Reyes, *El Curial del Parnaso* (Madrid: Librería de los Bibliófilos Españoles, 1909). This text reproduces the edition of 1624 (Madrid: Viuda de Cosme Delgado, 1624).

el Boccaccio en su *Fiameta* y el *Decameron* de sus novelas."[3] Cristóbal de Villalón lauds "aquella elegante industria de novelar del iminente orador Juan Bocacio."[4]

Individual tales were appropriated bodily for collections of stories and interpolated into novels of chivalry. The *novelle* provided the substance for sixteenth-century romances and suggested the plots for numerous Golden Age plays.[5] In most instances the popularity of a tale rested primarily on the content of the story rather than on the skill of the storyteller. The tales most often imitated were those of an exemplary nature, with a long history dating back to the oriental or classical tradition. The *Decameron*'s portrayal of the model wife (Griselda, X, 10), of sacrifices made for the sake of friendship (Tito and Gisippo, X, 8) or of the devoted vassal (Ruggieri, X, 1)[6] held particular appeal for an age which sought perfection in human and political dimensions.

Beyond the popularity of the individual tales, the *Decameron*'s structural exemplarity invited imitation. Boccaccio's *cornice* or frame design, modified by his successors though never surpassed, gave rise in Spain to a series of collections of short stories set in similar surroundings. Among the imitators were some of Spain's major literary figures: Tirso de Molina,

---

[3] Francisco de Lugo y Dávila, *Teatro Popular*, ed. Emilio Cotarelo y Mori (Madrid: Viuda de Rico, 1906) I, 26.

[4] Cristóbal de Villalón, *El Scholástico* (Madrid: Sociedad de Bibliófilos Madrileños, 1911), I, 31.

[5] For the trajectory of individual *Decameron* tales in Iberian letters see Caroline B. Bourland, "Boccaccio and the *Decameron* in Castilian and Catalan Literature," *RH*, 12 (1905), 1–232. Bourland's study includes a detailed description of the extant manuscripts as well as an introductory study on the influence of Boccaccio's work other than the *Decameron* in the evolution of Spanish letters. See also Florence Nightingale Jones, *Boccaccio and his Imitators* (Chicago: University of Chicago Press, 1910). This study includes imitators in English, French, German and Italian. For the influence of Boccaccio on the beginnings of Spanish prose fiction see Marcelino Menédez y Pelayo, *Orígenes de la novela*, 2nd ed. (Madrid: C. S. I. C., 1962), III, 1–29.

[6] For the specific sources of these stories see Vittore Branca, ed., *Decameron*, p. 1101, n. 1 (Ruggieri); p. 1164, n. 1 (Tito and Gisippo) and, pp. 1217–18, n. 5 (Griselda).

2

Pérez de Montalbán, Salas Barbadillo, Castillo Solórzano and María de Zayas.[7]

If the content and structure of the *Decameron* found favor with prose writers, it exerted no less an influence on the *comedia*. The tales, first introduced into the *loas*, were soon incorporated into the bodies of plays. The extent to which Boccaccio's *novelle* were known and imitated in Spain may be gleaned from the *loa* to Ricardo del Turia's *La burladora burlada*:

> La diversidad de asuntos
> Que en las loas han tomado
> Para pediros silencio
> Nuestros Terencios y Plautos
> Ya contando alguna hazaña
> De César o de Alejandro
> Ya refiriendo novelas
> Del Ferrarés[8] o del Bocacio.[9]

The attraction to these stories on the part of playwrights was guided primarily by their suitability for the stage as concerns form rather than content. Moreover, the flexible demarcation between prose fiction and drama in the sixteenth and seventeenth centuries encouraged genre transposition.[10] In her study of the *novela corta* as *comedia*, Florence Yudin calls attention to the constitutive elements of the short story which facilitated its adaptation to the stage:

The narrative develops from a single *enredo*. Although there is no

---

[7] See M. Menéndez y Pelayo, *Orígenes de la novela*, III, 27–28, for an enumeration of the Spanish collections of stories modelled after the *Decameron*.

[8] The term "Ferrarés" is a reference to the sixteenth-century Italian *novelliere* Giambattista Giraldi Cinthio (1504–1573), a native of Ferrara.

[9] Ricardo del Turia, *La burladora burlada*, in *Dramáticos contemporáneos de Lope de Vega* (Madrid: Atlas, 1951, *BAE*, XLIII), p. 213.

[10] Marcos A. Morínigo, "El teatro como sustituto de la novela en el Siglo de Oro," *RUBA*, 5ª Epoca, 2 (1957), 61. Morínigo underscores the facility with which the stories were adapted: "Por su parte los dramaturgos del tiempo transformaban en comedias cuantas novelas podían . . . y es curioso señalar que la lectura de tales no lleva más tiempo que el que se necesitaría para ver representada si en vez de la forma narrativa asumiera la dramática."

explicit textual division, the plot unfolds in a three part structure: the exposition and key motives given in the first section, the complication of the *intriga*, obstacles and misfortunes for the separated lovers to overcome builds Part II and the inevitable turn of events, made possible by a disguise and the merits of the protagonist, occupies the final sequence.[11]

In short, both genres are characterized by a tripartite structure, lively action, swift forward movement, and by dependence for success on an external pattern of scheme and counterscheme. They differ only in the manner of presentation.

The degree of affinity between *novela* and *comedia* was so deeply rooted in the minds of the authors and the public that Golden Age prose writers often used the terms interchangeably even when working directly with one or the other.[12] For example, Fernández de Avellaneda, pseudo-author of the apocryphal *Quijote*, alleges that "casi es comedia la historia de D. Quijote de la Mancha." In describing the structure of his own work, Avellaneda refers to it as "la presente comedia." In one of his diatribes against Cervantes, he challenges: "Conténtese Miguel de Cervantes con su Galatea y comedias en prosa, que eso son las más de sus novelas."[13] Lugo y Dávila, mentioned earlier regarding precepts for the *novela*, entitles his collection of tales *Teatro Popular*.[14] Playwrights were no less confused as to the distinction between *novela* and *comedia*. Witness the concluding verses of Tirso de Molina's *Amar por señas*:

> Invencionero ingenioso
> Es amor: esta novela

---

[11] Florence Yudin, "The 'novela corta' as *comedia*: Lope's *Las fortunas de Diana*," *BHS*, 45 (1968): 181–183.

[12] Marcos M. Morínigo, "El teatro como sustituto," p. 60, points out: ". . . la idea de que comedias y novelas son un mismo tipo de creación en moldes distintos estaba profundamente enraizada en el público y en los autores. Tanto que, aun teniéndolos los ejemplos ante los ojos, continuaban confundiéndolos."

[13] Alonso Fernández de Avellaneda, *Segundo tomo del ingenioso Don Quijote de la Mancha*, ed. Martín de Riquer (Tarragona: Felipe Roberto, 1614; rpt. Madrid: Espasa Calpe, 1972), pp. 7–12.

[14] See note 3, above.

Senado ilustre, lo diga
Y en ella el *Amar por señas*.[15]

Lope's own brief incursion into prose fiction was predicated on the assumption that facility with one genre could be easily transposed to the other: "Yo que nunca pensé que el novelar entrara en mis pensamientos, me veo embaraçado entre su gusto . . . y mi obediencia, pero, por no faltar a la obligación, y porque no parezca negligencia aviendo hallado tantas invenciones para mis comedias . . . serviré a vuestra merced con ésta . . . "[16] A similar defense of genre substitution may be found in *El desdichado por la honra*: "Demás yo he pensado que tienen las novelas los mismos preceptos que las comedias, cuyo fin es haber dado su autor contento al pueblo, aunque se ahorque el arte."[17] If, then, to the similarities in structure, execution and intent which facilitated adaptation, we add Boccaccio's long-standing reputation as a humanist scholar[18] and as a model for prose writers, it is not surprising that Lope de Vega should find the *Decameron* tales a most attractive foreign source during his early years as a dramatist. Nor is it less surprising that Lope's recourse to the *novelle* should have stimulated continued scholarly interest for more than one hundred years.

The verification of source and brief commentary on the derivative plays by nineteenth-century scholars Adolf von Schack,[19] Adolf Schaeffer[20] and Alfred W. von Wurzbach[21]

[15] Tirso de Molina *Amar por señas*, *Obras de Tirso de Molina* (Madrid: Impr. de la Publicidad, 1885, *BAE*, V), p. 481.

[16] Lope de Vega, "Las fortunas de Diana," *Obras de Lope de Vega* (Madrid: Atlas, 1950, *BAE*, XXXVIII), p. 1.

[17] Lope de Vega, "El desdichado por la honra," *Obras de Lope de Vega* (Madrid: Atlas, 1950, *BAE*, XXXVIII), p. 14.

[18] On Boccaccio's long-standing reputation as a humanist scholar see Catherine B. Bourland, "Boccaccio and the *Decameron*," pp. 10–22.

[19] Adolf Friedrich von Schack, *Geschichte der dramatischen Literatur und Kunst in Spanien* (Frankfurt am Main: Joseph Baer, 1854).

[20] Adolf Schaeffer, *Geschichte des spanischen Nationaldramas* (Leipzig: Blockhaus, 1898).

[21] Alfred Wolfgang von Wurzbach, *Lope de Vega und seine Komödien* (Leipzig: Seele, 1899).

constituted the first step in the process. It was not, however, within the scope of these studies to analyze the final product as to its originality. Rather, these works sought to point out the wide range of sources and plots which characterized Lope's production. Included among them were the eight Boccaccian plays. The untimely passing of Marcelino Menéndez y Pelayo deprived scholars of the customary erudite preliminary study to the *comedias novelescas* in the Royal Spanish Academy's edition of Lope's works. An indication of what he might have offered is found in Chapter IX of his *Orígenes de la novela* in which he discusses, in superb detail, the fifteenth-century translations of the *Decameron* and the Boccaccian sources for Lope's *El ejemplo de casadas* and *El halcón de Fededrico*.[22] The study by Caroline Bourland,[23] contemporary with that of Menéndez y Pelayo, examines the trajectory in Catalan and Castilian literature of the *Decameron* tales and treats each of the eight Lope plays clearly traceable to Boccaccio. The comprehensive rather than selective nature of the endeavor allowed for only a brief discussion of Lope's refurbishing. Commentary is limited, for the most part, to the notation of major points of amplification, deletion and recasting in plot or characterization. A subsequent study by Eugene Kohler in 1937 corroborates Bourland's observations but adds no new insights to the body of knowledge.[24] Interest in the subject, however, has continued to provoke scholarly consideration. Lope's technique of adaptation came under scrutiny by J. C. J. Metford in an article published in 1952.[25] Metford focuses on one or two significant episodes in each comedy which attest to Lope's power of invention and dramatic artistry. The nature of the

[22] Menéndez y Pelayo, *Orígenes de la novela*, III, 11–29, traces the introduction of Boccaccio's Griselda story (*Decameron* X, 10) into the mainstream of Spanish letters. In the case of *El halcón de Federico (Decameron* V, 9), Menéndez y Pelayo reproduces the entire medieval version of the Italian tale.

[23] See note 5 above.

[24] Eugene Kohler, "L'Art dramatique de Lope de Vega," *Revue des Cours et Conferences*, 13 (1937): 468–480.

[25] J. C. J. Metford, "Lope de Vega and Boccaccio's *Decameron*," BHS, 29 (1952): 75–86.

work, however, did not allow for an extensive evaluation encompassing the totality of the adaption. Nor was it within the purview of Metford's investigation to interpret thematic shifts in terms of Lope's epoch or to explore the complexities of adapting *novella* to drama. These two issues have been taken up in a recent contribution by Cesare Segre. Here, again, by the author's own admission, the analyses "hanno toccato aspetti tecnici e convenzioni più che il dominio su essi esercebato dall'artista (esso chiederebbe un'applicazione molto più protratta)."[26] The study which follows proposes to take up this charge.

Before moving to the main body of the text, however, it would be well to consider one final matter. A thorough assessment of Lope's Boccaccian plays is untenable without a careful examination not only of what he owes to his Italian source but also of what is characteristic to him. The obvious points of contact as well as the minor details or the barest hints of things which might have suggested to Lope many elements of expansion form the bases for contrast and comparison. They tell us much about Boccaccio's narrative talent and, more importantly, a great deal about Lope's creativity in surmounting the complexities of genre transposition.

Scholarship to date has shown a marked tendency to explain away Lope's innovations in recasting the *novelle* by viewing all shifts in theme, plot or characterization as part of a pattern of conformity to the dramatic conventions of the day. The point is not without basis in fact. However, excessive reliance on so facile an explanation tends to obsure or to thrust into the background several areas of discussion essential to Lopean scholarship: the merits of each play as a unique creation within the thematic framework inherited from the *Decameron*; the implications of the changes and their reconstruction to point up Lope's new conception of the theme and its dramatic restatement; the playwright's imaginative craftsmanship in

---

[26] Cesare Segre, "Da Boccaccio a Lope de Vega: derivazioni e trasformazioni," *Boccaccio: Secoli di vita* (Ravenna: Longo, 1975): 225–237.

adjusting the demands of literature to those of the stage; and, the presence in these plays of elements which are singularly Lopean. To address these issues requires, as Chapters II, III, and IV will show, a consideration of the Boccaccian material as more than just a written source. It demands an understanding of the spirit and vital forces which informed Boccaccio's era and which are an indelible part of his work. Unlike the *novella*, however, the *comedia* is intended for performance. While scholars are quick to call attention to the routine ploys, theatrical devices and stock characterizations which mark the genre, rarely do they acknowledge the source of a major portion of the techniques: the *Commedia dell'Arte*. To ignore the role of the Italian traveling players in the shaping of Lope's theater in general, and the Boccaccian plays in particular, as Chapter V suggests, is to ignore one of the *comedia*'s constituent elements. As for Lope's talent in bringing this life-giving energy to the Spanish stage, I shall merely observe for the moment, that it is not so much a question of the playwright's ability to harness the merry spirit of the *Decameron* and the *Commedia dell'Arte* within the limits of Spanish conventions, but rather, of his capacity for manipulating the corpus of preordained modes to suit his own needs while apparently conceding to those requisites, a talent which assured him more than four decades of success.

No study of Lope's theater, even of so small a portion as the Boccaccian plays, can remain aloof from the socio-historic context in which the plays were engendered. Despite ·the revival of interest in Boccaccio in the latter half of the sixteenth century, the *Decameron* tales are, nonetheless, tied to a four-teenth-century world view. The themes which dominate the *Decameron*—*Fortuna, Amore, Ingegno*—though equally attractive to Lope's era, cannot escape a new configuration, one deriving from a Counter-Reformation view of man's position in relation to his fellow man, his monarch, and his God. In this light, Lope's adaptations are more than a routine reshaping of eight delightful tales.

The plays are exemplified by a unique blend of stylistic innovations: the careful apportionment of major and minor characters, of powerful drama offset by moments of diminished tension or comic relief, of multilevel linguistic representation, and of animated dialogue balanced by fine lyrical interludes. All of these qualities are given added vitality by the use of numerous external contrivances, even to the humorous intervention of the author in his own plays. These elements of Lope's *privatum jus*, the personal, magical substance which he brought to the raw material of his predecessors, were to inspire dramatists for many years to come. Cervantes' words are most appropriate: "entró luego el monstruo de la naturaleza, el gran Lope de Vega y alçóse la monarquía cómica."[27]

[27] Miguel de Cervantes Saavedra, *Comedias y entremeses*, eds. Rodolfo Schevill y Adolfo Bonilla (Madrid: Imprenta de Bernardo Rodríguez, 1915), p. 7.

I. Textual Sources

Two extant manuscript translations attest to Spanish interest in the *Decameron*. The earliest, dated 1429, is a Catalan version by an anonymous author of San Cugat des Valles.[1] The manuscript is a literal translation of the *Decameron* except for the last *novella,* that of the patient Griselda. The latter is based, oddly enough, not on the Italian original, but on Bernat Metge's Catalan version executed from Petrarch's *De obedientia ac fide uxoria,*[2] a Latin transcription of Boccaccio's tale. Metge's version, *Historia de las bellas virtuts,* also known as the *Historia*

[1] Johan Boccaci, *Decameron*, traducció catalana, publicada segons l'unic manuscrit conegut (1429) per J. Massó Torrents (New York: Hispanic Society of America, 1910). This is the first printed edition of the Catalan translation.

[2] Francesco Petrarca, *Historia Griseldis* (Cologne: Ulrich Zel, ca. 1469). This is considered to be the earliest printed edition of Petrarch's Latin translation. It is the property of the Lilly Library, Indiana University, Bloomington, Indiana.

de Valter e de la pacient Griselda,[3] was in circulation as early as 1403.[4] The second manuscript, a fragmentary work containing fifty *novelle*, is a Castilian version in the Escorial library[5] and is presumed to date from the middle of the fifteenth century.[6] The manuscript does not follow the order of the stories in the *Decameron*. Instead, the division into days is eliminated and almost all that is not narrative has been deleted. The capricious ordering appears to have been dictated by personal taste, or, as Menéndez Pelayo suggests, by an incomplete source, i.e., individual stories circulating in *cuadernos sueltos*.[7] The same admixture characterizes the first Spanish edition which appeared in Seville in 1496 and which was reprinted four times

---

[3] *Historia de valter e de la pacient Griselda* escrita en llatí per Francesch Petrarcha: e arromançada per Bernat Metge. Estampada en Barcelona per n'Evarist Villastres en l'any M.DCCC.lxxxjjj. See also Martín de Riquer, "Il Boccaccio nella letteratura catalana medievale," in *Il Boccaccio nelle culture e letterature nazionali*, ed. Francesco Mazzoni (Firenze: Olschki, 1978), pp. 107–126).

[4] Regarding the Catalan translation, Menéndez y Pelayo points out: "No se conoce exactamente la fecha de esta versión, que en uno de los manuscritos que la contienen lleva el título de *Historia de las bellas virtuts*, pero de seguro es anterior a 1403, en que el mismo autor compuso su célebre *Sueño*, donde atestigua la gran popularidad que la novela . . . había adquirido ya, hasta el punto de entretener las veladas del invierno, mientras hilaban las mujeres en torno del fuego . . . ." (p. 7).

[5] The only printed edition of the Escorial manuscript is that of F. DeHaan, "El *Decameron* en Castellano, Manuscrito del Escorial," *Studies in honor of A. Marshall Elliott* (Baltimore: The Johns Hopkins University Press, n.d.), II, 1-235.

[6] Menéndez y Pelayo, (*Orígenes de la novela*, III, 15), calls attention to the record of two other fifteenth-century manuscripts of the *Decameron* whose fate is unknown: "En el inventario de los libros de la Reina Católica, que estaban en el Alcázar de Segovia . . . en 1503, figura con el número 150 'otro libro en romance de mano, que son las novelas de Juan Bocacio'; . . . Y en el inventario . . . (1440), de la biblioteca del Conde de Benavente . . . publicado por Fr. Liciniano Saez, se mencionan 'unos cuadernos de las cien novelas en papel cebtí menor,'."

[7] See Menéndez y Pelayo, *Orígenes de la novela*, III, 16. Boccaccio's Introduction to Day IV (*Decameron*, p. 450), suggests that the stories circulated individually prior to their collection into one volume. The relevant portion reads: "Sono adunque, discrete donne, stati alcuni che, queste novellette leggendo, hanno detto che voi mi piacete troppo."

before the Council of Trent forbade further publication in 1559.[8]

The first of Boccaccio's stories to enter the mainstream of Spanish letters, as I noted earlier, was that of Griselda (X, 10). In addition to its rendering in Catalan by Bernat Metge, the story was retold in an anonymous fifteenth-century Spanish work, *Castigos y dotrinas que un sabio dava a sus hijas*. In this version, however, there is no direct reference either to specific characters or to the author except to note that "Léese en un libro de las cosas viejas que en parte de Italia en una tierra que se llama de los Salucios . . . "[9]

A second *Decameron* tale, the tragic love story of Ghismonda and Guiscardo (V, 1),[10] was equally well-known in the fifteenth century, as indicated by allusions to it in several texts. The main points of the tale are briefly: Tancredi, Prince of Salerno and father of Ghismonda, orders her lover killed. He sends the lady Guiscardo's heart in a golden goblet. Ghismonda, adding poison to the goblet, drinks its content and dies, but not before she extracts a promise from her father that she and her lover will be buried together. A late fifteenth-century version of the chivalric romance *El conde Claros* contains an appended story in which the heart of a lover is pre-

[8] See Antonio Palau y Dulcet, *Manual del librero hispano-americano*, 2nd ed. (Barcelona: Palau, 1948), II, 291. The bibliography records the four subsequent editions of the Spanish translation as being those of Toledo, 1524; Valladolid, 1539; Medina del Campo, 1543; and Valladolid, 1550. For a study of the contents of the Spanish edition of Toledo, 1524, see José Blanco Jiménez, "L'eufemismo in una traduzione spagnola cinquecentesca del *Decameron*," in *Il Boccaccio nelle culture e letterature nazionali*, ed. Francesco Mazzoni (Firenze: Olschki, 1978), pp. 127–147. I have examined the copy held by the Huntington Library, San Marino, California and presumed to be that of Medina del Campo, 1643 (the first six folios are missing). After close examination of the text and *errata* therein in accordance with the detailed notations of Caroline B. Bourland (pp. 64-67), I am of the opinion that the copy at the Huntington Library is, in fact, that of Valladolid, 1550.

[9] "Castigos y dotrinas que un sabio dava a sus hijas," in *Dos obras didácticas y dos leyendas* (Madrid: Sociedad de Bibliófilos Españoles, 1878), XII, 255–265.

[10] Boccaccio, *Decameron*, p. 461. The caption reads: "Tancredi, prenze di Salerno, uccide l'amante della figliuola e mandale il cuore in una coppa d'oro; la quale, messa sopr'esso acqua avvelenata, quella si bee, e così muore."

sented between two golden plates to the beloved.[11] The tale appears to echo not only the story of Ghismonda but also the equally grisly episode of Guiglielmo Rossiglione (IV,9).[12] In this story, the lady's husband has the lover's heart prepared for dinner. When the source of the viand is announced, the lady commits suicide by hurling herself from the window. *Curial y Guelfa*, a Catalan tale of the fifteenth century, contains a specific reference to the Ghismonda story. Laquesis, admonished by her mother for being in love with a knight beneath her station, reminds her: "recordats vos, senyora, de les paraules que dix Ghismonda, a Tancredi son pare, sobre lo fet de Guiscart e de la descripció comendat la dona de seny e de virtut."[13] The story was so popular to the point of being suggested as the illustration for a pack of playing cards.[14]

Multiple reminiscences of the *Decameron* inform Joan Martorell's *Tirant lo Blanc*,[15] the Catalan prototype of the chivalric novel. In Chapter CCLXV, the hero, Tirant, recounts the adventures of the shipwrecked merchant, a tale which parallels that of Landolfo Rufolo (II,4).[16] The opening lines of the

---

[11] See "Romance del Conde Claros-II (de Antonio de Pansac)," in *Romancero General*, ed. D. Agustín Durán (Madrid: Atlas, 1945, *BAE*, X), pp. 222–23.

[12] Boccaccio, *Decameron*, p. 548. The caption reads: "Messer Guiglielmo Rossiglione da a mangiare alla moglie sua il cuore di messer Guiglielmo Guardastagno ucciso da lui e amato da lei; il che ella sapiendo, poi si gitta da una alta finestra in terra e muore e col suo amante e sepellita."

[13] *Curial e Guelfa*. Text del XV[en] Segle reproduhit novamente del Codex de la Biblioteca Nacional de Madrid per R. Miguel y Planas (Barcelona: R. Miguel y Planas e Anfós Par, 1932), p. 235, vv. 7959–7980; vv. 8042–8049.

[14] See C. B. Bourland, "Boccaccio and the *Decameron*," p. 25, n.1. Bourland refers to a fifteenth-century manuscript pointed out to her by Ramón Menéndez Pidal, entitled "Envinción tomada sobre el juego de las naypes por Fernando de la Torre." In the manuscript, the author, suggesting the design of one of a pack of playing cards says: "Ha de ser la figura del caballero la Ystoria de Guysmonda." The manuscript is from the Biblioteca de Palacio, Madrid, Ms. 2-F-5, fol. 71, a–6.

[15] Joanot Martorell e Martí Joan de Galba, *Tirant lo Blanc*, ed. Martí de Riquer, 2[a] ed. (Barcelona: Seix Barral, 1970). This edition reproduces in its entirety the first edition of Valencia, 1490. The orthography is modernized, as is capitalization and punctuation.

[16] Boccaccio, *Decameron*, p. 160. The introductory résumé reads: "Landolfo Rufolo, impoverito, divien corsale e da genovesi *(continued on page 14)*

"Replica que fa Plaerdemavida a Tirant," (Chapter CCCLV) are a candid reproduction of Boccaccio's proem to the *Decameron*. The Catalan adaptation reads: "Humana cosa és haver compassió dels afligits, e majorment d'aquells qui en algun temps han tenguda prosperitat, e dolre's d'aquells miserables que en llur temps han trobat alguns qui els han sabut donar remei en ses passions e congoixes, entre les quals, si jamés ne fon neguna, jo só estada una d'aquelles."[17] The shipwreck and separation of Plaerdemavida and Tirant, their subsequent adventures among the Saracens and eventual reunion (Chapter CCCLXXIII) are analogous to those of Boccaccio's Gostanza and Martuccio (V,2).[18]

The sporadic allusions and reiterations which characterize Spanish interest in the *Decameron* in the fifteenth century gave way, over the course of the next hundred years, to conscious, direct imitation.[19] Sixteenth-century incursions into Boccaccio's world coincide with a revival of interest in the *Decameron* throughout Europe. The revival was spurred by a

---

(continued from page 13) preso, rompe in mare, e sopra una cassetta di gioie carissime piena scampa; e in Gurfo [Corfù] ricevuto da una femina, ricco si torna a casa sua." For a study of the parallels between Boccaccio's text and its counterpart in *Tirant lo Blanc* see Arturo Farinelli, "Note sul Boccaccio in Ispagna nell'Età Media," *Archiv*, 117 (1906): 114–141. The notation in brackets is mine.

[17] Boccaccio, *Decameron*, p. 3. Boccaccio's Proem begins: "Umana cosa è l'aver compassione agli afflitti; e come che a ciascuna persona stea bene, a colora è massimamente richesto li quali già hanno di conforto avuto mestiere, e hannol trovato in alcuni: fra' quali, se alcuno mai n'ebbe bisogno, o gli fu caro, o già ne ricevette piacere, io son uno di quegli."

[18] Boccaccio, *Decameron*, p. 597. The caption to this tale reads: Gostanza ama Martuccio Gomito, la quale, udendo che morto era, per disperata sola si mette in una barca, la quale dal vento fu trasportata a Susa: ritruoval vivo in Tunisi, palesaglisi; ed egli grande essendo col re per consigli dati, sposatala, ricco con lei in Lipari se ne torna."

Plaerdemavida, (*Tirant lo Blanc*, Chap. 350), like Gostanza, takes refuge in a fisherman's boat, moves her captives to pity and manages to be reunited with her male companion. Tirant (Chap. 373) like Martuccio, is the prisoner of a Saracen king, obtains his freedom, riches and king's favor and succeeds in defeating a powerful rival. At the end of her adventure, Plaerdemavida recounts her fortunes to Tirant just as Gostanza relates her story to Martuccio.

[19] For a detailed discussion of fifteen additional *Decameron* tales and their adaptation in the sixteenth and seventeenth centuries by writers other than Lope, see Caroline B. Bourland, "Boccaccio and the Decameron," pp. 69–189.

new image of the work which developed as Italian grammarians of the *Accademia della Crusca* fought to put the vernacular on an equal footing with Latin as a serious literary medium. It is the latter effort which eventually established the *Decameron* as a *testo di lingua*[20] and made possible the first expurgated edition, that of the *Deputati*, in 1573.[21] A second expurgated edition, with further emendations, was published in 1582.[22] All editions which conformed to that of 1573 were approved for circulation in Spain by the *Indice de Quiroga* (1583).[23] As far

[20] On the establishment of the *Decameron* as a *testo di lingua* see Ugo Foscolo, "Boccaccio," *Critical Perspectives on the Decameron*, ed. Robert S. Dombroski (New York: Barnes and Noble, 1976). See also Bartolomeo Gamba da Bassano, *Serie dei testi di lingua* (Venezia: Co' Tipi del Gondoliere, 1839), pp. 58–59.

[21] *Il Decameron di Messer Giovanni Boccacci cittadino fiorentino*, Ricorretto in Roma, et Emendato secondo l'ordine del Sacro Conc. di Trento, et riscontrato in Firenze con Testi Antichi e alla sua vera lezione ridotto da'Deputati di loro Alt. Ser. Nuovamente Stampato . . . In Fiorenza, Nella Stamperia de i Giunti MDLXXIII. The annotated emendations were published separately the following year: *Annotationi et discorsi sopra alcuni luoghi del Decameron di M. Giovanni Boccacci*; fatte dalli molto magnifici sig. deputati da loro altezze serenissime, sopra la correttione de esso Boccaccio, stampato l'anno MDLXXIIIJ. Fiorenza, Stamperia de i Giunti, 1574. Gamba da Bassano, *Serie di testi di lingua*, pp. 58–59, notes that, "Non ostante le mutilazioni a questa edizione, fatto secondo l'ordine del Sacro Concilio di Trento, essa è riputatissima . . . Nel testo le badesse e le monache, innamorate de' loro ortolani furono mutate in matrone e damigelle; i frati, impostori di miracoli in negromanti; i preti adulteri delle comare, in soldati; e sono non poche altre transformazioni . . . ."

[22] Menéndez y Pelayo, *Orígenes de la novela*, III, 24, asserts: "La Inquisición Española . . . autorizó el uso de esta edición en el índice de Quiroga (1583), donde sólo se prohiben las *Cien Novelas* . . . 'Boccacii Decades sive Decameron aut novellae centum, nisi fuerunt expurgatis et impressis ab ano 1572,' fórmula que se repite en todos los índices posteriores. A la traducción española . . . nadie pensó expurgarla, ni hacía mucha falta, porque el *Decameron* italiano corría con tal profusión y era tan fácilmente entendido." See Antonio Palau y Dulcet, *Manual del librero*, II, 291, for confirmation of the lack of expurgated Spanish editions. The bibliographer notes: "La Inquisición . . . suprimió todas las tiradas en lengua castellana, pero autorizó la lectura de las italianas conformes a la de 1573; si bien es cierto que durante tres siglos no se reimprimió el *Decameron* en castellano, no se echaba de menos puesto que la lengua italiana ha sido siempre familiar a los españoles."

[23] *Il Decameron di messer Giovanni Boccacci, cittadino fiorentino*, di nuovo ristampato e riscontrato in Firenze con testi antichi e alla sua vera lezione ridotto dal Cavalier Lionardo Salviati, Deputato del Sere- (continued on page 16)

as I am able to determine, neither of the expurgated texts was ever translated into Spanish, although the Italian versions, easily understood by Spanish readers, enjoyed widespread distribution. Why Lope chose to recast only eight of the *Decameron* tales remains a mystery. It may be explained by the fact that Lope's career as a dramatist began at a time when the popularity of the tales, though not their artistry, was being supplanted by a taste for the more violent or sensational stories which emerged from Italy during the latter part of the sixteenth century, especially those of Matteo Bandello[24] and Giambat-

---

(continued from page 15) nissimo Gran Duca di Toscana. In Venezia, del mese di Agosto per li Giunti di Firenze MDLXXXII. The latter is more properly labeled an expurgated edition since, in addition to the suppression of references to clerics, guilty or innocent of wrongdoing, all passages deemed corruptive by the editors are deleted and marginal admonitions are inserted where necessary to underscore the Counter-Reformation interpretation. For a discussion of Salviati's revisions see Herbert G. Wright, "The Characteristics of Salviati's Edition of the *Decameron*," in *The First English Translation of the Decameron, Essays and Studies on English Language and Literature*, No. XIII (Cambridge, Mass.: Harvard Univ. Press, 1953).

[24] The Dominican friar, Matteo Bandello (1485–1561) accumulated, over a period of almost forty years as secretary in specific Italian courts, two hundred and fourteen tales. They were published in four parts: the first three in 1554 (Lucca: Busdrago) and the fourth part, posthumously, in 1574 (Lyons). By 1559 they had begun to be translated into French and shortly thereafter into English (1567). A Spanish translation of fourteen tales based on the French version, appeared in 1589. For general studies on Lope's indebtedness to Bandello see Eugene Kohler, "Lope et Bandello," in *Hommage à Ernest Martinenche* (Paris: Editions D'Artrey, 1939), pp. 116–142; Antonio Gasparetti, *Las novelas de Mateo Maria Bandello como fuentes del teatro de Lope de Vega Carpio* (Salamanca: Univ. de Salamanca, 1939) and Raymond L. Scungio, "A Study of Lope de Vega's use of Italian *Novelle* as Source Material for his Plays, Together with a Critical Edition of the Autograph Manuscript of *La discordia en los casados*" (Unpublished doctoral dissertation, Brown University, 1966). For Lope's recourse to the Spanish translation of 1589 see Charles Leighton, "La Fuente de *La quinta de Florencia*," *NRFH*, 10 (1956), 3, n. 9. For studies of individual Bandello-based plays see: Alfred Wolfgang von Wurzbach, *Ausgewählte Komödien von Lope de Vega: Castelvines y Monteses* (Vienna: H. Scholl, 1917); William L. Fichter, ed. Lope de Vega's *El castigo del discreto* (New York: Instituto de las Españas, 1925); Maria Goyri de Menéndez Pidal, *La difunta pleitada*, in *De Lope de Vega y del Romancero* (Zaragoza: Librería General, 1953); N. L. D'Antuono, "Genoese History and Lope's *El genovés liberal*: Sources and Implications," *AION-SR*, 18 (1976): 9–13; N. L. D'Antuono, "La configuración ambivalente de *El Mayordomo de la Duquesa de Amalfi* de Lope de Vega," *Actas*

16

tista Giraldi Cinthio.[25] Interest in Boccaccio's tales may have been further subverted by the appearance, in Spanish translations, of collections of stories by other Italian *novellieri* such as Doni,[26] Guicciardini (Luigi)[27] and Straparola,[28] as well as

---

del Coloquio sobre el teatro del Siglo XVII. La influencia italiana (Roma: Instituto Español de Cultura, 1981), pp. 325–345; and Marina Scordilis Brownlee, "Belleforest's *Histoire Tragique* II, 19 as Model for Lope's *El mayordomo de la Duquesa de Amalfi*: A note on the Poetics of Adaptation," *Crítica hispánica*, 3 (1981): 17–20.

[25] The *Hecatommithi* of Giambattista Giraldi Cinthio (Monte Regale: L. Torrentino, 1565), reprinted six times (Venezia, 1576; 1574; 1580; 1584; 1593 and 1608) enjoyed immediate success in Spain. According to Menéndez y Pelayo, *Orígenes de la novela*, III, 26–38, "Los *Hecatommithi* de Giraldi Cinthio . . . tenían para nuestra censura, más rígida que la de Italia, y aún para el gusto general de nuestra gente, la ventaja de no ser licenciosos, sino patéticos y dramáticos, con un género de interés que compensaba en parte su inverosimilitud y falta de gracia en la narrativa. . . ." A portion of the *Hecatommithi* was translated into Spanish in 1590. For a brief description of its content and the reproduction of the translator's prologue see Menéndez y Pelayo, *Orígenes de la novela*, II, 38–39, n. 1. Lope's indebtedness to Giraldi Cinthio has been studied by Antonio Gasparetti, "Giovan Battista Giraldi Cinthio e Lope de Vega," *BH*, 32 (1930): 372–403; E. H. Templin, "The Source of Lope de Vega's *El hijo venturoso* and (Indirectly) of *La esclava de su hijo*," *HR*, 2 (1934): 345–348; Joseph G. Fucilla, "La discordia en los casados de Lope de Vega y una novela de G. B. Giraldi," *MLJ*, 18, (1934): 280–83, reprinted in *Relaciones hispanoitalianas* (Madrid: C. S. I. C., 1953), pp. 163–168; Edwin S. Morby, "Gli Ecatommiti, El favor agradecido and Las burlas y enredos de Benito," *HR*, 10, (1942): 325–28; and, Eugene Kohler, "Lope de Vega et Giraldi Cinthio," *Études Litteraires: Mélanges*; 1945, II, Publications de la Faculté des Lettres de l'Université de Strasbourg, Fasc. 105 (Paris: Les Belles Lettres, 1946), pp. 169–220.

[26] See Antonio Palau y Dulcet, *Manual del librero*, IV, 512. The entry concerning the Spanish translation reads: "Doni (Antonio Francesco). *La zucca del Doni En Español*. (Al fin:) In Venetia Per Francesco Marcolini. Il Mese d'Ottobre MDLI (1551) 8, letra cursiva, 166 p. 5 h. grabs."

[27] Luigi Guicciardini's collection of tales and anecdotes, as noted by Palau, VI, 464, was translated as "Horas de recreación. Traducidas de lengua Toscana. En que se hallarán dichos, hechos y exemplos de personas señaladas con aplicación de diversas fábulas, de que se puede sacar mucha doctrina. En Bilbao, por Mathías Mares, 1586, 8, 16h. 192 fols."

[28] According to Palau y Dulcet, *Manual del librero*, XXII, 181, Francesco di Caravaggio's (Straparola) *Piacevoli notti* appeared in Spanish as *Honesto y agradable entretenimiento de damas y galanes*. Compuesto por el señor Joan Francesco Carvacho, Cavallero Napolitano. Y traduzido de lengua toscana en la nuestra vulgar, por Francisco Truhado, vezino de Baeça. En Bilbao, por Mathias Mares. A Costa de Juan Ruelle, mercader de libros, 1580, 12, 264 fols." Spanish translations of all or part of the work continued *(continued on page 18)*

17

those of Bandello and Giraldi Cinthio. Of these, only Bandello and Giraldi Cinthio appear to have contributed directly to Lope's theatre.

In conjunction with Lope's dramatization of the eight *Decameron* stories, the question necessarily arises as to whether Lope worked from the Spanish translation of the *Decameron*, an Italian text, or from a combination of the two. The playwright's reference to his knowledge of Italian in a letter to the Duke of Sessa[29] and in *La Dorotea*[30] as well as his conscious use of the language textually in several plays[31] either to define character or for comic effect argues, most scholars agree,[32] for an Italian text as source. Yet the very same scholars show surprisingly little interest in particularizing the Italian source. For instance, one might ask if Lope was indebted to a pre-1559 edition of the *Decameron*[33] or to one of the later, expurgated versions (1573; 1582). The difficulty of establishing source is complicated by several factors. First, more often than not, the brief Italian narrative was insufficient for an entire play and much of what was added was Lope's own invention. Second, owing to the wide diffusion of the *Decameron* stories, could not Lope have drawn on his book of recollections rather than have adhered exclusively to a specific source, or even have combined both founts? Finally, no investigation would be complete without the consideration of inter-

---

(continued from page 17) to be printed until 1611. For specifics concerning the subsequent translations see Palau's entry as noted above.

[29] See Agustín G. de Amezúa, *Epistolario de Lope de Vega*, 4 vols. (Madrid: Real Academia Española, 1935–43), III, 122.

[30] See Lope de Vega, *La Dorotea*, ed. Edwin S. Morby (Madrid: Castalia, 1958), p. 288.

[31] See Joaquín Arce, "Italiano e italianismi cinque-secenteschi in Lope de Vega," *Il Rinascimento: Aspetti e problemi attuali* (Firenze: Olschki, 1982); and "Boccaccio nella letteratura castigliana: panorama generale e rassegna bibliográfico-crítica," *Il Boccaccio nelle culture e letterature nazionali*, ed. Francesco Mazzoni (Firenze: Olschki, 1978), pp. 63–105.

[32] See Introduction, ns. 20, 21 and 24.

[33] On the editions of the *Decameron* in Italy see Vittore Branca, ed., Boccaccio, *Decameron*, pp. xxxvii-liv. For additional commentary on the expurgations see G. Biagi, *Annedoti letterari* (Milano, 1887) and A. Sorrentino, *La letteratura italiana e il Sant'Ufficio* (Napoli, 1935).

mediate sources (i.e., those stories retold by writers prior to Lope: Juan de Timoneda,[34] Antonio de Torquemada,[35] Melchor de Santa Cruz[36] and Pedro Navarro[37]), and the degree to which they influenced Lope's refurbishing. While the question of a precise source can only be answered by the author himself, I believe a case can be made for the expurgated edition of 1582 as the basic, though not exclusive, source. I will confine my comments to those points of contact between the source material, Spanish and Italian, and the derivative plays which may hold the key to the concretization of source. In each instance, a brief résumé of the Italian plot is offered for the reader's convenience.

In delimiting Lope's sources, we may discount both manuscript translations, since the Catalan version was probably inaccessible to Lope and the Spanish manuscript of fifty *novelle* contains only two of the dramatized stories: X, 1 and X, 8.[38] Despite the inexplicably jumbled order of the Spanish printed edition, it remains a faithful translation of the content of each *Decameron* tale, with only an occasional liberty taken. (I

---

[34] Juan de Timoneda, *El patrañuelo*, in *Obras de Juan de Timoneda* (Madrid: Sociedad de Bibliófilos Españoles, 1947), XIX, Series 2. Timoneda reproduces the following tales from the *Decameron*: X, 10—Patraña II; II, 9—Patraña XV; X, 8—Patraña XXII. Three additional tales were incorporated into the *Sobremesa y alivio de caminantes* (*Obras*, XIX, Series 2), VII, 7—Parte I, Cuento LXIX; X, 1—Parte I, Cuento XLVII; VI, 4—Parte II, Cuento XLV.

[35] Antonio de Torquemada, *Colloquios satíricos* (1553) recounts *Decameron* X, 1. See George Davis Crowe, ed., Antonio de Torquemada, "*Los colloquios satíricos* con un colloquio pastoril" (Unpublished doctoral dissertation, University of Texas, Austin, 1953).

[36] Melchor de Santa Cruz de Dueñas, *Floresta española* (Madrid: Sociedad de Bibliófilos Españoles, 1953), XXIX, Series 2. Melchor de Santa Cruz retells *Decameron* X, 1 in Parte II, No. 1xxi.

[37] Pedro Navarro, *Comedia muy exemplar de la Marquesa de Saluzia llamada Griselda* (1603), ed., Caroline B. Bourland, *RH*, 9, (1902): 331–354.

[38] On the popularity of this tale see Louis Sorieri, *Boccaccio's Story of Tito and Gisippo in European Literature* (New York: Institute of French Studies, 1937), pp. 232–268. See also Grace E. Megiwinall Andreu, "G.X.8 del *Decameron*: Posible fuente de *La boda entre dos maridos*, de Lope de Vega, o mito de Apolo, fuente común," in *Lope de Vega y los orígenes del teatro español*; Actas del I Congreso Internacional sobre Lope de Vega, ed. Manuel Criado de Val (Madrid: EDI-6, 1981), 179–202.

refer only to those stories which found their way into Lope's theater). To cite an example: Novella XII of the Spanish translation recounts the story of Rinaldo d'Esti (*Decameron* II, 2) who, robbed and left to survive a wintry night clad only in a shirt, finds lodging and a mistress as well. The Spanish translator expands the role of the lady's servant in urging her mistress to take advantage of what fortune has sent her way—a handsome young nobleman instead of the elderly Marquis who failed to keep his assignation. The expansion may have suggested to Lope the characterization of Fenisa, the maid who offers similar counsel in *El llegar en ocasión*. There is, however, no textual correspondence and Lope's character amplification could just as easily have been suggested by literary antecedents such as Trotaconventos or Celestina. In both the Spanish translation and the Italian editions through 1573 (the date of the first expurgated edition), Rinaldo's conversation with the robbers posing as merchants centers on his daily prayer to St. Julian for a safe journey and a good night's lodging.[39] In the expurgated edition of 1582, reference to St. Julian is deleted and the conversation focuses, instead, on which arms to bear while traveling. In Lope's play, neither St. Julian nor weapons are mentioned: the travelers take turns telling stories to pass the time.[40] These departures from the original *novella* which, in fact, provided no more than the basis for Act I and the first scene of Act II, render elusive any attempt to concretize the source.

Similarly, while the Spanish title of Novella liij (*Decameron* V,4) "de ricardo y catalina como tomo el ruy senor" (sic) recalls immediately the title of Lope's comedy, *El ruiseñor de Sevilla*, it is not sufficient evidence to indicate a direct borrowing from the Spanish text. Boccaccio's title, "Ricciardo Ma-

---

[39] For the medieval belief in the "Paternoster di San Giuliano l'Ospitaliere," see Arturo Graf, *Miti, leggende e superstizioni del Medio Evo* (Torino: Chiantore, 1925), pp. 383–391.

[40] On the provenance of these stories see Cesare Segre, "Due racconti del *Novellino* nel *Llegar en ocasión* di Lope de Vega," *Travaux de Linguistique et de Littérature*, Université de Strasbourg, 16, no. 1, 483–487.

nardi è trovato da messer Lizio da Valbona con la figliuola, la quale egli spose, e col padre di lei rimane in bona pace," makes no reference to a nightingale. The story, however, centers on a play on words concerning *l'usignolo*[41] and could easily have prompted Lope to incorporate it into the title. In both, the heroine is a sprightly young girl who, on the pretext of wishing to sleep outdoors in order to hear the nightingale sing, makes it possible for her lover to visit her. There is, however, a correspondence between deletions made in the expurgated edition of 1582 and those made by Lope in his play. Neither contains mention of specific bodily parts when the lovers are found in bed. Also omitted is the Italian narrator's description of the lovemaking and references to the lovers' quantitative sexual activity which, strangely enough, is retained in the expurgated edition of 1573. The omission, in both cases, however, was more likely a matter of propriety than one of direct derivation.

There are no visible changes between the Spanish translation and the Italian editions up through 1573 in the story of Federico degli Alberighi (*Decameron* V, 9), the source for *El halcón de Federico*. Boccaccio's hero, having spent his fortune in pursuit of a beautiful and virtuous married woman, retires in poverty to a small estate. His only wealth is his falcon which he kills to serve to the lady, now widowed, when she calls on him. Recognizing his devotion and ignoring his poverty, the lady marries him. The 1582 edition, however, carries a marginal note which shifts the meaning of the term "Fortuna" from its association with providential intervention to its secular aspect as chance-change. The recasting, which throws the onus of responsibility for determining one's fate on the indi-

---

[41] The sexual connotation of "l'usignolo" is clear in the father's description of the position in which the lovers are found: "Su tosto, donna, lievati e vieni a vedere, che tua figliuola è stata si vaga dell'usignolo, che ella è stata tant alla posta che ella l'ha preso e tienlosi in mano . . ."(p. 623). Lope was undoubtedly familiar with the double meaning and must have depended on some recognition of the same from his audience. The association was not beyond the imagination of most of the spectators.

vidual and on his capacity for self reliance,[42] is entirely in keeping with Lope's dramatic vision. Lope's Federico recognizes his lack of courage as he bids farewell to a former servant who has made a successful career for himself in the army:

> Vos con plumas de esperanzas
> De una justa pretensión
> Y yo con los de un halcón
> Que me enseña sus mundanzas.
>
> Y esto no por la fortuna
> Que sólo virtud ha sido,
> Por haverla vos tenido
> Y no tener yo ninguna.
>
> (469b)

As in Boccaccio, Lope's heroine marries Federico in recognition of his constancy and devotion.

The genesis of *El ejemplo de casadas y prueba de la paciencia* (X, 10) is complicated by the fact that all Spanish translations and pre-Lopean Spanish versions of the Griselda story are based on Petrarch's Latin transcription rather than on Boccaccio's original. The trials Griselda endures at the hands of her husband is retold, as I noted earlier, by the anonymous author of *Castigos y dotrinas que un sabio dava a sus hijas*, by Narciso Viñoles (*Suma de todas las crónicas del mundo*),[43] and by Juan de Timoneda (*El Patrañuelo*).[44] The two latter versions, in turn, served as basis for the play by Pedro Navarro, the *Comedia muy exemplar de la Marquesa de Saluzia, llamada Griselda*. Lope's play, in which the characters are hispanized, offers no means of

---

[42] See R. Hastings, *Nature and Reason in the Decameron* (Manchester, G.B.: Manchester University Press, 1975), p. 102.

[43] The story of Griselda is recorded in Jacopo Filippo Foresti's Latin chronicle, *Supplementum chronicorum orbis ab initio mundi* (Venetia: Bernardinus Rizus, 1490). The work was translated by Narciso Viñoles as *Suma de todas las crónicas del mundo* (Valencia: Jorge Costilla, 1510). C. B. Bourland reproduces Viñoles' version of the Griselda story in "Boccaccio and the *Decameron*," pp. 333–335.

[44] See José Romera Castillo, "Un tema boccacciano (D. X, 10) en Lope de Vega y Joan Timoneda," *Lope de Vega y los orígenes del teatro español. Actas del I Congreso Internacional*, ed. M. Criado de Val (Madrid: EDI-6 (1981), pp. 203–216.

determining whether he worked with both Boccaccio and Petrarch or either one exclusively. The passages in which the Italian masters diverge are either deleted or so modified as to make the establishment of a specific source impossible. There are, however, several points of contact with Navarro's play in addition to the similarity of focus in both titles. A decided pastoral flavor characterizes both works. In each, the nobleman and the shepherdess meet in a wood. Moreover, a number of passages in *El ejemplo de casadas* find their counterpart in the *Comedia muy exemplar*. In both plays the heroine refers to herself as having been raised without a mother:

Griselda:	Laurencia:
Quedad con Dios, señor padre,	Padre mió,
que yo haré lo que deuo,	Como os habéis cegado desa
y esso en cargo me lo lleuo,	suerte.
y aunque criada sin madre	Pues a un hombre, y en traje
la bondad será mi ceuo.	cortesano
(fol. 3ᵛ)	Que no visteis jamás, dais
	vuestra hija,
	criada tan sin madre,...
	(21a)

Laurencia's lament over the removal of her son is not unlike that of Navarro's Griselda when she gives up her daughter:

Griselda:	Laurencia:
y que ha hecho esta criatura?	Hijo, ¿por qué naciste tan aprisa,
	Para poner mi vida en
Galisteo:	contingencia?
Por ser de prosapia exura	Parece que de un parto y de una
y de pastoril linage.	suerte
	Nacieron vuestra vida y vuestra
Griselda:	muerte.
Hija, a quién fuyste homicida?	Hijo, ¿queréis saber vuestro
que apenas estás nacida,	delito?
y en naciendo delinquente?	Sabed que os matan porque
tú mueres, hija, innocente!	fuistes nieto
yo viviré triste vida!	De la humildad de un viejo a
(fol. 14ʳ)	quien imito,...
	(31a)

There is also a resemblance between the two personages

23

as they compare the cares of an exalted, worldly position to the peace and tranquility of a humble existence:

Griselda:
El mundo con sus engaños
me levantó de cimiento
pues he viuido diez años
puesta en áspero tormento
para muy mayores daños.
Mas quisiera el ornamento
y no me fuera tormento,
se mi çimarra y çurrón
que no ver tan gran passión
y mi hija en perdimiento.
(fol. 19ᵛ)

Laurencia:
Palacios ricos, ¿dónde está el
contento?
¿Está en vuestros tesoros y
riquezas,
O en la seguridad del
pensamiento?
¡Oh, cuán seguro estado es la
pobreza,
Pues no puede temer que humille
el viento
su miserable estado á más bajeza!
(26a)

The words of the protagonist to the servant as they prepare for the arrival of the nobleman's new bride are also similar:

Griselda:
Ama, y en amor hermana,
barred essas losas duras,...
(fol. 21ʳ)

Laurencia:
Haz, Fenisa, que esta sala
Se limpia y ponga muy bien.
(44b)

A less obvious parallel may be found in the dramatic intent of both authors. Navarro, following closely the postscript of the *Supplemento*,[45] offers the story of Griselda as an example for all women in moments of adversity:

Damas de merecimiento
casadas y por casar,
no se os deue de oluidar
Griselda del pensamiento,
que es digna de memorar.
De Griselda os acorda,
esta Griselda imita;

---

[45] Narciso Viñoles, *Suma.* . . The postscript reads: "Esta historia he querido aqui escrivir: por enxemplo de todas las mugeres. Afin que cuando algun perverso marido o tuviere alguna adversidad o mala dicha que se sepa conservar con paciencia y ser umildes y magnánimas en todos sus afanes y fatigas y les sepan sobrar y vencer: como Griselda hizo con grandeza de ánimo."

24

mirad lo que ha padecido
no lo pongays en oluido
su paciencia remira!
(fol. 24ᵛ)

While Lope does not exhort his feminine public directly, it is clear from the final passages that he, too, is setting before the wives of his day a perfection to be imitated:

Enrique: Da los brazos á tus hijos,
             Y mí, que te doy el alma,
             Por la mujer más famosa,
             Más perfecta y más honrada,
             Más humilde y obediente
             Que en las historias se halla
             Fuera de aquellas que tiene
             La Iglesia en nombre de santas . . .
             . . .   .
             Vasallos, hagamos fiestas
             Y puede hacellas España,
             De que hubo en ella mujer
             De las nueve de la fama.

Tibaldo: No dudes de que en su gloria
             Resulta alabanza tanta
             Entre las muchas matronas
             Que por su virtud se alaban.
                               (45b)

The textual similarities noted above would indicate that Lope knew the work of his predecessor and admired it sufficiently to follow his lead, if only in part, in the dramatization of the Griselda story. I am disinclined to conclude, however, that Lope's source like Navarro's, was the Petrarchan version. Rather, I suggest that the widespread diffusion of the Griselda story, both in the Boccaccian original and the Petrarchan transcription rendered unnecessary the consultation of a specific source. While Navarro's play, close at hand, may have suggested elements of expansion, the hispanization of the protagonists, the contrastive presentation of the court and the countryside, and the amplification of the role of Griselda's father and those of her companions are the product of Lope's fertile imagination.

Concerning the source of *El anzuelo de Fenisa* (VIII, 10), *El servir con mala estrella* (X, 1) and *La boda entre dos maridos* (X, 8), the text of the Spanish translation differs so slightly from the original that I am unable to discern a preference in any one of the three plays for one source over the other. Nor are any major changes reflected in either of the expurgated editions. The Italian source for *El anzuelo de Fenisa* relates the adventures of a Florentine merchant who falls prey to the wiles of a Sicilian cortesan and who is able to avenge himself later with a similar deceit. The expurgated text of 1582 surpresses two words, "in paradiso," which describe the hero's reaction to bathing with the cortesan, but does not eliminate the episode. Lope, understandably, discards the scene. He adds a Spanish subplot involving a *caso de honor* which is carefully woven into the main plot and eventually assumes a dominant role, thereby relegating the Italian material to an accesorial, though no less dynamic, role. One aspect of Lope's plot expansion however, suggests a strong preference for Italian materials. A Spanish servant, Fabio, in an effort to trick a fellow countryman, speaks Italian on three separate occasions, even to the point of singing an Italian song which was probably in circulation at the time and known to the Spanish soldiers on duty in Italy.[46]

The story of the Italian knight (X, 1) who is never properly rewarded for his service by Alfonso, King of Castile, is recast three times by Spanish authors between 1553 and 1574. The brief, intermediary versions in which the main character is either an old servant (Torquemada and Timoneda) or a page (Santa Cruz) appear to have had no effect on Lope's rendition. The latter adheres closely to the original tale, even to the retention of the main character's name as Rugero.[47] Lope's

---

[46] See Eugenio Mele, "Una canzone popolare siciliana in una commedia di Lope de Vega," *BH*, 35 (1933): 454–456; and Joaquín Arce, "Italiano e italianismi . . ," pp. 14–15.

[47] See S. Griswold Morley and Courtney Bruerton, "Addenda to the Chronology of Lope de Vega's *Comedias*," *HR*, 15 (1947): 58. Morley and Bruerton note that a card dated February 18, 1946, from Marcel Bataillon mentions a *rapprochement* with the French court after the death of Henry IV (1610).

plot amplifications, taken from Spanish history and legend deal, in part, with the events surrounding the birth of Estefanía, whose subsequent history is the basis of another play, *La desdichada Estefanía*.[48]

The relationship of intermediate sources may not be dismissed so easily for *La boda entre los maridos*. In this instance, although the basic Lopean source is clearly Boccaccio's story of Tito and Gisippo (X, 8), several details of the dramatic refurbishing suggest a familiarity with Juan de Timoneda's earlier version. Boccaccio's protagonist Gisippo, a Greek, allows his best friend Tito, a Roman, to substitute for him on his wedding night because of a melancholy which Tito has conceived for Sofronia, Gisippo's intended bride. In Timoneda and subsequently in Lope, the exchange of husbands is made on the day of the wedding. The friend substitutes for the groom at the signing of the marriage contracts thereby making him the lady's lawful spouse from the outset. The second half of Boccaccio's story centers on Tito's willingness to sacrifice his life for Gisippo who, having fled to Rome penniless, stands mistakenly accused of murder and condemned to be crucified. The versions of Timoneda and Lope make two adjustments: Gisippo's counterpart is robbed on his way to Rome, and his friend does not immediately recognize him when he is brought to court. The similarities noted above, however, are not sufficient to make a case for direct borrowing. Beyond these points, Lope's rendition remains faithful to Boccaccio's basic plot. Those revisions which are uniquely Lopean—the shift to main characters representing Spain and France; the complication of the changes which bring Gisippo's counterimage to trial; and, the addition of a *gracioso* figure—are made in the interest of theatricality and dramatic impact.

Given the fact that there is no significant difference between the original Italian tales and the Spanish translation as

---

[48] *La desdichada Estefanía,* in *Obras de Lope de Vega,* VII, 329–363. For the historical sources of this play see Menéndez y Pelayo's introductory study to the volume, pp. lxviii–lxix.

sources for *El anzuelo de Fenisa, El servir con mala estrella* and *La boda entre dos maridos*, it would be presumptuous to settle on one or the other as source at this point. The indebtedness to Timoneda for the latter play brings an added dimension to the question.

La discreta enamorada (III, 3), on the other hand, clearly indicates an Italian source and, in particular, an expurgated text. Boccaccio's gullible friar, made to serve as go-between by an unscrupulous married lady and the man she desires, becomes, in Lope's play, a blustering soldier. The change corresponds to those prescribed for the expurgated *Decameron* of 1573, but, oddly enough, not in this tale. In this version, the friar as unwitting dupe is allowed to stand because he is innocent. The expurgated edition of 1582, however, more thorough in its deletions and emendations, casts Boccaccio's "frate montone" as a pedagogue. Moreover, the heroine is now a young lady who, about to be wed by her parents to one she does not love, manages to end up married to a man of her own choosing. With the exception of the friar-pedagogue transition, the changes in plot correspond exactly to those found in Lope's adaptation.

In sum, then, while the issue of Lope's precise sources can never be resolved definitively, I believe sufficient evidence has been presented to confirm earlier speculation regarding an Italian source and to consider specifically the expurgated Italian edition of 1582 as the most likely source. Lope's indebtedness to secondary sources is, for the most part, negligible except for the occasional detail taken from Timoneda for *La boda entre dos maridos* and the textual similarities between Navarro's *Comedia muy exemplar* and Lope's *El ejemplo de casadas*. In the latter instance, Boccaccio's story of Griselda was so well known as to preclude the need to consult the original. On the other hand, the strong Italianate orientation and textual use of Italian in *El anzuelo de Fenisa;* the deletions and emendations in *El ruiseñor de Sevilla;* and the parallel shift in attitude toward *Fortuna* in *El halcón de Federico* support the first assertion. The changes in plot and characterization for *La discreta enamorada*, which correspond to those of the 1582 edition, and the fact that

Lope was hardly one to consciously peruse a variety of *Decameron* editions in his search for plot lines, argue for serious consideration of the expurgated Italian *Decameron* of 1582 as the basic though not exclusive source for Lope's Boccaccian plays.

II. *Fortuna*

It has been noted that part of Boccaccio's admiration of human intelligence stems from the recognition that it is man's only protection against the vagaries of Fortune; it is the only palliative with which to confront adversity. From the outset of the *Decameron*, in the description of the plague, the power of *Fortuna* over men's lives is accentuated.[1] The flow and ebb of all worldly things is emphasized again as the subject matter for Day II is agreed upon: " . . . con ciò sia cosa che dal principio del mondo gli uomini sieno stati diversi casi della fortuna menati, e saranno infino alla fine, ciascun debba dire sopra questo: 'Chi, da diverse cose infestato, sia, oltre alla sua speranza, riuscito a lieto fine,'."[2] This is not to suggest, however,

---

[1] Relevant to Boccaccio's concept of Fortune see: Howard R. Patch, *The Goddess Fortuna in Medieval Literature* (Cambridge, Mass.: Harvard Univ. Press, 1927); Vincenzo Cioffari, "The Conception of Fortune in the *Decameron*," *Italica*, 17 (1940), 129–137; "The Function of Fortune in Dante, Boccaccio and Macchiavelli," *Italica*, 24 (1947), 1–13; Vittore Branca, *Boccaccio medievale* (Firenze: Sansoni, 1970), pp. 20–21; and R. Hastings, *Nature and Reason in the 'Decameron'*, pp. 91–98.

[2] Boccaccio, *Decameron*, p. 118.

that man could ultimately subdue Fate to his will but rather that man, through experience, might learn how to adapt himself to circumstances as they occur.

For Boccaccio, man's chances against Fortune are only fifty-fifty. There are some mishaps which no amount of foresight can prevent (the plague, for one), and even the most prudent man may come to grief when least expected. On the other hand, by judicious behavior and wise choices, one may learn how to become resilient, to ride out the storm and be alert to opportunities when they present themselves, so that we may learn to make the best of those occasions of good fortune which come our way from time to time. Thus, the stories of Days II and III center on those who manage to survive ill fortune and emerge successful either by luck (Day II) or by their own efforts (Day III). Although the second and third days are devoted specifically to *Fortuna*, Boccaccio reveals a constant preoccupation with the theme throughout the *Decameron*. It surfaces time and again as a secondary motif in matters of love (Days IV and V), the celebration of intelligence (Days VI, VII and VIII), or magnificence (Day X).

While Boccaccio does not discount the possibility of divine intervention in human affairs (the plague may have been punishment for the wickedness of the Florentines),[3] Fortune is not generally characterized as an instrument of Divine Providence. It is most often a blind and arbitrary force, the workings of pure chance, treacherous, fickle, rewarding man one minute and punishing him the next without apparent justification. In this capacity, *Fortuna* becomes a convenient figure on which to blame all unexplained reversals as well as the goddess to be thanked for favors granted.

It is this view of Fortune which undoubtedly attracted Lope. Although he takes from all three *Decameron* motifs, Lope

---

[3] Boccaccio, *Decameron*, pp. 13 and 18. In the Introduction to Day I, the plague is: ". . . o per operazione de' corpi superiori o per le nostre inique opere da giusta ira di Dio a nostra correzione mandata sopra i mortali, . . ." and a few pages later, ". . . l'ira di Dio a punire le iniquità degli uomini con quella pestilenza . . . ."

is particularly inclined toward *Fortuna*, which is the basis for four plays: *El llegar en ocasión* (*Dec.*, II, 2), *La discreta enamorada* (*Dec.*, III, 3), *El servir con mala estrella* (*Dec.*, X, 1) and *El ejemplo de casadas* (*Dec.*, X, 10). Lope's fascination with the theme of Fortune would appear to parallel that of Boccaccio since it emerges as an auxiliary motif in the remaining four plays though their main focus is love: *El ruiseñor de Sevilla* (*Dec.*, V, 4), *El halcón de Federico* (*Dec.*, V, 9) and *La boda entre dos maridos* (*Dec.*, X, 8); or intelligence: *El anzuelo de Fenisa* (*Dec.*, VIII, 10). As an irrational, illogical force, Fortune is ideally suited to the constantly shifting action of Lope's theater. The progression of each source tale from unforeseen mishaps to equally unexpected happy resolutions is consonant with the playwright's dramatic vision. Moreover, the theme of *Fortuna* and the attendant motives of *Occasio* and *Tempus* enjoyed a spirited revival in the drama and prose fiction of Lope's time.[4]

The respective sources for *El llegar en ocasión* and *La discreta enamorada* deal with the irrationality of Fortune and with man's choice either to succumb to its reversals (as do Rinaldo, the Marquis and the widow of *Decameron* II, 2) or to attempt to circumvent its course (as does the unhappy young wife of III, 3). In each instance, Lope alters the theme, focusing on the power of man to meet the challenge of Fortune and turn the tide in his favor by seizing the occasion or by using prudence and discretion.

El llegar en ocasión

In the source story for *El llegar en ocasión*, Boccaccio's protagonist, Rinaldo d'Esti,[5] is robbed by highwaymen posing as merchants and takes refuge in a doorway just outside the walls of Castel Guglielmo. Due to a fortuitous combination of

[4] For the appearance and significance of Fortune in Spanish literature from its beginnings to the time of Lope de Vega see: Helen L. Sears, "The Concepts of Fortune and Fate in the *Comedia* of Lope de Vega" (Unpublished doctoral dissertation, University of California, Los Angeles, 1949), pp. 28–59.

[5] Boccaccio, *Decameron*, pp. 135–145.

circumstances, which the narrator attributes to Rinaldo's unswerving faith in God and St. Julian,[6] he is admitted to the house where he finds not only lodging but a mistress as well. The lady, angered by the failure of her lover, the Marquis of Ferrara, to keep the evening's assignation and impressed by Rinaldo's handsome appearance, grants the latter her favors. The next morning, swearing Rinaldo to secrecy, she gives him clothes and money with which to return home.

Lope absorbs Boccaccio's narrative elements, which are insufficient for an entire play, into Act I in such a way that the remainder of the play seems a natural outgrowth of those components. The unexplained detention of the Marquis, for example, becomes an assassination plot linked to the theme of honor. Rinaldo emerges as Otavio, the young son of a Ferrarese senator. Lope's widow is a woman of independent means who has been, thus far, unsuccessfully pursued by the Marquis. Boccaccio's widow changes lovers for one night; Lope's heroine, Laura, sets about to make the substitution permanent. In Boccaccio, it is the lady who makes the advances. Lope reverses the pattern so that Otavio is the pursuer. Then, having won the lady's favors with the promise of marriage, Otavio suspends his departure the next morning and remains on the premises disguised as a shepherd. From this point on the play diverges entirely from the Italian tale. The remainder of the play is taken up with Laura's efforts to conceal Otavio from her servants and from the Marquis until her former suitor accepts the lady's change of heart. In the interest of propriety, Lope deletes Boccaccio's allusion to divine intercession and

---

[6] Arturo Graf, *Miti, leggende e superstizioni*, pp. 383–391. According to Graf, the prayer to St. Julian was often extended to include female companionship for the night. On the veneration of St. Julian as patron of boatsmen, innkeepers and travelers, see *The Book of Saints. A Dictionary of Persons Canonized or Beatified by the Catholic Church* (Ramsgate, New York: St. Augustine Abbey, 1966), p. 412. That the veneration to, or at least respect for St. Julian persisted to Lope's time is evident in a subsequent play by Lope, *El animal profeta, San Julián*, in Ac. IV, 395 ff. Lope's authorship of the play has been questioned by Morley and Bruerton, *Cronología*, p. 420. Menéndez y Pelayo, on the other hand, found no reason to doubt the authenticity. See his *Estudios sobre el teatro de Lope de Vega* (Madrid: C. S. I. C., 1949), IV, ciii.

focuses instead on the pagan concept of Fortune as chance-change. Through the careful expansion of characterization, Lope renders the indiscriminate rewards and punishments of Fortune, as exemplified in Boccaccio's narrative, compatible with the principle of poetic justice.

It is Boccaccio's treatment of the lady, however, and the notion of *ocasión* presented therein which suggests to Lope the principal motif for his play. Boccaccio had focused exclusively on the two men, one a loser and the other a gainer, reversing their fortunes by the end of the story. Lope shifts the emphasis to the woman who is about to make a change in her life and is determined to make the best of a good opportunity. *Fortuna* as chance-change left no room for human interference; *Occasio* offered that measure of flexibility essential to the realization of the work. To give the theme added impact, Lope associates it with what appears to be a popular adage,[7] "Quien pierde la ocasión, tarde y mal la cobra,"[8] and repeats it with variations throughout the play. The choice of maxim is not without significance. In conjunction with the title, the proverb brings into play an entire complex of associations—*Tempus, Occasio, Fortuna*—popular in classical antiquity,[9] and one which had

---

[7] See Francis C. Hayes, "The Uses of Proverbs as Titles and Motives in the *Siglo de Oro* Drama: Lope de Vega," *HR*, 6 (1938): 303–323. Hayes avers that Lope allowed proverbs to influence his thinking to such a degree that he built thesis plays out of them . . . and in many instances made up titles which have a definite proverbial ring."

[8] Pertinent to the *refranes* associated with *ocasión*, see: Gonzalo Correas, *Vocabulario de refranes y frases proverbiales* (Madrid, 1924), p. 369; Francisco Rodríguez Marín, *Más de 21,000 refranes castellanos* (Madrid, 1926), p. 350; Julio Cejador y Frauca, *Refranero castellano* (Madrid, 1929), p. 103; and, Luis Martínez Kleiser, *Refranero general ideológico español* (Madrid: Real Academia Española, 1953), pp. 538–539, entries 46.977–47.190.

[9] Callistratus, *Descriptions*, in Philostratus: *Imagines*. Callistratus: *Descriptions*, trans. Arthur Fairbanks (New York: G. P. Putnam, 1931), p. 399. The description by Callistratus of the statue of Kairos, the Greek god of Time later associated with Occasion, reads: ". . . the lock of hair on his forehead indicates that while he is easy to catch as he approaches . . . when he has once passed by, the moment for action has likewise expired, and that, if opportunity has been neglected, it cannot be recovered." See also Posidippus, "On a Statue of Time by Lysyppus," *The Greek Anthology*, ed. W. E. Paton (New York: G. P. Putnam, 1918), V, 324–325. Although the statue by Lysyppus is

gained currency in Lope's time.[10] Lope's recourse to the theme, then, is not an isolated phenomenon but part of a sustained interest in the motif.

The opening lines focus immediately on Fortune's mutability, implicitly affirming the notion that while man has no control over changes which occur, it is within his power to use those changes to full advantage when the opportunity presents itself. As the play progresses this view is reinforced by the behavior of the major characters, each of whom, having been provided with an *ocasión*, determines to make the most of it:

> La mudanza espera el sabio;
> Que pocas veces verás
> Gran bien sin ajeno agravio.
>   Cuando un reino se arruina
> Otro á las nubes confina
> Y hasta el sol llegar intenta,
> Porque un estado se aumenta
> Con lo que el otro declina.
>   Hereda el mancebo tierno
> Al viejo avaro, que está
> Por ventura en el infierno;

---

called *Tempus* it has all the attributes of *Occasio;* a razor in the right hand, a long forelock and a bald occiput. On the expansion of the meaning of *Fortuna* in the late Latin classical period to include the elements of *Tempus* and *Occasio* see Patch, *The Goddess Fortuna*, p. 12.

[10] On the renewal of interest in the *Fortuna-Tempus-Occasio* motif in the sixteenth and seventeenth centuries see: J. E. Matzke, "On the Source of the Italian and English Idioms Meaning 'To Take Time by the Forelock,' with specific reference to Bojardo's *Orlando Innamorato*, Book II, Canto vii–ix," *PMLA*, 8 (1894): 303–331; Rudolph Wittkower, "Chance, Time and Virtue," *JWI* (1937–1938): 313–321; and, Samuel C. Chew, "The World of Time: *Tempus-Occasio-Fortuna*," *The Pilgramage of Life* (New Haven, Conn.: Yale University Press, 1962), pp. 12–34. For the visual concretization of the newly revived allegory in sixteenth-century emblem literature see: Andrea Alciati, *Emblemata Fontes Quattor*, Holbein Society Facsimile, No. 4, ed. Henry Green (Manchester, England: A. Brothers, 1970); the *Hecatomagrafie* of Giles Corrozet (1540; rpt. Paris: H. Champion, 1905); Jean Cousin, *The Book of Fortune*, trans. H. Mainwaring Dunstan (London: Remington, 1883). This text reproduces the plates of the original French edition, *Le Livre de Fortune* (Paris: Kervet, 1568). See also Achille Bocchi, *Symbolicarum Quaestionum* (Bologna: Societatem Typographie Boniense, 1574), p. 152.

La guerra la paz nos da,
Como el verano al invierno.
    Si no hubiera noche oscura
No fuera tan claro el día;
No hay, Fabio, cosa segura.
                    (349a)

The *sabio*, in this instance, is the Marquis of Ferrara, who is congratulating himself over the sudden death of Rugero, Laura's husband. Chance has now made it possible to pursue the lady openly, and success seems within reach. The ensuing conversation, however, from which the nobleman emerges as an unfeeling man impelled only by sexual desire, suggests that he is unworthy of his good fortune and hints at a reversal. Nevertheless, to maintain dramatic tension, Lope allows the Marquis to savor a measure of success as a servant brings news that Laura has agreed to receive him.

If chance motivates the Marquis' action, it also plays a significant role in Laura's acceptance. The nobleman's request, delivered at precisely the right moment, finds Laura unbearably lonely and susceptible to the advances of any man. No hypocrite, Laura admits she enjoys masculine attention and that she sees no point in remaining faithful to one who is dead. Yet despite the hard, practical tone of these lines, the playwright is careful to indicate a certain hesitancy on the part of the widow, a hesitancy which paves the way for Laura's change of heart a few scenes later.

The dramatist now moves abruptly to two scenes which fully illustrate the fickleness of chance. As Otavio journeys to Ferrara, he is despoiled by robbers posing as merchants and left to brave the wintry night clad only in a shirt. At the same moment, the Marquis, who is on his way at last to a rendezvous with Laura, becomes aware of an assassination plot against him and returns home. Fabio, a servant, is sent ahead to make his apologies to Laura.

It is here that Lope introduces the notion of *ocasión*. The failure of the Marquis to keep his appointment provokes an angry, vengeful response from the young widow which reflects a change in emphasis. To Fenisa's query, "¿ . . . le dió algún mal . . . / que le obligó a perder . . . / esta ocasión?",

Laura retorts: "Pues tenlo por sin duda; / Que quien la pierde, tarde y mal la cobra," (359a). The Marquis has failed to seize the opportunity, and the spectator, through Laura's words, is alerted to possible complications.

Lope now shifts quickly back to Otavio. Chance, which moments earlier had been antagonistic, brings Otavio to Laura's door only minutes after Fabio's departure. Although the audience is well aware of the importance of Otavio's timely arrival, Lope teases the spectator by making Laura at first unreceptive to his cries. When told that a man hovers outside trembling from the cold, Laura snaps: " . . . morir le deja / Basta ser hombre no más / Ya lo aborrezco,"(359b). Upon the insistence of Fenisa, however, the widow admits him.

Having broached the theme of *ocasión* in an earlier scene, Lope is now ready to develop it fully. The servants are the first to fall under Otavio's spell. Fenisa, convinced that he is a gentleman, persuades Laura to give him a suit of clothes belonging to her late husband. Sirena, equally animated by the presence of a man in the house, is quick to suggest that he be invited to dinner. Lope uses Sirena's musing about this stranger who suddenly replaces the Marquis at the dinner table to elicit from Laura a second reference to *ocasión*:

> La ocasión es alcahuete
> Que suele hacer en una hora
> Más que pueden en mil días
> Diligencias y porfías.
> (361a)

The fusion of Fortune, Time and Occasion as treated by Patch, Wittkower, and Chew is evident in these lines. *Ocasión*, the subject of the verses, is personified as a go-between, a role normally assigned to the Fortune of Love.[11] Fortune is also the goddess of the opportune moment. The juxtaposition of "Que suele hacer en una hora" and "Más que pueden en mil días" emphasizes once more the idea of chance-change. Fortune has deprived Laura of one lover but also provided her with another within the hour. Otavio, on whom Fortune has

---

11 See Patch, *The Goddess Fortuna*, p. 94.

smiled, comes to enjoy "en una hora" what the Marquis has been unable to attain in "mil días" of "diligencias y porfías." Although *ocasión* immediately calls to mind the notion of "seize the occasion," the emphasis here seems to be on timing, specifically on the fortuitous arrival of Otavio in time to enjoy the bath and meal planned for the Marquis. In addition, the use of the word "alcahuete" clearly suggests that Otavio may derive additional benefits. Lope employs a second reference to *ocasión* in the same scene to state the title and principal motif of the play. When questioned by Fenisa as to whether Otavio will stay the night, Laura, unsure of her emotions, answers with exasperation: "No sé, ¡Por Dios! Mucho puede / El llegar en ocasión," (362b).

Lope consciously plays on Laura's hesitancy for he does not wish to equate Laura's behavior with that of her Italian counterpart who has no qualms about seducing Rinaldo while still mistress to the Marquis. If Lope's heroine is to maintain her dignity, if she is to conform or at least appear to conform to the prevailing moral code, it is Otavio, not Laura, who must seize the occasion. While this shift does not in itself absolve Laura of responsibility, Otavio's promise of marriage renders the widow's behavior less offensive and secures from the audience a measure of approval.

Once the main characters are brought together, chance acquires growing importance as a dramatic device. Two scenes merit attention in this regard. The unexpected arrival of the Marquis the following morning allows Lope a splendid opportunity to display his skill as a farceur. The nobleman, intent upon arranging a second assignation, comes upon Laura conversing with Otavio who is disguised as a shepherd. Lope makes excellent use of the *engañar-con-la-verdad* technique as Otavio, his jealousy aroused by the presence of the Marquis, channels his anger into an extemporaneous *pleito* concerning the arrival of a second *pastor* (the Marquis). Ostensibly addressing the Marquis in words reminiscent of "Suelta mi manso mayoral extraño,"[12] Otavio reproaches Laura for her

---

[12] See Lope de Vega, *Rimas*, ed. Gerardo Diego (Madrid: Palabra y Tiempo, 1973), p. 264.

fickleness, reminding her "Que si en ocasión llegué, / No salgo sin ocasión" (370b). The comic value of the situation rests on the confusion of the Marquis as he interprets Otavio's words literally while Laura, recurring to allegory, assures Otavio that he is the only *pastor* she wishes to keep.

As tension builds, chance precipitates a second encounter between the Marquis and Otavio (Act III). Suspicious of Laura's numerous postponements, the Marquis, as Laura's sovereign, orders her back to Ferrara. Otavio overhears the command and reacts instantly, with surprising resourcefulness. He bursts upon the scene, pretends to have been bitten by a rabid dog, and menacingly approaches Laura who, cued *sottovoce* by Otavio, suddenly claims to be similarly afflicted. Frightened by the prospect of contamination,[13] the Marquis and his servants depart hastily. Lope consciously plays on the folkloric heritage of his public to give the episode credibility. The reference to witchcraft or demonic endeavors and their palliatives are too numerous to be ignored. The rabid dog is black.[14] Tirso suggests sending for "El sacristán señor, / Que conjura los nublados." Otavio urges, "Llamad a un saludador," (386b). Fenisa opts for " . . . agua bendita," as Tirso labels Otavio a "nigromante," (387a). The humor of the scene derives primarily from the multilevel connotations of *rabiar*[15] which the dramatist cleverly fuses with the folkloric tradition to amplify the significance of the episode. The "madness" which overcomes Otavio stems from his desperation in the face of the order by the Marquis that Laura return to Ferrara.

Having used chance to intertwine the lives of the three major characters, Lope returns to the key theme of *ocasión* and the attendant idea of *mudanza* to cue the dénouement. Otavio

---

[13] On the bite of the huntsman's dog which in turn drives other dogs mad, see Stith Thompson, *Motif-Index of Folk-Literature* (Bloomington, Indiana: Indiana University Press, 1958), II, 469.

[14] See John Esten Keller, *Motif Index of Mediaeval Spanish Exempla* (Knoxville, Tenn.: University of Tennessee Press, 1949), p. 13.

[15] For the multiple meanings of *rabia/rabiar* in the seventeenth century, see the *Diccionario de Autoridades*, Edición facsímil, Real Academia Española (Madrid: Gredos, 1963), III, 478-479.

accidentally comes upon Federico, the escaped assassin, who has hidden in a nearby room. The chance meeting, in which Federico claims to be a *pastor* whom Laura is hiding, precipitates Otavio's denunciation of the lady. In an impassioned diatribe against women, Otavio cautions all men to love if they must but to have little faith in the object of their love. Thus, Lope brings the spectator full circle back to the theme of *mudanza* which informed the opening lines.

> ¿Quién estará seguro de mudanza?
> ¿Quién de lealtad, aunque en presencia sea?
> ¿Quién de quien nunca sus agravios vea?
> ¿Quién puso en la mujer toda esperanza?
> Si es fuerza amar, amar sin confianza
> Ataja el mal que el crédito rodea;
> Ame quien es amado, mas no crea
> Que nunca el daño al desengaño alcanza.
> Es esfera de tantos movimientos,
> Que ni la experiencia ni las artes
> Han reducido su mudanza á nombre;
> Que son de la mujer los pensamientos,
> Como un espejo que, quebrado en partes,
> En cada parte puede verse un hombre.
> (389,a-b)

The resolution now rests with the Marquis. Federico, the unsuccessful assassin, had secretly married the nobleman's sister, Diana. If he is to accept Federico as a brother-in-law, the Marquis must restore his honor by marrying Federico's sister, Camila, whom he had previously seduced. Recognizing that Fotune, which has deprived him of Laura's love, now offers an opportunity to recapture the love and respect of his subjects, the nobleman agrees to marry Camila. By the singular act of self-conquest, he is restored to dignity and indeed becomes the *sabio* of the opening lines.

Although Boccaccio's *novella* provided the substance for *El llegar en ocasión*, Lope's thematic revisions give the play an entirely new dimension. Whereas Rinaldo remains "l'uomo trastullo della Fortuna,"[16] the Spanish characters triumph

---

16 Vittore Branca, "Giovanni Boccaccio," *Letteratura Italiana: I Maggiori* (Milano: Marzorati, 1956), I, 222.

over Fortune in their capacity to use the mutability of chance to personal advantage. Lope expands Boccaccio's concept of *Fortuna* to include the notions of *Occasio* and *Tempus*. The subsequent fusion of all three with the principle of poetic justice renders the Italian tale less a question of man's victimization by Fortune than one of man rewarded or punished according to the moral validity of his acts.

La discreta enamorada

The protagonists of Boccaccio's Day III are labeled "vittoriosi della Fortuna[17] 'per loro industria'."[18] They are successful, through their own initiative and cleverness, in turning bad fortune to good. This approach is decidedly appealing to the dramatist since it mandates constant reaction on the part of the characters and provides the necessary motivation for plot development. Hence, it is not surprising that Lope should be attracted to the third story of the third day in which a young woman of Florence, married by her parents to an elderly wool merchant whose only interest is business, takes a young lover through the aid of an unsuspecting friar who is a friend of the man she desires.[19]

Given the nature of the content, however, Lope was constrained to make certain basic changes. Consequently, although she possesses all the guile and determination of her Italian counterpart, Lope's heroine is a sprightly young girl whose only desire is marriage. Fenisa, *la discreta enamorada*, who has accepted the marriage proposal of middle-aged Captain Bernardo to please her mother, is secretly resolved to marry the Captain's son, Lucindo. The plot is complicated by the presence of Gerarda, a cortesan and former lover of Lucindo; Belisa, the heroine's mother, who also wishes to marry

---

[17] Ibid. p. 222.

[18] Boccaccio, *Decameron*, p. 311. The introduction to the Third Day reads "Incomincia la terza nella quale si ragiona . . . di chi alcuna cosa molto da lui desiderata con industria acquistasse o la perduta recoverasse."

[19] Boccaccio, *Decameron*, pp. 336–348.

Lucindo; and, Estefanía, an identity assumed by Hernando as a ploy of Lucindo to arouse Gerarda's jealousy.

Whereas Boccaccio posed *industria* as a palliative against adverse fortune, Lope offers *discreción*. The shift from *industria* to *discreción* is predictable in light of two factors: the negative connotation which *industria* carries both in Italian and Spanish and the extent to which the words *discreto/discreción* informed the literature of Lope's time. *Industria*,[20] as a faculty of the will, directs the talents of the rational faculty toward the accomplishment of a specific goal. However, it also suggests the achievement of personal gains at the expense of or to the detriment of others. For example, Boccaccio's heroine satisfies her lust without regard for the sanctity of her marriage vows or for the office of the friar whom she dupes into serving as go-between.

Lope's objective is to create a comedy of intrigue, a love story from which the heroine emerges, according to the conventions of the *comedia*, married to the man she loves. If marriage is the goal set for Fenisa by her literary creator, she must be more than extraordinarily clever; whatever *industria* she employs must be directed to the achievement of that morally acceptable end lest she provoke censure. Fenisa may at times be "algo desenvuelta; pero no de modo que descubriese algún género de deshonestidad."[21] The subterfuge perpetrated to

---

[20] Sebastián de Covarrubias y Orozco, *Tesoro de la lengua castellana o española* con privilegio. En Madrid, por Luis Sánchez Impressor del Rey, N. S. Año del Señor MDCXI. p. 503 ⱽ. Covarrubias defines *industria* as maña, diligencia y solercia con que alguno haze cualquier cosa con menos trabajo que otro. Hazer una cosa de industria, hazerla a sabiendas, y adrede para que de allí sucede cosa que para otro sea a caso y para él de propósito, puede ser en buena y en mala parte. The *Diccionario de autoridades* interprets *industria* as "destreza o habilidad en cualquier arte . . . se toma por ingenio y sutileza maña u artificio." The *Vocabolario degli accademici della Crusca* (Firenze: Cellini, 1899), VIII, 780, defines *industria* similarly: "Diligenza ingegnosa usata per conseguire chechessia mediante lavoro o fatica . . . E per sagacità, Avvedimento, Accorgimento, overo Artifizio, Destrezza . . . posti in conseguire chechessia, ovvero in riuscire a qualche fine o intento desiderato." The text cites the *Decameron*, Day III, to substantiate this meaning.

[21] Miguel de Cervantes Saavedra, *Novelas ejemplares: La gitanilla* in *Obras completas*, ed. Angel Valbuena Prat (Madrid: Aguilar, 1965), p. 775.

bring her plans to fruition will be overlooked provided Fenisa evidence flawless *discreción* without which she would not be considered worthy of the sacrament of marriage.[22]

While *discreción* implies *industria*, it does not carry the negative linguistic charge often associated with the second word. *Discreción* reflects a discriminating, intelligent approach to situations; *industria* implies the use of surreptitious and less than exemplary means to achieve a specific end. *Discreción* is a desirable trait, almost a virtue. In its association with prudence,[23] it involves an aspiration to perfection and is its own reward. Although discretion may at times focus on gains of an immediate or temporal nature, there remains the idea of the eventual attainment of a greater good.

That Lope's era attached great importance to *discreción* may be gleaned from the number of works dedicated to the examination of that faculty and its social manifestations. To cite the most important ones: Baldesar Castiglione's *Il Cortegiano* (1528), termed a "manual de discreción" by Menéndez y Pelayo[24] and translated into Spanish by Juan Boscán in

---

[22] James E. Holloway, Jr., "Lope's Neoplatonism: *La dama boba*," *BHS*, 49 (1972): 236–355. In his discussion of Lope's neoplatonism, Holloway takes as point of departure a well known sonnet from *La dama boba*, "La calidad elemental resiste" which Lope published separately with *La Filomena* (1621), and *La Circe* (1624). Holloway deals with the functional relationship of the sonnet to the rest of the play and as a separate entity reflecting the essence of Lope's understanding of the universe, a view strongly influenced by Lope's reading of Pico della Mirandola and Marsilio Ficino.

[23] Damasio de Frías, "Diálogo de la discreción," in *Diálogos de diferentes materias inéditas hasta ahora*, ed. Francisco Rodríguez Marín (Madrid: G. G. Hernández y Galo Saez, 1929). Frías notes that, "No se puede decir que la discreción tenga en el hombre algún fin que distinto sea de sí mismo . . . tiene, no el conocimiento de la verdad por fin, que éste es de los hábitos especulativos, sino la perfección de su propia forma." See Frías, p. 42, for a discussion of the distinction between *discreción* which is almost a virtue and *prudencia*.

[24] Baldesar Castiglione, *Il Cortegiano*, ed. Bruno Maier (Torino: Editrice Torinese, 1955) pp. 199–200. Castiglione offers these "regole universali . . . consideri ben che cosa è quella che egli fa o dice e 'l *loco* dove lo fa, in *presenza* di cui, a che *tempo*, la *causa* perchè la fa, la *età* sua, la *professione*, il *fine* dove tende e i *mezzi* che a quello condur lo possono; e così con queste avvertenze s'acomodi *discretamente* a tutto quello" (The emphasis is mine.) *(continued on page 44)*

1534;[25] Damasio de Frías' *Diálogo de la discreción* (1579); and, Baltasar Gracián's *El discreto* (1645).[26] Although Cervantes did not devote a particular text to the study of *discreción*, the range and frequency of the word and its derivatives in his works attest to its importance in the Spanish Golden Age.[27]

These works, however, deal exclusively with *discreción* as applied to the male member of society in his contact with others. When they treat of women the attitude varies significantly. Damasio de Frías, for example, asserts that woman is to be seen but rarely heard:

> Porque la discreción no ha de ser una y la misma en todos. . . . La discreción de un mancebo bien hablado sería necedad y bachillería en una doncella. . . . Lo que en el hombre es despejo y desenfado, en la mujer es desvergüenza o desenvoltura. . . . En las hijas no ha de haber otra discreción que la honestidad y saber responder preguntadas . . . calladas y muy vergonzosas en lo demás todo.[28]

(continued from page 43) Margaret Bates, in *"Discreción"* in the *Works of Cervantes: A Semantic Study*, (Washington, D. C.: Catholic University of America, 1945), p. 36, cites the prologue of the 1873 edition of *El Cortesano* as the source for Menéndez y Pelayo's classification of *Il Cortegiano* as a "manual de discreción." To date, I have been unable to examine the 1873 edition.

[25] Baldassare Castiglione, *El Cortesano*, trans. Juan Boscán (1534; rpt. Madrid: Cª Ibero-Americana de Publicaciones, 1931). The translation of the portion cited above in note 24 appears on page 146.

[26] Baltasar Gracián, *El Discreto*, in *Obras completas*, ed. Arturo del Hoyo (Madrid: Aguilar, 1960), pp. 70–145. Although the work was intended as a manual of instruction for the young prince Baltasar Carlos, its didactic value far exceeded those limitations. As the "Aprobación" points out, "Enseña a un hombre a ser perfecto en todo, por eso nos enseña a todos." In comparing *El discreto* with its predecessors, *El Héroe* and *El Político*, Arturo del Hoyo observes: "Pero sin discreción no resulta posible ni un héroe, ni un político, ni un prudente, ni una representación novelesca veraz de la vida y de la sociedad. Al configurar el tipo del discreto, Gracián . . . propuso el hombre ideal de su tiempo . . . nos ha dado la imagen ideal del hombre español del siglo XVII. Y en ese sentido, aportó un retrato universal como en el Renacimiento había hecho Castiglione," (p. cli).

[27] The best general discussion on *"discreción"* in the *siglo de oro* remains that of Margaret Bates (see n. 24, above). The range of Ms. Bates' inquiry is not limited to Cervantes' literary production but takes into account the major philosophical, religious and moralist texts which may have influenced Cervantes' view of discretion.

[28] The use of the word "bachillería" to describe that amount of discretion

If Lope's age did not normally grant the quality of *discreción* to women, how could Lope justify his use of the adjective *discreta* to characterize his heroine? Is he in complete disagreement with his contemporaries? I do not believe so. Lope's purpose is to entertain, to offer his public, caught up in the pressures of day-to-day living, a glimpse of an earthly paradise[29] only to return at the end of the play to the preordained resolution demanded by the society for which he wrote. Within these limits, Lope is free to grant his heroine the same degree of *discreción* normally accorded the male provided the objectives are sanctioned by the society it represents.

Lope's title, then, is chosen with precision and deliberation. The seeming incompatibility of the terms *discreta* and *enamorada* was, no doubt, intended to fire the spectator's curiosity. A study of the play, however, reveals that Lope was aiming at more than a clever title to attract attention. Fenisa is *discreta* in the fullest sense of the word throughout the comedy. The nature of the theme, *Fortuna* coupled with *discreción*, mandates that Fenisa be in full possession of her faculties, that she be *cuerda y de buen seso* if she is to turn the course of Fate rather than merely sidestep it as her Italian predecessor had done.

The examination of a few key episodes in the play will show that Fenisa indeed exemplifies these qualities and that *discreción* may well serve as a remedy against adverse fortune. In a matter of a few scenes at the play's inception Fenisa manages to attract the attention of the man she secretly loves through the ploy of the dropped hankerchief; to fend off her

---

acceptable in a male but unacceptable in a young woman is corroborated in the opening lines of *La discreta enamorada*. When Fenisa counters her mother's reprimands, she is silenced with "No repliques, bachillera," (395a).

[29] Francisco Ruiz Ramón, *Historia del teatro español* (Madrid: Alianza Editorial, 1971), pp. 196–197. Ruiz Ramón characterizes the world of Lope's theater as "un mundo donde todo acaba bien porque es la voluntad de su creador. Voluntad puesta al servicio de la ilusión, que, sin evadirse de la esencia problemática del vivir del hombre, . . . mediante el reflejo estético de la realidad cotidiana, descubre todas las salidas que el ser humano, apresado en su tiempo, tiene hacia el reino de la felicidad."

mother's hypocritical reproaches with learned arguments as well as common sense;[30] and, to trick Captain Bernardo into delivering a message to Lucindo. The latter pays tribute to her cleverness in the final verses of Act I:

> Pues con discreción tan alta
> Supo engañar a dos viejos
> De edad y experiencia tanta;
> Y enamorada de quien
> Apenas le vió la cara,
> Ha dicho su pensamiento,
> Y se le ha entendido el alma,
> Bien la podemos llamar
> *La discreta enamorada.*
>
> (409b)

Fenisa is both "discrete" and "discreet."[31] She is sepa-

---

[30] In the opening scene, Fenisa counters her mother's reprimands for raising her eyes from the ground with a learned argument concerning man's upright form:

> Crió Dios derecho al hombre
> Porque al cielo ver pudiera;
> Y de su poder sagrado
> Fue advertencia singular,
> Para que viese el lugar
> Para donde fue criado.
>
> (395a)

The theme of man's upright form was popular in sixteenth-century religious literature. An example may be found in Frey Heitor Pinto's, *Imagen de la vida cristiana*, ed. Edward Glaser (Barcelona: J. Flors, 1967), p. 223. The text reads: ". . . Teniendo todos los otros animales la cabeza inclinada para la tierra, el hombre solamente la tenía levantada para el cielo. Quiso Dios que nuestra mesma figura y composición nos significasen que no éramos criados para la tierra sino para el cielo . . .". For further discussion of the theme see C. A. Patrides, "Renaissance Ideas on Man's Upright Form," *JHI*, 19 (1958): 256–258.

[31] *The Oxford Universal Dictionary on Historical Principles*, ed. C. T. Onions (Oxford: Clarendon Press, 1955), p. 523, offers the following definitions of "discreet" and "discrete": "Discreet (ME. discret, discrete, A. F. Ad L. discretus, in the late L. sense. A doublet of discret. 1. showing discernment in the guidance of one's own speech and action; judicious, circumspect, cautious; often esp. when speech is inconvenient. Discrete (ME and L. discretus, 'separate, distinct,' pa. pple. of discernire, a doublet of discreet). 1. separate, detached from others, distinct." For further discussion of the *discreto* as a man apart see Monroe Z. Hafter, *Gracián and Perfection* (Cambridge, Mass.: Harvard University Press, 1966), pp. 148–149. In relation to this second connotation,

rate and distinct from the two other *enamoradas*, Gerarda the cortesan and Belisa. In fact, Belisa might better be termed *enamoradiza*. The lack of judiciousness and circumspection on the part of Gerarda and Belisa points to their *necedad* and, by contrast, serves to amplify the portrait of Fenisa as *discreta*. I cite briefly two instances. In Act I, Gerarda's jealous tantrum provokes a quarrel which eventually destroys Lucindo's love for her. In Act III, Belisa, so eager for love, listens to Hernando's parody of a love speech as if the words were courtly love lyrics.[32] By contrast, during the initial nocturnal interview with Lucindo, Fenisa weighs her words and actions carefully. Having declared her love but before taking further steps, Fenisa insists: "pero tratadme verdad / o desengañadme aquí. . . ." (416a). It is only after she receives Lucindo's pledge of affection that Fenisa boldly sets her plan in motion. Despite the audacity of her scheme, however, Fenisa never steps beyond the bounds of discretion. At any given moment, she may withdraw from the game with her reputation intact, although she does at times push the situation to the limit.

Her invitation to Bernardo to bring Lucindo to the house so that she may give him her blessing results in one of the play's most delightful episodes. The air is charged with excitement as Bernardo, conscious of Lucindo's youth and handsome good looks, experiences uncontrollable pangs of jealousy. Lucindo's lofty homage to Fenisa provokes constant, angry interruptions:

Margaret Bates (*Discreción,* p. 94) notes that in the seventeenth century the second connotation of *discreto* encompassed the notions of modesty, equanimity, accommodation (which includes *disimulo* and propriety), inventiveness (tempered with *cordura*) and foresight." For a concise explanation of the evolution of the second meaning of "discreto" as "discriminating," "intelligent," see Yakov Malkiel's review of Bates' study in *Word,* 2 (1916): 99.

[32] Fenisa may well be said to possess that quality of *cuerda intrepidez,* the *audacia discreta* advocated by Gracián in Chapter II of *El Discreto:* "No hablo aquí de aquella natural superioridad que señalamos por singular realce al *Héroe,* sino de una cuerda intrepidez, contraria al deslucido encogimiento, fundado, o en la comprensión de las materias, o en la autoridad de los años, en la calificación de las dignidades, que en fe de cualquiera dellas puede uno hacer y decir con señorío." (p. 81).

Lucindo.	Como á madre que sois mía
	Me manda ¡Oh bien soberano!
	Qué os bese esa hermosa mano.
Capitán.	¡Que superflua cortesía!
	La mano basta decir;
	¿Para qués decir hermosa?
Lucindo.	Quiere mi boca dichosa
	Este epíteto añadir. . . .
Capitán.	Levántate; que no gusto
	Que beses con epítetos.

Fenisa's benediction, while her elderly suitor continues to grumble, is a fine example of the *engañar-con-la-verdad* technique. The blessing is indeed within the bounds of discretion. The previous night's interview, however, renders the words a simultaneous pledge of love:

> Dios te bendiga y prospere;
>   Dios te dé mujer que sea
> Tal como la has menester;
> En efecto, venga á ser
> Como tu madre desea.
> Dios te dé lo que á este punto
> Tienes en el corazón;
> Quien te da su bendición,
> Todo el bien te diera junto
> . . .   .
>   Y te dé tanto sentido
> En querer y obedecer,
> Que te pueda yo tener
> Como en lugar de marido.
>   (419a)

Lope accentuates the degree to which Fenisa has successfully duped both parents through Bernardo's congratulatory speech to Belisa the next day, upon learning that Lucindo wishes to marry her. The marriage proposal is a lie invented by Fenisa to keep Bernardo, in his jealous anger, from sending Lucindo to Portugal. Lope's use of the word "discreción" in this context heightens the absurdity of the situation:

> Casado con quien es madre
> De mi bien, como confío
> De vos misma, el hijo mío

48

Vengo yo á tener por padre;
Y Fenisa, mi mujer,
Y vuestra hija, tendrá
Padre en Lucindo; y dará
A todo el mundo placer
    La discreción del trocar
Las edades por los gustos.
                    (428b)

Lope's *discreta enamorada*, however, unlike her silly
mother, Belisa, or the pompous Captain, never loses her grip
on the surrounding reality. With cool, deliberate actions she
foils each and every obstacle to her happiness: an elderly
suitor, an avaricious mother, and an intriguing former lover of
Lucindo. In one final maneuver, she arranges for Lucindo to
visit her at night and tricks Bernardo into going to Belisa's
room where he is not recognized until it is too late. That
Fenisa's behavior is less than exemplary matters little. Lope's
audience was more than willing to overlook the circumvention
of the moral code in the name of love, especially if the object of
the subterfuge was matrimony.

In this light, Boccaccio's tale becomes less of a joke perpetrated by a married woman on an unsuspecting dupe than a
love story which ends in lawful marriage. Lope captures all of
the spontaneity, humor, and liveliness of the Italian story and
translates it into a play which reflects the standards, cultural
values, and aspirations of the world around him. Lope retains
the fundamental theme of *Fortuna* coupled with *industria* but
reproduces it within a moral context, emphasizing Fenisa's
discreción in turning the course of Fate in order to marry the
man of her choice.

If Lope espoused the view that man can control his fate
by the intelligent application of free will coupled with discretion and prudence or by the quickness to seize the occasion, he
also recognized that man might sometimes be helpless in the
wake of adverse circumstances. No amount of forethought or
planning could avert Ruggieri's poor treatment at the hands of
Alfonso, king of Spain (*Decameron*, X, 1) or Griselda's at the
hands of her husband (*Decameron*, X, 10). Lope, however,
eschews a fatalistic vision and focuses, in these instances, on

man's ability to ride out the storm by opposing to it virtue, constancy, and patience in keeping with the Christian stoic ideals of his time.[33] *El servir con mala estrella* and *El ejemplo de casadas y prueba de la paciencia* form part of this tradition as Lope offers, respectively, a knight exemplar and a perfect Christian wife.

El servir con mala estrella

Boccaccio's Ruggieri de Figiovanni faithfully serves Alfonso VII of Spain for many years but is never rewarded, even though other knights have been regaled handsomely. When the knight asks for permission to return to Italy, he is given a mule as a parting present. The king also sends along a servant who, unknown to Ruggieri, is to report on anything the knight may say against the sovereign. The same afternoon, as Ruggieri and the servant water their horses at a river, Ruggieri's horse relieves itself, whereupon his master exclaims: "Deh! dolente ti faccia Dio, bestia, che tu se' fatta come il signore che a me ti donò." Other than these words, he speaks kindly of the king. The next morning the servant insists that Ruggieri return to court on the king's orders. When asked to explain the comparison, Ruggieri openly admits: "Signor mio, per ciò ve l'assomigliai, perché, come voi donate dove non si conviene e dove si converrebbe non date, così ella dove si conveniva non stallò e dove non si conveniva sì." The king exonerates himself for the lack of remuneration by arguing that his seeming neglect is due not to lack of recognition but rather to the knight's personal *Fortuna* which has kept the king from rewarding him: "Messer Ruggieri, il non avervi donato come fatto ho a molti li quali a comparazion di voi da niente sono, non e avvenuto perché io non abbia voi valorossissimo cavalier conosciuto e

---

[33] On the penetration of Stoic ideals in the literature of Spain's Golden Age see: K. A. Blüher, *Seneca in Spanien. Untersuchungen zur Geschichte der Seneca-Rezeption in Spanien vom 13. bis 17. Jahrhundert* (Munich: Franck, 1969) and Henry Ettinghausen, *Francisco de Quevedo and The Neostoic Movement* (Oxford: Oxford Univ. Press, 1972). See also Anthony Levi, *French Moralists. The Theory of the Passions, 1585–1649* (Oxford Univ. Press, 1964), pp. 429–455.

degno d'ogni gran dono, ma la vostra fortuna, che lasciato non m'ha . . . ," (p. 1103). As proof, the king presents Ruggieri with two coffers; one containing the crown jewels, while the other holds dirt. He then orders Ruggieri to select one of the two coffers. Ruggieri's choice falls on the box filled with earth. To counter this, the king voluntarily gives Ruggieri the jewels as a token of his esteem.

Although Lope does not alter the basic points of the story, it is now imbedded in an episode from Spanish history: Alfonso VII's love affair with Doña Sancha and the legend surrounding their daughter Estefanía. The historic context, rather than detract from the main thrust of the action, permits the dramatist to bring forth with greater intensity the injustice of Fortune, the knight's worthiness, and the ingratitude of the king.

Boccaccio's tale centers on the concept of *Fortuna* as a personal lot,[34] an individual destiny that guides the movement of each human being. Although Fortune is personified, it represents not the goddess herself but the events or those circumstances which the goddess brings about. Underlying the concept of a personal *Fortuna* is the notion of astral influences, a notion which held as much appeal for Lope's epoch as it had held for that of Boccaccio. As a cleric,[35] Lope could only agree with Saint Thomas (*Summa* I–II, Q. 9, art. 5) and Saint Augustine (*De Civitate Dei*, V, 6) that the stars could incline the will; they could not force it. As a dramatist in pursuit of a specific artistic effect, he found astral influences a convenient device. Moreover, Lope's public, like their medieval predecessors,[36] never abandoned faith in one or more occult and irresistible powers, distinct and separate from the Divine Will and variously designated as destiny, fortune or astrological influ-

---

[34] See Vincenzo Cioffari, "The Concept of Fortune in the *Decameron*," pp. 135–136, and Howard Patch, *The Goddess Fortuna*, pp. 112–113.

[35] For the opinions of Lope's contemporaries on this issue, see Félix J. Olmedo, S. J., *Las fuentes de "La vida es sueño"* (Madrid: Editorial Voluntad, 1928), pp. 192–198.

[36] See Arturo Graf, *Miti*, p. 276, and Frank Halstead, "The Attitude of Lope de Vega Toward Astrology and Astronomy," *HR*, 7 (1939): 205–219.

ence. The extent and commonplace nature of the belief may be gleaned from the playwright's own correspondence. Angered by poor treatment at the hands of his patron, the Duke of Sessa, Lope, not unlike Ruggieri, complains: "Esta negra casa . . . me obliga a ocupaciones agenas de mi natural condición pero nacimos algunos hombres con estrella que la misma cuna nos sirvió de galera, desde entonces vamos en la vida. . . ." On a positive note, in response to gossip concerning himself and Lucía de Salcedo, Lope remarks, "gracias a mi fortuna . . . no me han hallado otra passión viziosa fuera del natural amor. . . ."[37]

The references to "mi estrella" and "mi fortuna" are not to be taken, however, as manifestations of a deep-rooted belief in astrology. In Lope's theater, we may find as much evidence to the contrary as we would find in favor of belief in astral influence.[38] Sometimes, both views are evident in the same play. *El servir con mala estrella* suggests credence in the power of the stars. Yet within the text, don Fernando, a nobleman, in conversation with Turín, Rugero's servant, insists that the keys to Fortune's coffer are "pluma . . . espada . . . industria" accompanied by "la prudencia y la paciencia," (542a). The lines are especially pertinent since Rugero will have to choose between two coffers at the end of the play just as his Italian predecessor had done. Turín's refutation, "Que industria, pluma y espada, / si no hay estrella no son nada," returns to the theme as expressed in the title except for a subtle shift in emphasis as he summarizes his master's accomplishments. Rugero, he maintains, does not lack talent and his "estrella" is not against him. What stands between Rugero and his reward is the human obstacle of an unfeeling and ungrateful king:

> Tres llaves tiene gallardas:
> Pero pienso en parte alguna
> Que el arca de la fortuna
> Le ha mudado el Rey las guardas.
> (542a)

---

[37] See Amezúa, *Epistolario*, III, 92.
[38] See Halstead, "The Attitude of Lope de Vega," p. 206.

Thus, while Lope retains the *fortuna/estrella* concept, the vigorous presentation of Rugero's allegiance and faithful service as opposed to the king's prolonged insensitivity to his vassal's needs suggests strongly that Lope was merely giving lip service to the theme as good theater and may even have been ridiculing outright the accuracy with which such influences could be predicted. What emerges is a *comedia palaciega* in which a faithful knight patiently suffers the callous unconcern of his sovereign until the knight feels forced to withdraw, a gesture which brings the king to his senses.

From the play's inception, Lope focuses on Rugero's honesty and openness:

> Que los hombres de mi ley,
> Con esta lengua que empuño,
>   Que es de acero, han de servir.
> . . .   .
> No con lengua lisonjera,
> No con hablar ni fingir.
>
> (530a)

Nor is Rugero a coward. When offered the choice either to fight against the Moors or to be part of Alfonso's council, Rugero chooses to fight. He is humble and not given to exaggerated speech. Upon returning triumphant from the war, his simple greeting and reaction to Alfonso's praises stands in sharp contrast to the excessive verbal exchanges between the king and the other knights. Although disappointed by the lack of remuneration, he is unfailing in his devotion, hoping for some recognition in the future:

> Cordura de Alfonso fué:
> No hay sino esperar callando,
> Porque servir murmurando
> Sólo en gente vil se ve.
>
> (539a)

To his servant's insistence that even a small recompense is better than none, Rugero counters: "Servir por interés es cosa infame." He prefers to remain silent, believing that "Obligar con servir es buena estrella." Nonetheless, Turín's rejoinder, "Guárdate el cielo de servir sin ella," (540b), alerts the spectator to the possibility of continued ill fortune.

The entire second act is devoted to accentuating Rugero's fidelity and self-sacrifice which goes consistently unrewarded. Rugero's allegiance extends even to accompanying the king on his nocturnal visits to Doña Sancha to avert suspicion. As the play progresses, it becomes increasingly evident that Lope's Rugero is much more human and will not bear the king's neglect with the same patience shown by his Italian counterpart. Moreover, a seventeenth-century Spanish audience, steeped in the *honra* tradition, would have found the Italian knight's docility unconscionable. The astonishment of Act I slowly gives way to impatience and, finally, to genuine anger. When the king presents Rugero with a horse with which to leave Spain, the polite form of Rugero's thanks barely conceals his sarcastic intention. This is not to suggest a diminution of the monarchical ideal. Neither Rugero, nor the Cid, with whom Rugero is paralleled at the beginning of Act III, directly confronts his liege. He simply backs away to avoid further offense.

The musician's verses which recall the valor of the Cid and the subsequent ingratitude of his king, Fernando I, are intended to arouse spectator sympathy for Rugero who has endured similar disregard:

> Cuando el Cid vió que su Rey
> No le hacía ningún favor,
> Quiso volverse á Vivar;
> Pero consejo tomó.
> Díjole Martín Peláez:
> "Acertáis, Cid, mi señor;
> Que quien serve á dueño ingrato,
> Merece tal galardón.
> Quien sirviendo se envejece,
> Al leal perro imitó,
> Que viene á morir de·hambre
> A puertas de su señor.
>   (555b)

When the king finally offers a suitable reward, his excuse for the previous lack of recognition—an occult force which seems to prevent the gesture—falls limp in view of Rugero's long-suffering dedication and service. In Boccaccio, the king's gesture is seen as an act of magnificence which contradicts the dictates of Fortune. On the other hand, Lope's portrayal of the knight and the stress on his valor and discretion stand in such great contrast to Alfonso's verbal but intangible recognition that the king can only emerge as remiss and unappreciative.

Whereas the title of the play, *El servir con mala estrella* suggests a continuance of the medieval belief in astral influences and man as a plaything of Fortune, Lope's refurbishing, in fact, makes a case for the importance of human endeavors and for man's capacity to shift the winds of fate, however slightly, by righteous deeds. Although Rugero is in the end dependent upon Alfonso's generosity as visible acknowledgment of his service, he is, in and of himself, an exemplary knight. In serving Alfonso he acts independently, of his own free will. As such, we see him not so much as a victim of "mala estrella" as of the monarch's thoughtlessness.

El ejemplo de casadas y prueba de la paciencia

The shaping of *El ejemplo de casadas*, Boccaccio's Griselda story, though similar in approach, required substantial revision to make it a successful vehicle of entertainment. Rugero, as a knight, possesses considerable mobility and occasion for actively opposing ill fortune. Boccaccio's Griselda, as an exemplary Christian wife, is denied this latitude of movement. Patience, constancy and forebearance are her only weapons against the trials imposed upon her by her husband. While these palliatives could hardly fail to appeal to an age beset by economic, social and ideological disorder, their embodiment in Griselda and her resultant superhuman impassivity were unsuited to drama where conflict is the essence of success. It is to Lope's credit that he was able to recast this exemplary tale, more suited to the pulpit than to the theater, into a dynamic play without sacrificing the spirit of the original work.

In Boccaccio's tale, Gualtieri, Marquis of Saluzzo, constrained by his vassals to marry, chooses Griselda, daughter of a shepherd. Shortly after the birth of their first child, a daughter, Gualtieri is struck by a strange desire to test Griselda's patience by several intolerable deeds. On the pretext that his vassals are displeased with his choice of a humble wife and of consequent offspring of lowly birth, Gualtieri deprives Griselda first of her daughter and later, of her son. In each case, he pretends to order them killed, but in fact sends them to Italy to be reared by relatives. As a final test, he tells Griselda that their marriage was a hasty act and that he has asked for an annulment so that he might marry a younger woman of noble birth. Griselda is sent home to her father only to be recalled to the castle to prepare for the new bride's arrival. Satisfied that her patience and loyalty have been sufficiently tested, Gualtieri announces to Griselda, during the festivities, that the young girl and her brother are their children and that he wishes only Griselda as a wife. He explains that he has not meant to treat her with cruelty but only to teach her to be a good wife; to show his subjects how to choose and keep a good mate; and, to assure himself of a peaceful existence as long as they should live together.[39]

Though Lope's immediate predecessors in the adaptation of the Griselda story, Juan de Timoneda and Pedro Navarro, make several alterations to the material, it remains essentially an Italian tale. Timoneda, undoubtedly affected by the popularity of the theater, focuses on the literary rather than on the exemplary aspect of the work. Navarro attempts to vitalize the material through rudimentary psychological penetration. It remained for Lope, however, to give the tale its definitive dramatic form and to bring it into the mainstream of Spanish letters by hispanizing the content.

Boccaccio's Gualtieri becomes Enrico, Count of Barcelona;[40] Griselda is now Laurencia, a Spanish shepherdess

---

[39] Boccaccio, *Decameron*, p. 1231–1232. Boccaccio's Gualtieri explains: ". . . ciò che io faceva, ad antiveduto fine operava, vogliendo a te insegnar d'esser moglie e a loro di saperla torre e tenere, e a me partorire perpetua quiete mentre teco a vivere avessi: il che, quando venni a prendere moglie, gran paura ebbi che non mi intervenisse, e per ciò, per prova pigliarne, in quanti modi tu sai ti punsi e trafissi."

[40] Lope appears to have chosen Enrico as the protagonist's name simply to distinguish the Catalonian from the Spanish "Enriques." The historical

whose beauty, humility and discretion attract Enrico. Lope enlarges the role of Laurencia's father, emphasizing his refusal to come to court to live or to accept gifts from his daughter when she becomes a Countess. The expansion, coupled with the introduction of several minor characters from the countryside, enables the dramatist to make ample use of the *alabanza de aldea* theme. The plot is given historical relevance as Enrico (at the end of Act II) joins the armies of Richard of England and Alfonso VIII of Castile on their way to the Holy Land.

The playwright's recourse to the Griselda story is motivated by more than a passing interest in a well-known tale. Its appeal for both the dramatist and the spectator must be seen as part of a sustained interest in the stoic precepts of self-dominion and indifference to externals through the exercise of reason and will, within the bounds of Christian philosophy. The stoic resonance of the title *El ejemplo de casadas y prueba de la paciencia* is striking but not unusual. Spanish enthusiasm for Seneca had been considerable since at least the thirteenth century and was especially strong during the latter half of the fifteenth century.[41] The vogue for Senecan philosophy continued into Lope's era and was given new life by the work of Justus Lipsius, chronicler to Philip II, and subsequently, by Francisco de Quevedo.[42]

Lope's own attraction to Senecan precepts was life-long. Beneath the unceasing buoyancy and zest for life—as manuals of literature are wont to describe him—lay an incipient pessimism which became increasingly pronounced during his later life. We need only examine his correspondence to discover the strain of continuous sadness which, as the years passed, be-

---

references throughout the play are jumbled. On the title page Enrico is Conde de Barcelona; on page 9b, he is the Conde de Ruisellón. On 38a, Enrico speaks of going on a crusade with Richard of England and Alfonso VIII of Castile, to whom Richard has promised the hand of his daughter Leonor. Leonor, however, is not Richard's daughter, but the child of Henry II. On the latter see Luis Suárez Fernández, *Historia de la Edad Media* (Madrid: Gredos, 1970), p. 245.

[41] See K. A. Blüher, *Seneca in Spanien*, pp. 258–259.

[42] See Ettinghausen, *Francisco de Quevedo and the Neostoic Movement*, and n. 32, above.

came "una melancolía profunda, absorbente, densa y constan-
te."[43] Perhaps in recasting the Griselda story Lope sought to
persuade himself as well as the spectator that the chaos which
surrounded him could be endured and even conquered by
self-knowledge and control. Lope's appearance in the work,
as Belardo,[44] a favorite device, argues strongly for a personal
as well as professional affinity for the material.

In this connection, Lope, like his predecessor Navarro,
was closer in spirit to Petrarch's interpretation than to Boccaccio's *novella*. Boccaccio's Gualtieri, as noted above, offers a
threefold explanation for sounding Griselda's forebearance.
Petrarch's Gualtherius merely wishes to test his wife. The
latter version, however, ends with Petrarch's comment that he
has not retold the story in order to set before the wives of his
day an almost unattainable ideal but, rather, to encourage all
men to meet the suffering sent them by God with a constancy
equal to Griselda's in bearing the trials laid upon her by her
spouse.[45]

The Christian stoic thrust of the postscript is unmistakable, as is that of Lope's play. The repeated use of *constancia*,

---

[43] See Amezúa, *Epistolario*, II, 271–279.

[44] On the Lope/Belardo disguise see José María de Cossío, *Lope, personaje
de sus comedias* (Madrid: Real Academia Española, 1948), and S. Griswold
Morley, *Pseudonyms*, p. 429–430.

[45] Francesco Petrarca, *Historia Griseldis*, p. Cliij (sic). Petrarch's Gualthe-
rus announces to his assembled guests that he had merely wished to try his
wife: "Sciant qui contrarium credidere me curiosum atque experientem esse,
non impium, probasse coniugem, non damnasse. . . ." The postscript reads:
"Hanc historiam stylo nunc alio retexere uisum fuit, non tam ideo, ut ma-
tronas nostri temporis ad imitandam huius uxoris patentiam, que mihi uix
imitabilis uidetur, quam ut legentes as imitandam saltem femine constantiam
excitarem, ut quod haec uiro suo prestitui, hoc prestare deo nostro audeant,
qui licet ut Jacobus ait apostolus intemptator sit malorum et ipse niminem
temptet." The reference to James concerns his letter to the twelve tribes of the
Dispersion—those Jewish Christians living in the Graeco-Roman world—
which begins: "My brothers, you will always have your trials but, when they
come, try to treat them as a happy privilege; you understand that your faith is
only put to the test to make you patient, but patience too is to have its practical
results so that you will become fully developed, complete with nothing." See
The Jerusalem Bible: New Testament, ed. Alexander Jones (New York: Double-
day, 1966), p. 396.

paciencia, obediencia, humildad, alegría, to describe Laurencia's reactions is as Senecan as it is Christian. The degree to which Senecan principles had been adapted to orthodox Christian beliefs by the seventeenth century is evident from the description of the impassivity and joy with which Jesuit missionaries faced death in Japan: "Echóse bien de ver su constancia, quán de gana, con quánto ánimo y espíritu yvan a dar su vida por Christo . . . passaron todos . . . su gloriosa carrera con increyble y marabillosa fortaleza."[46] The fusion of joy and impassivity in anguish is no less dear to Lope.

When Laurencia is asked to give up her son, she replies:

> Que a ejemplo, gran señor, de mi paciencia,
> Con ella te daré tu prenda cara;
> Si conviene tu vida, tu Excelencia
> Crea que con la misma alegre cara
> Esperaré la muerte suya y la mía.
>
> (30b–31a)

Lope repeats the imagery in Enrico's aside: "¡Qué notable paciencia y alegría!" (31a); "¿Hay humildad como ésta? ¿Hay obediencia?" (31b).

Laurencia's fortitude is underlined through its opposite, the tears and disbelief of her lady-in-waiting, Fenisa:

> De tu paciencia me espanto,
> Condesa y señora mía,
> Pues muestras el alegría
> Cuando me deshago en llanto,
>   Tus hijos muertos, ¿estás
> En aquesa compostura?
> No sé qué piense de ti;
> De piedra tus ojos son,
> De bronce tu corazón.
>
> (31b–32a)

---

[46] The passage is taken from Juan de Santa María, *Relación que seys Padres descalços franciscos, tres hermanos de la Compañía de Iesus, y diecisiete Iaponeses christianos padecieron en Iapón* (Madrid, 1601), fols. 135ʳ–139ʳ, as cited in Ettinghausen, *Francisco de Quevedo,* p. 7 n. 30. On the Spanish missionaries in Japan in the sixteenth and seventeenth centuries, see the introduction by J. C. Cummins to his edition of Lope's *Triunfo de la fe en los reynos del Japón* (London: Tamesis, 1965).

In Act III, Lope, as Belardo, a fellow shepherd, recapitulates Laurencia's constancy and humility which by now has become legend:

> Vamos, que no es posible
> Que la fortuna adversa mude el pecho;
> Que al bien más imposible
> Estuvo humilde.
>
> (37b)

So famous is she in her devotion to Enrique that

> Llámanla en todas sus tierras,
> En extranjeras ciudades,
> De las casadas ejemplo
> Único, santo, admirable.
>
> (39b)

Laurencia faces the ultimate humiliation—Enrico's request that she make ready the house for the new bride—with customary good spirit. Lope underscores her patience, once again, through the opposite reaction in the servants. Tibaldo reports to Enrico:

> Ya por tu casa con placer camina;
> Las salas cuelga, y limpia hasta donde
> Se ponen los manteles de cocina,
> Tan contenta y alegre, que con vella
> Lloran los que le ayuden sólo en vella.
>
> (44a)

The success of Lope's play, however, stems not from the solace one may take in Laurencia's exemplary patience but, rather, from the warm humanity with which Lope infuses his heroine. Laurencia is not unquestioning in her acceptance of the torments to which she is subjected. She is an example of perfection, but hers is a human excellence, born not out of innate patience but of the obedience implicit in her marriage vows:

> Yo prometí esta obediencia
> Al estado que tomé;
> Sólo pido á Dios me dé
> En tantos males paciencia.
>
> (45a)

Although Laurencia capitulates to her husband's will, we are made to feel her conflicting emotions as she is tested time and again. In this, Laurencia evidences an independence of spirit not found in her Italian prototype. For example, when Enrico's impatience drives her friends away, she ventures a mild criticism. Enrico's feigned regret that he has married beneath his station is countered by a reminder that his vassals have often commended his choice of a wife. Laurencia does not conceal her sadness over the loss of her children. A tinge of bitterness is perceptible toward the end of the play when Tibaldo approaches with Enrico's last request: "¿Hay más pruebas de paciencia? / ¿Hay nueva persecución?" (42b) Yet despite these misgivings, Laurencia does not falter in her devotion. When she returns to Enrico, it is of her own free will; her choice as a thinking, independent woman. Virtuous in prosperity and forebearing in adversity, Laurencia meets the Christian stoic challenge of good and ill fortune.

Just as the submissiveness of Griselda was unsuited to the dramatic medium, the tyranny of the husband also lacks credibility. Lope attempts to soften the hardness through several introductory scenes which underscore Enrico's fear of marriage. Despite these additions, the nobleman's comportment throughout the play suggests that, at heart, Lope, like Boccaccio's narrator, saw the behavior of this character as "una matta bestialità" (p. 1218). The repeated but unheeded warnings of a loyal servant, Tibaldo, accentuate Enrico's obsessive pursuit. Lope appears to be creating in this instance, not a loving husband, but a *curioso impertinente* who takes to hiding behind doors in order to ". . . saber del todo / De aquella condición heroica el centro, . . ." (31b). Enrico's excesses, however, are deliberately intended by the playwright to thrust into sharp focus Laurencia's exemplary patience which, if it is to assume heroic proportions, must be severely tested.

A parallel may be drawn between the major characters of *El ejemplo de casadas* and *El servir con mala estrella*. Both Laurencia and Rugero are victims of adverse fortune. Their plight seems all the more unjust since they apparently have done nothing to deserve the misfortunes but have, rather, given unselfishly at every turn. While the reward, in each instance, depends solely on the magnanimity of an outside party, Lope builds a case for the worthiness of each protagonist so that the character does, in fact, affect the outcome, if only by the exemplary behavior which renders him deserving of the act of generosity. As a consequence, when the magnanimous gesture is put forth, it appears as no great gift but rather as something rightfully due each of the protagonists. In contrast to *El llegar en ocasión* and *La discreta enamorada*, where Lope entertained the notion of "seize the occasion," *El ejemplo de casadas* and *El servir con mala estrella* shift the accent to man's subservience to the wiles of Fortune for which the remedies are patience and right deeds.

III. Amore

Love in the *Decameron* is forthright, honest, spontaneous and natural, youthfully amoral and committed to its satisfaction by any and all means.[1] It is a part of the natural order of life, Boccaccio explains to his feminine readers: ". . . gli altri e io, che vi amiamo, naturalmente operiamo,".[2] Since love is natural, it is an instinctive, irrational force which transcends all barriers—age, social station or parental authority. Boccaccio's characters love by accident, not force: ". . . niuno secondo debita elezione ci s'innamora ma secondo l'appetito e il piacere."[3] As a God-given instinct,[4] there is neither guilt nor

---

[1] Aldo Scaglione, *Nature and Love in the Middle Ages* (Berkeley: University of California Press, 1963), pp. 49–82. See also Luigi Russo, *Letture critiche del Decameron* (Bari: Laterza, 1961), pp. 176–177; Azzurra B. Givens, *La dottrina d'amore nel Boccaccio* (Messina-Firenze: Casa Editrice D'Anna, 1968), pp. 141–192 and Robert Hollander, *Boccaccio's Two Venuses* (New York: Columbia University Press, 1977).

[2] The passage cited is from the Introduction to Day IV, Boccaccio, *Decameron*, p. 459.

[3] Boccaccio, *Decameron*, X, 7, p. 1161.

[4] R. Hastings, *Nature and Reason in the 'Decameron,'* p. 27, n. 7. Hastings calls attention to the story of Rinieri and Elena, *(continued on page 64)*

remorse attached to its satisfaction because, "Le leggi d'amore son di maggior potenzia che alcune altre: elle rompono non che quelle della amistà, ma le divine."[5] Love makes Boccaccio's characters quickwitted (as it does Lope's) and the intelligence derived therein has one objective: the satisfaction of the erotic instinct. Even when we find no explicit reference to it, as in the story of Federico and Monna Giovanna (V, 9), there is no reason to assume that it is absent.

As part of the natural law, love is superior to the laws of man and society. To stand willfully in the way of its fulfillment is to sin against nature and to court disaster.[6] Witness the tragic outcome of parentally thwarted love in the stories of Girolamo and Salvestra (IV, 8) and of Ghismonda and Guiscardo (IV, 1). How different is the outcome of V, 4, where a practical father, accepting the ways of nature and young girls, resolves the matter of his daughter's seduction by her quick marriage. In this world in which love reigns supreme, Boccaccio's stance is unequivocal: all is fair in the pursuit of love. There are no moral judgments to be made; there is no sense of sin.

It must be added, however, that Boccaccio's position is not to be viewed as condoning promiscuity and indiscriminate free love but rather, as an implicit criticism of the arranged marriages of the Middle Ages which denied love its rightful expression for the sake of political or financial expediency. It is a reaction against the excesses of Medieval spirituality with its emphasis on the mortification of nature and the flesh. We may view it as a plea for that balance between mind and body, spirit

---

(continued from page 63) *Decameron*, VIII, 7. Although the tale ends on a bitter note, the opening lines unequivocally assert the legitimacy of love as something divinely bestowed and sanctioned: ". . . e seco estimo colui potersi beato chiamare, al quale Iddio grazia facesse lei potere ignuda nelle braccia tenere."

[5] Boccaccio, *Decameron*, X, 8, p. 1168.

[6] Boccaccio, *Decameron*, IV, 8, p. 539. Boccaccio's narrator tells the story of Girolamo and Salvestra to point up the foolishness of those who would presume to oppose their logic to love; a presumption from which unhappiness springs, since love, as many other natural things, brooks no counsel or resistance.

and flesh, which characterized the Classical world; a plea which would find its fulfillment in the Renaissance. Love in the *Decameron*, then, its playful and delightful nature aside, is not to be taken lightly. It most often ends in a serious manner, i.e., marriage or tragedy. Thus, while Boccaccio appears to stand on the side of gratification of the senses, he is also suggesting that it be tempered with reason and discretion[7] (as does the widow in *Decameron* II, 2). For Boccaccio, marriage, the logical crowning of love, should be a free choice; marriage imposed from without is the mortal enemy of love.

Lope was no stranger, certainly, to love thwarted for the sake of monetary gain. We need but recall the scandalous affair with Elena Osorio and the lady's subsequent liaison with a wealthy Spanish gentleman who had made his fortune in the New World. As for love as a natural, irresistible force, Lope's multiple affairs of the heart, both in and out of wedlock, would indicate a kindred spirit, a predilection for love in all its naturalness not unlike that of his Italian source.[8]

The plays to be considered below, like their Boccaccian counterparts, turn the tables on those social conventions which would deny love's fulfillment: Lucinda, in *El ruiseñor de Sevilla*, emerges married to a man of her own choosing; Celia marries Federico ignoring his poverty, as reward for his selfless love and hospitality (*El halcón de Federico*); and Lauro,

---

[7] In conjunction with the use of the word *ragione* as applied to the use of reason in the regulation of human behavior and the control of natural instincts, see R. Hastings, *Nature and Reason*, pp. 38–39. On "discrezione" see Scaglione, *Love and Nature*, pp. 86–87.

[8] Most appropriate are the comments of Bruce W. Wardropper in "Lope de Vega's Short Stories: Priesthood and the Art of Literary Seduction," *Medieval and Renaissance Studies*, 2 (1968): 57–73. Wardropper maintains that "This penchant for disorder is Lope's greatest weakness as a man and as a poet. It was such a great weakness because it was only late in life that he recognized it. In . . . *Fortune's Remedy*, he asserts his opposition to art and to the disciplined life in the clearest possible terms: "El hacer versos y amar / naturalmente ha de ser . . ." (*El remedio en la desdicha*, Ac. IX, 178a). For the first fifty years of his life, Lope makes a virtue of spontaneity. From this irrational belief he infers, for his craft, the superiority of a first draft over a published one, and, for his life, the superiority of an illicit passion over conjugal love."

through a clever subterfuge, makes it possible for Febo to marry the woman he loves (in this case, Lauro's fiancée, Fabia) in *La boda entre dos maridos*.

Lope's wholehearted support of the lovers, similar to that of Boccaccio, must not be construed as open defiance of the prevailing social norms. The Spanish dramatist could not have been the success he was were it not for his consummate artistry in securing public approbation for the cause of love while ostensibly complying with social and moral directives. It is to Lope's credit that he could recast the three tales to meet the strictures of his epoch without losing the fullness and the spontaneity of love as expressed in the *Decameron*.

In selecting these tales for dramatization, we cannot help but wonder why Lope avoids the stories from Day IV, which treat of those whose love ends tragically. Certainly, these are the more powerful tales; stories in which unwelcome or ill-matched suitors are killed by the lady's father (IV, 1), brothers (IV, 5) or husband (IV, 9). Indeed, the tales would seem to encourage dramatization. The motivation for violence could easily be enjoined to the honor code which by Lope's own admission was good theater, for it stirred the hearts of all men.[9] The dramatist's subscription to this principle suggests that he was intuitively aware of the ritualistic function served by the theater and the obligation of the playwright to consciously celebrate, in that theater, the values of his nation. Yet Lope's attitude toward the honor code and its exigencies is not easily delimited and is rarely the same for very long. In his book on Lope's honor plays, Donald Larson notes that while in his later plays Lope treats the plight of the dishonored protagonist with evident sympathy, in the early plays, Lope "advocates forbearance and understanding in the face of personal dishonor." These early plays, Larson establishes, have certain distinguishable traits:

(1) a tendency to attribute the ultimate responsibility for the protagonist's dishonor to the protagonist himself;

---

[9] See Lope Félix de Vega Carpio, *El arte nuevo de hacer comedias en este tiempo*, ed., Juana de José Prades (Madrid: C.S.I.C., 1971), p. 298.

(2) A propensity, resulting from the preceding, to regard the actions of the offenders as partially excusable; and

(3) a concomittant disinclination to allow the offenders to suffer any extreme form of vengeance, thus permitting them to be rehabilitated at the end of the piece and the play to achieve a happy or "comic resolution."[10]

In light of the foregoing, and given the dates for the Boccaccian comedies as established by Morley and Bruerton, the motivation for Lope's choice of love stories is quite clear. At this stage Lope prefers those tales of lovers who, after fierce or unfortunate accidents, find happiness, rather than those whose love is doomed from the start.

While the plays to be discussed below may not properly be termed honor plays, they do form part of Lope's early theater and as such partake of the characteristics noted above. Camilo's lies, in *El halcón de Federico*, provide the occasion for what he imagines to be an act of infidelity on the part of his wife. Lucinda's father in *El ruiseñor de Sevilla*, all too indulgent toward his daughter's whims and equally stubborn as concerns her marriage, encourages deceit. Lope's attitude toward the main characters, in conjunction with the second point, is lenient. We are reminded that Federico's pursuit of Celia, though she is married, is motivated by love, an exemplary love which will be borne out by the sacrifice of the falcon. Lucinda of *El ruiseñor de Sevilla* is a healthy, lusty woman in need of a husband. Febo's only offense in *La boda entre dos maridos* is his great love for Lauro, whom he allows to secretly marry his own fiancée. In all three plays the protagonists come to no harm and are restored to their positions in society through marriage, or in the case of *La boda entre dos maridos*, through the generosity of a friend.

El ruiseñor de Sevilla

Ernest J. Templin describes the lover in the *comedia* as a "sort of adolescent who has not reached the age of discretion,"

---

[10] Donald R. Larson, *The Honor Plays of Lope de Vega* (Cambridge, Mass.: Harvard University Press, 1977), p. 24.

a most appropriate description of the lovers in these three plays. Here love is a temptation of the flesh, sudden in its inception and one to which the young, lacking experience, easily succumb. It is for this reason that their transgressions are viewed indulgently. Lope, like Boccaccio, seems to be arguing for the naturalness of love, especially in the young, and the wisdom of applying less rigid criteria for the restoration of honor wherein "the vagaries of youth come within the control of marriage." Marriage in the *comedia*, Templin avers, is not only the "*remedio* for youthful irregularities and brainlessness, but also the *enmienda* which annuls all past errors, thereby rendering condonement possible and vengeance unnecessary."[11] The indulgent attitude, common among the earlier *siglo de oro* playwrights, is ascribable in part to the influence of Lope and is best exemplified by a line from the Conde Claros ballad, "Que los yerros por amores-dignos son de perdonar, . . ."[12] The frequency of reference in Lope's plays to the *yerros* and their extenuation, Templin asserts, may well be said to

---

[11] Ernest H. Templin, *The Exculpation of "Yerros por Amores" in the Spanish Comedia*, University of California Publications in Languages and Literatures, I. no. 1 (Berkeley: University of Californis Press, 1933), pp. 1–50. The degree to which this formulistic resolution dominated comedies of intrigue in the seventeenth century is noted by Arturo Farinelli: "El público . . . estaba mal acostumbrado: quería la absolución para todos los desafueros . . . quería tener la pareja casada al terminar la comedia, lo mismo si este desenlace concordaba con los sucesos expuestos, como si no concordaba . . . Que la moral salga de ello perjudicada, ¿qué le importa al autor, qué le importa al público? El amor todo lo perdona; a él y a la tradición se ha de sacrificar todo" (*Lope de Vega en Alemania*, pp. 254–255). Ricardo del Arco y Garay shares this view: "Cualesquiera que sean las excepciones derivadas de la índole de los personajes o de la disposición particular de la trama, el amor tenía por punto de mira, por aspiración general, y por desenlace artístico, la honesta solución del matrimonio," (*La sociedad española*, p. 333). Lope himself affirms this pattern in *Lo fingido verdadero* (Ac., IV, 59a):

> Y aunque es comedia de amor,
> Si el autor no la remedia,
> No tendrá fin de comedia,
> Pues no ha de parar en bodas.

[12] See the "Tratado de los romances viejos," II, in Vol. VII of the *Antología de poetas líricos castellanos*, Vol. XXIII of the *Edición nacional de las obras completas de Menéndez y Pelayo* (Santander: Aldus, 1944), 292–297.

represent "an ethical attitude arising from personal experience and . . . for that matter . . . , posterity . . . can find no more suitable epitaph to inscribe on certain episodes of his life."[13]

This is most certainly the case in *El ruiseñor de Sevilla* where the *yerros por amores* theme is imbedded in what I perceive to be not just another *comedia* but, rather, an exultant tribute to the consummation of Lope's love for Micaela de Luján. To my knowledge the play has not previously been seen in this light. I cannot help but wonder if Catherine Bourland did not perhaps intuit the special nature of this play when she commented: "The characters are well thought out and life-like, and those added by Lope are consistent with the spirit of the original story."[14]

Boccaccio's story of Caterina and Ricciardo Manardi, and the sudden discovery of their love nest by the lady's father, while pleasantly diverting, is too brief an episode to hold the interest of a seventeenth-century audience for two hours. Lope's expansion includes the addition of Riselo, a servant and friend of the gallant; an unwelcome suitor forced upon the lady by her father; Fabio, the father's elderly friend whose daughter, Lisarda, appears disguised as a man throughout the play; and Adrián, the heroine's brother, whom Lisarda loves. Lope's approach to this play is similar to that for *La discreta enamorada*; in the name of love all subterfuges, deceits,

---

[13] See Templin, *The Exculpation*, p. 41, n. 15. On Lope's assumption of the name "Conde Claros" as a literary disguise, see S. Griswold Morley, *Pseudonyms*, p. 440. Morley comments: "Among the prefatory poems to the *Rimas humanas y divinas del Licenciado Tomé de Burguillos*, 1634, is a sonnet, 'España, de poetas que te honoran,' said to be written by 'El Conde Claros al Licenciado Tomé de Burguillos.' The legendary hero of Spanish balladry surely did not resuscitate in order to compose it. It is undoubtedly a composition by Lope to himself."

[14] See Catherine B. Bourland, "The *Decameron*, p. 122. Bourland's commentary includes the following evaluation: "The action throughout the play is extremely lively, the situations are humorous, and the dialogue easy and often witty. . . . Lope was evidently keenly alive to the droll humor of the original *novella* which he has succeeded marvelously well in recalling in his *comedia*. We cannot but admire the fine skill with which he has adapted for the stage a story, which, upon first consideration would seem wholly unfit for dramatic representation."

schemes and plots are pardonable provided order is restored at the end of the comedy and the couple legally married.

Lope's recourse to the tale of *l'usignolo*, as I posited earlier, goes beyond the recognition of its dramatic potential. The Italian tale struck a very precious, intimate chord to which Lope could not fail to respond. For one, the nightingale is the bird with which Lope associates his poetizing throughout his lifetime. We need only consult the dedicatory letter of *El ruiseñor de Sevilla*, addressed to Francisco Herrera Maldonado, to confirm the relationship. Writing at the time of the play's first edition in 1621, Lope responds in gratitude: "En mí, por lo menos, emplea vuesa merced un censo de alabanza perpetua, y aunque tan desigual mi Ruiseñor, sirva por la paga de este año, para que todos los de mi vida continue su voz y pluma este reconocimiento."[15] The title of a second work, *La Filomena*, written the same year, underscores the Lope/*ruiseñor* association.[16]

These texts, however, belong to Lope's mature years. At the time *El ruiseñor de Sevilla* was written (1603–1608), the Lope/*ruiseñor* configuration was already in force and enjoyed a unique context. It was an inseparable part of Lope's passion for Micaela de Luján.[17] *El Peregrino en su patria*, conceived and

---

[15] According to Castro y Rennert, *Vida*, p. 14, n. 4, D. Francisco de Herrera Maldonado, a close friend of Lope's family, was the canon of the Royal Chapel of Arbas de León and the author of *Libro de la vida y maravillosas virtudes . . . de Bernardino de Obregón* (Madrid, 1633), in which he provides information concerning the rare Christian spirit of Lope's father. Castro and Rennert note an epistle addressed to D. Francisco in the *Obras sueltas*, I. 309.

[16] S. Griswold Morley, *Pseudonyms*, comments: "In the second part of *La Filomena*, 1621, Lope reviewed his life and accomplishments at some length. He identified himself with the Nightingale, *El ruiseñor*, (Filomena), ..." (p. 471). On the poet/nightingale association in general see Albert R. Chandler, *Larks, Nightingales and Poets* (Columbus: Ohio University Press, (1938) and A. de Vries, *Dictionary of Symbols and Imagery*, 2nd ed. rev. (Amsterdam: North-Holland Publishing Company, 1976),p. 341.

[17] On Lope's relationship with Micaela de Luján, the Camila Lucinda of his poetry, see Castro y Rennert, *Vida*, pp. 401–430; Cayetano de la Barrera, *Nueva biografía de Lope de Vega* (Madrid: Atlas, 1973, *BAE*, CLXII), pp. 299–312; Joaquín Entrambasaguas, *Vivir y crear de Lope de Vega* (Madrid: C.S.I.C., 1946), pp. 211–247; and, Emilio Cotarelo y Mori, "La descendencia de Lope de Vega," *BRAE*, 2 (1915); 21–56. For additional bibliography on the topic see José

executed at about the same time, or shortly before *El ruiseñor de Sevilla*, contains an exquisitely tender poem in tercets, "Serrana hermosa que de nieve helada," which recounts with painful delicacy, the separation of Lope (el ruyseñor) from Micaela ("Lucinda") and the children ("mis dulzes paxarillos"):

> No suele el ruyseñor en verde selva
> llorar el nido de uno en otro ramo
> de florido arrayán y madreselva
> con más doliente voz que yo te llamo
> ausente de mis dulzes paxarillos
> por quien en llanto el coraçón derramo.
> . . .   .
> Lucinda, sin tu dulze compañia
> y sin las prendas de tu hermoso pecho
> todo es llorar desde la noche al día,
> que con sólo pensar que está desecho
> mi nido ausente me atraviesa el alma,
> dando mil nudos á mi cuello estrecho; . . .[18]

The same *ruyseñor*/*nido*/Lucinda imagery is repeated, with a slight temporal shift, in *El ruiseñor de Sevilla*. Here, Félix prays for night to fall quickly so that he may make his way to Lucinda's side for the first time:

> Para que el ruiseñor mas venturoso
> Que desde su tragedia tuvo amores,
> Entrando en su jardín, cante á Lucinda
> Y entre los dos un nido fabriquemos
> Que conserve este amor por largos años.
> (72b)

At the risk of unduly pressing the point, there are, beyond the *ruiseñor*/Lucinda imagery, several verses which allude to autobiographical reality. The hero's name is Félix, Lope's own middle name and a pseudonym employed by him from time to time.[19] To this potpourri add another name

Simón Díaz y Juana de José Prades, *Ensayo de una bibliografía de las obras y artículos sobre la vida y escritos de Lope de Vega* (Madrid: C.S.I.C., 1955).

[18] See Lope de Vega, *El peregrino en su patria*, Myron A. Peyton, ed., University of North Carolina Studies in Romance Languages and Literatures, no. 97 (Chapel Hill: University of North Carolina Press, 1971), pp. 349–356.

[19] See S. Griswold Morley, *Pseudonyms*, pp. 446–447, for further data on the Lope/Félix relationship.

frought with reminiscence—that of Dorotea, long recognized as the literary disguise of Elena Osorio. Is it unresolved rancor which prompts Lope to cast Dorotea in the role of Lucinda's cousin and confidant only to have her function, in the love scenes, as a *criada* and counterfigure to Riselo, Félix's manservant? That the emotional scars of the Elena Osorio episode were still tender and in need of soothing is evident in two portions of dialogue. After a misadventure with Don Juan over the affections of the cortesan Lucrecia, Don Félix asks Riselo to help him avoid such women. Riselo's offer to "ven conmigo, /Que a enseñarte a amar me obligo", however, is cut short with "No amar, que yo me lo sé; / Olvidar no más querría," (55a). But the ghost of Elena lingers persistently. It emerges once more in one of the subplots. When Lisarda (disguised as Pedro) is constrained to tell her story, she recalls the happy times in Mexico until:

> Vino el rico mercader
> De los famosos de Lima,
> Á dar agrio al dulce pecho
> En que yo entonces vivía.

The "rico mercader" is Filiberto, chosen for Lisarda by her family. Were these lines not sufficient to recall Francisco Perrenot de Granvela, Lope's wealthy rival for the affections of Elena, Lisarda goes on to relate:

> Servíame Filiberto
> Dentro de mi casa misma;
> Adrián sólo en la calle,
> Los dos al igual porfían,
> Aunque el que en mi casa estaba
> Lejos del alma vivía,
> Y el de la calle tan cerca,
> Que se me entró por la vista.
> (81b)

While the allusions have their basis in fact, the conclusion of the episode, in Lope's play at least, is pure fiction. A duel between the two men, Adrián's escape and Lisarda's subsequent flight to Sevilla and eventual reunion with Adrián is a long cry from the facts of the matter. It may well be that Lope, in reliving the past offers it to us not as it was, but as he wished it could have been.[20]

Elena Osorio, however, is not the only evocation from the past. A later love, Celia, is also part of the cast. The identity of this lady, known literarily as Celia has prompted several hypotheses.[21] She is generally believed to be Antonia de Trillo de Armenta, prosecuted for concubinage, along with Lope, in 1596. According to Donald McGrady, Lope proceeded with extreme prudence in this case and, contrary to his usual pattern, refrained from making public any details which might offend the lady's sensitivity. This is ascribed to the fact that the lady was from an upper class family attached to the court, in contrast to Lope's other loves, actresses from the lower classes who were accustomed to being in the public eye. Lope's restraint holds true for the lady's portrayal in *El ruiseñor de Sevilla*. She remains offstage throughout the play. We know only that she is Fabio's niece and that Fabio has arranged for her to marry Adrián. When Don Juan is rejected by the heroine at the end of the play, Fabio offers him Celia's hand and a large dowry as recompense.

---

[20] On Lope's constant evocation of his past and present love life through the names of his characters, see S. Griswold Morley and Richard Tyler, *Los nombres de personajes en las comedias de Lope de Vega*, University of California Publications in Modern Philology, 55, (University of California Press: Berkeley, 1961), pp. 17–18. Castro and Rennert, *Vida*, call attention to Canto XIX of "La hermosura de Angélica" in which Lope, in a poem celebrating Micaela de Luján, we find Lope/Lucindo relating in detail his earlier loves. On the same topic see also S. Griswold Morley, *Pseudonyms*, p. 460. As for the familiarity of Lope's contemporaries with his penchant for reliving the past, the protagonist in Alonso Fernández de Avellaneda's *Don Quijote de la Mancha* boasts: "Yo lo escribo . . . más heroicas poesías que . . . ha hecho Lope de Vega a su Filis, Celia, Lucinda ni a las demás que tan divinamente ha celebrado . . ." (pp. 45–46).

[21] On the possible identity of Celia see María Goyri de Menéndez Pidal, "La Celia de Lope de Vega," *NRPH*, 4 (1950): 347–390. According to this study, Celia = Lucinda = Micaela de Luján. See also S. Griswold Morly and Courtney Bruerton, "Lope de Vega, Celia, y *Los comendadores de Córdoba*," *NRPH*, 6 (1952): 56–78. Donald E. McGrady, in "La Celia de Lope de Vega: un misterio resuelto," concludes that Celia is Antonia de Trillo de Armento [*Lope de Vega y los orígenes del teatro español. Actas del I Congreso Internacional* (Madrid: EDI-6, 1981), 179–202].

Elena and Celia, however, belong to the past. The present play, if we may confide in the dates established for it by Morley and Bruerton,[22] is a song to Lope's newest love, Micaela de Luján. In this context, Riselo, go-between and message bearer for the lovers, also assumes extratextual dimensions. He may well be the fictional disguise of Gaspar de Barrionuevo,[23] intermediary for the Lope/Micaela liaison. A sonnet written at approximately the same time as the play attests to the close friendship. Lope, writing from Toledo, asks Gaspar, who was in Seville at the time, to assure the lady of his devotion:

> Gaspar, si enfermo está mi bien, dezilde
> Que yo tengo de amor el alma enferma,
> Y en esta soledad desierta y yerma,
> Lo que sabéis que passo persuadilde.
>   Y para que el rigor tiemple, aduertilde
> Que el médico también tal vez enferma;
> Y que segura de mi ausencia duerma,
> Que soy leal quanto presente humilde.
>   Y aduertilde también, si el mal porfía,
> Que trueque mi salud á su accidente,
> Que la que tengo el alma se la embía.
>   Decilde que del trueco de contente;
> ¿Mas, para qué le ofrezco salud mía?
> ¡que no tiene salud quien está ausente![24]

What Lope offers, then, in *El ruiseñor de Sevilla* is not just another love story, but the story of Lope and Micaela, illicit, to

---

22 Morley and Bruerton, *Cronología*, pp. 265–266, establish the dates of the play as being between 1604 and 1608.

23 On Lope and Gaspar de Barrionuevo see Castro y Rennert, *Vida*, p. 141 and p. 141, n. 37. Riselo as a character in Lope's writings was also a well known pseudonym for Pedro Liñán de Riaza, another close friend of Lope. On Lope's friendship with the latter see Castro y Rennert, *Vida*, p. 63, n. 14; J. F. Montesinos, *Poesías líricas de Lope de Vega*, Clásicos castellanos no. 68 (Madrid: Espasa Calpe, 1925), I, 214; J. de Entrambasaguas, "Cartas poéticas de Lope de Vega y Pedro Liñán de Riaza," *Fénix*, I (1935): 227–261; and, Agustín G. de Amezúa, *Epistolario*, II, p. 88. Also see Myron A. Peyton, ed., *Peregrino*, p. 473, n. 112.

24 See Lope de Vega, *Rimas*, fol. 313 as cited by Castro y Rennert, *Vida*, p. 141, n. 37.

be sure, but none the less passionate and all consuming. In the name of love Lope asks us to look indulgently upon his protagonists, literary as well as real-life, and to grant them pardon. I would venture further, if we are to judge by the unbridled sensuality which pervades the work, that the play was written at the height of the Lope/Micaela passion which, like the play's setting, flowered in Seville.

In this spirit, Lope reminds us from the outset that love is natural, and that it is a strong, unrelenting emotion which will not be denied. Lucinda's melancholy is readily diagnosed by the elderly Fabio as "El ordinario mal de las doncellas: / El inmortal deseo de casarse," (57a). Love is accidental in its inception, more passionate and therefore less tempered by reason. As such, it is deserving of disculpation. Lucinda explains her passion for Félix insisting that, "No ha sido, prima, elección / Sino accidente y pasión / Que de mi estrella ha nacido . . ." (56b). Fortune and the stars have willed it so and she is powerless to resist:

> No hayas miedo que resista
> Al principio en que me veo,
> Porque es ya resolución
> Que de consejo carece.
> (56b)

The inseparability of *Fortuna/estrella* from matters of love is repeated as Lucinda, about to sign the contract of marriage to don Juan, is suddenly aware of don Félix's feelings toward her: "Pues, si don Félix me quiere, / ¿Qué estrella o fuerza podrán / Darme por dueño a don Juan?" Lucinda's subsequent action suggests that Lope, like Boccaccio, disapproved of loveless marriages and believed that one should do everything in one's power to resist. And resist she does. Making irreverent use of a church argument, (on fleeing the occasion of sin), the lady sidesteps the marriage by fainting dead away:

Lucinda. Quiero un desmayo fingir
          Y pasará la ocasión.
Dorotea. Siempre nuestras armas son
          Y nuestros pies para huir.
                    (61b)

75

Lucinda's swoon occasions a second reference to the swift violence with which love strikes as Riselo reports to Don Félix: "Desta torre fuiste el rayo, / Tú diste con ella en tierra," (62b).

Lope reminds us again, a few pages later, that love, like nature, will have its way: "Que rinda amor libertades, / no es milagro, es natural;" (64b) especially if it is given a hearty assist by Riselo, whose efficacious *salmo*, which restores the lady from her daily swoons, serves as a means of communication between the lovers and by an overly protective father who gives in to his daughter's every whim. The unrestrained emotional crescendo of these lines at the end of Act II, as Félix appears for the first nocturnal meeting with Lucinda, could not have escaped Lope's specatator:

> Lucinda del alma mía,
> Si soy vuestro ruiseñor
> Y he de cantaros mi amor
> Antes que amanezca el día,
>   Advertid que he de comer
> Picado ese corazón,
> De la amorosa pasión
> Con que me habéis de querer.
>   (75b)

Act II finds *el ruiseñor* at the center of the action. Lope can barely contain his exuberance as we are regaled with one instance after another of the *engañar-con-la-verdad* technique. The moments are delightful not only in their patent deceptiveness as concerns the other characters but also in the barely disguised erotic overtones which emanate from the Lope/*ruiseñor* parallel. While the latter may have escaped the censor, the audience was surely not oblivious to the implications of the nightingale's song which Lucinda claims to have heard:

> Lucinda, ten alegría,
> Que habrá en tus cosas mudanza;
> Espera, que el fin alcanza
> Quien esperando porfía.
>   Aquí estoy yo para darte
> Todas las noches placer,
> Y mis deseos contarte.
>   (77a)

Nor could the spectator have failed to chuckle at Justino's credulity: "Echad todos bendiciones / Al pajarillo galán, / Á su pico y sus canciones," (78a). Lope seems determined, in fact, to parade his identity before all and does not hesitate to indulge in a little self-adulation. The musician who has been called in to cheer the lovesick Lucinda, we are told, "Canta apaciblemente á lo moderno, / Con tonos de Juan Blas,[25] letras de Lope," (70a). Justino's request, "Y tú, pues letrillas pones, / Haz una del ruiseñor . . . ", is countered by "Yo la pediré, señor, / Á un hombre cuya poesía / Le ha enseñado el mismo amor, . . . " (78a).

As Lope sets the stage for the rendezvous-marriage, Lucinda's response to the good wishes of Félix is a shameless confirmation of their love, to which Félix responds with equal candor and not a little tongue-in-cheek, all in the presence of Justino and Don Juan:

Lucinda.   Señor, mi padre ha mandado os diga
             Vengáis cuando sabéis, y ansí os guardo,
             Sin que haya falta, porque importa mucho;
             Que sin duda es mañana el desposorio.
Félix.   Vendré á serviros como está tratado,
             Y á la hora que fuere conveniente;
             Que deseo en extremo vuestro gusto,
             Y yo sé que vendré primero que otro,
             Que estoy más cerca, como soy vecino; . . .
                          (83a)

The lovers can barely contain their passion as they react to the musician's song with imagery reminiscent of Lope's "Serrana hermosa . . . ", again within earshot of Lucinda's father and of Don Juan, the intended groom:

---

[25] Ricardo del Arco y Garay, *La sociedad española en las obras dramáticas de Lope de Vega* (Madrid: Real Academia Española, 1942), p. 730. Arco y Garay points out that "En muchas de las obras de Lope se cantaban bellísimas tonadillas, cuyas letras eran del poeta y la música la componía Juan Blas de Castro, gran amigo de Lope, músico y cantor de la Real Capilla desde 1605." See also J. F. Montesinos, "Notas sobre algunas poesías de Lope de Vega, *RFE*, 13 (1926), 151. On the occasion of Juan Blas de Castro's death, Lope composed his "Elogio en la muerte de Juan Blas de Castro," fragments of which are reproduceed by Castro y Rennert, *Vida*, pp. 396–397.

Félix.	¡Dichoso el ave que os da,
	Señora, tanto contento!
Lucinda.	Todo el que de oírlo siento
	Es pena cuando se va.
Félix.	¿Qué os dicen aquellas quejas?
Lucinda.	Que hemos de anidar los dos.
Félix.	¡Plegue a Dios!
Lucinda.	¡Quiéralo Dios!

(83b-84a)

The question of honor is conspicuous by its absence. In fact, the word appears textually in reference to Lucinda and Félix only after the lovers are discovered, and then it is the primary concern of the lady's outraged brother rather than of her father. The latter, recognizing his own hand in the deception, prefers a less violent resolution. Justino's order "¡Tente, que no importa nada!", as Adrián unsheathes his sword, is clearly a plea for benevolence and understanding. All that matters is love, and in the pursuit of it all errors are pardonable. Justino's tolerant view and the playing down of honor once the seduction has occurred, places Lope's father figure squarely in the same camp as Boccaccio's Lizio di Valbona. There is no moral outrage, no sense of culpability; only a desire to remedy the irregularity through marriage.

In sum, the numerous biographical allusions, the lively, droll humor, the witty dialogue and the indulgent spirit with which the liaison of Lucinda and Don Félix is resolved, point to more than a passing fascination for a Boccaccian theme. Lope recognized a kindred view of life and love in the persistence of Caterina and Ricciardo in fulfilling their need for love beyond the dictates of social convention. *El ruiseñor de Sevilla* is not just another dramatic reshaping; it is the story of Lope and Micaela unabashedly told. Lope revels in the exuberant sensuality of that love and asks us to look indulgently upon it:

Aquí *El ruiseñor* se acaba:
Si cual debe no cantó
El señor será el senado,
Y el autor el ruiseñor,
Pues el señor, al que es ruin
Bien puede dalle perdón.

(88b)

El halcón de Federico

In his discussion of courtly love in Spanish literature, Otis H. Green recalls those elements of the convention which were still operative for the *siglo de oro* dramatist. The components, present in fully developed or adumbrated form throughout the sixteenth and seventeenth centuries are:

> . . . that love is ennobling, the business of courteous and gentle hearts; that it is born of the contemplation of a beautiful woman; that suffering for its sake is or has been thought to be blessed; that the beloved is superior to the lover, . . . that desire is the essence of love . . . that such a love is . . . unholy, a truancy, from which a return must be made, either through marriage, or through the designation of oneself as a warning to others.[26]

That this codified medieval tradition still held sway in Lope's time, Green maintains,[27] is apparent from the comments of two sixteenth-century moralists: Alonso de Cabrera and Juan de Pineda. Cabrera, court preacher to Philip II, berates those husbands who behave in a manner reminiscent of medieval courtiers, urging them "not to enter, not to engage in conversation, not to hover about her house at night, not to make presents nor receive them, . . . all of which things, no matter how pure you make them, . . . are not as holy as partaking of the Body of Christ."[28] Fray Juan de Pineda's *Agricultura christiana* is even more specific. Here Spanish gentlemen are reproached for their dissolute living, excessive eating, gambling and parading through the streets "gathering unto yourself eager glances from attractive windows, coveting what is behind them . . . . "[29]

Yet these very elements, so severely condemned by

---

[26] See Otis H. Green, *Spain and the Western Tradition* (Madison: The University of Wisconsin Press, 1963), I, 96.

[27] Ibid., p. 236.

[28] Fray Alonso de Cabrera, *Consideraciones en los evangelios* (Barcelona, 1609) as cited in Luys Santa María, *La vida cotidiana en nuestros clásicos* (Barcelona: C.S.I.C., 1948), p. 50.

[29] Fray Juan de Pineda, *Los treynta y cinco diálogos familiares de la agricultura cristiana* (Salamanca, 1589), II, fol. 26 as cited and translated by O. H. Green, *Spain and the Western tradition*, I, 235.

moralists, are those in which the Golden Age theater abounds. Sacrifices made in the name of love are as appealing to Lope's audience as they had been to that of Boccaccio. In Spain the tradition had at its source, Macías, the persistent lover and poet of *cancionero* fame. The versions of the legend are multiple. The principal components, however, are few: Macías' intense and impossible love for a married lady who begs him to desist, his imprisonment for his own safety, and his eventual death at the hands of the offended husband. The latter, angered beyond endurance by Macías' songs to the lady, supposedly hurled a lance through the barred window of the poet's cell. In another version, Macías is killed on the spot for refusing to move from the ground on which his lady has stepped. Despite the fact that in both versions the love is illicit, impossible and punished by death, Macías remains, "a great and virtuous martyr of Cupid."[30]

Lope, too, was susceptible to the lure of the Macías legend and dramatized it as *Porfiar hasta morir*. Since historical data concerning the lover was largely nonexistent, playwrights were free to elaborate on the portrayal in any way which seemed appropriate. According to Menéndez y Pelayo, Lope drew primarily form the *Nobleza de Andalucía* for the facts of Macías' life.[31] In relation to *El halcón de Federico*, *Porfiar hasta morir* stands at the opposite end of the spectrum. A brief consideration of the latter, however, will serve to bring into sharper focus the approach to courtly love as expressed in *El halcón de Federico*.

Porfiar hasta morir is a late honor play. Hence, the treatment of love is markedly different from that of Lope's earlier plays. Love is no longer a temptation of the flesh attributable to the youth of the protagonists. It is now an obsessive passion lightning-swift in its onset and growth, sweeping all obstacles

---

[30] See O. H. Green, *Spain and the Western Tradition*, I, 237 and M. Menéndez y Pelayo, *Estudios sobre el teatro de Lope de Vega*, 2nd ed. (Madrid: C.S.I.C., 1949), V, 9.

[31] For a review of the sources for Lope's version of the legend see Menéndez y Pelayo, *Estudios*, V. 7–13.

before it, oblivious to conventions, scruples or shame. It is a disease for which there is no remedy save death, a blessed sacrifice. Yet we are moved to pity for Macías, the otherwise perfect lover who, in his human weakness, is unable to stem the tide of his passion and in the end must be punished. Alongside the pity we feel for the lover, it is obvious that Lope is moved by the plight of the dishonoured protagonist and that he does not entirely condemn the violent resolution to which the husband resorts.

As a play of Lope's mature years, *Porfiar hasta morir* differs considerably in technique from *El halcón de Federico*, written before 1605. Here, the playwright's attitude toward courtly love, offense and castigation, right and wrong, is not so clearly formulated. Rather, we are acutely aware of its vacillating, inconsistent nature. For one, we may not expect to find in this early play, though the theme be courtly love, the precise, carefully ordered development of plot as in *Porfiar hasta morir*. *El halcón de Federico* reflects that inclination already seen in *El ruiseñor de Sevilla* toward leniency and pardon for the follies committed in the name of love and toward a non-sanguine resolution as concerns honor. This, however, is not easily effected. In fact, it is only with the greatest awkward-ness that Lope unites Federico and Celia at the end of the piece. A number of elements leave the reader with a sense of disease, one which stems, at base, from Lope's own discom-fort in adjusting Boccaccio's tale of courteous love and sacrifice to the exigencies of his craft. Thus, while Lope's Federico appears to mouth the customary courtly phrases in Act I, we also perceive him as cruel and unkind in relation to a former love, Julia. While Celia, the heroine, responds at times with equally courtly sentiments, she also engages in an unseemly altercation with Julia over Camilo. And ironically, it is Camilo, Celia's husband, whose life is sacrificed to honor.

Lope's awkward handling of the chivalric theme may be explained in part by the fact that despite the public's continued interest in tales of courtly gallantry, the stilted, refined senti-ments were, during the dramatist's early years, incompatible with his view of human relationships and of the literary profession. For Lope, "el hacer versos y amar / naturalmente ha de ser",[32] a sentiment we find repeated in *El halcón de Federico*:

> Yo escribo Perote amigo,
> Enseñado de mi amor,
> Sin más arte que el dolor
> Del imposible que sigo.
> (452b)

As a consequence, although Lope adheres to the stylized ideals of courtly love, it is soon apparent that the adherence is more cosmetic than ethical and that the veneer of gallantry, despite protestations of respect and humility, is marred by the simultaneous desire to effect an assignation.[33]

The uneasiness with courtly gallantry not withstanding, Lope found Boccaccio's tale too enchanting to resist and set about transposing it to the Spanish stage. Boccaccio's narrator tells of Federico degli Alberighi who, having squandered his fortune in hopeless pursuit of Monna Giovanna, a virtuous married lady, retires to a tiny estate where he ekes out a living by farming and by hunting with his most treasured possession, a falcon. He kills the bird and serves it to the lady, now widowed, when she calls on him. Disregarding Federico's poverty and in recognition of the love and devotion he has shown, the lady marries him.

Prolonged, hopeless courtships, however, are incompatible with a genre which demands a rapidly unfolding action. In order to enliven a plot which might easily deteriorate into a succession of love scenes without resolution, Lope adds a number of minor characters who interact with all three protagonists. These are: Julia, a cortesan, former lover of Federico, recently visited by Camilo and subsequently threatened by Celia; Ludovico, who arranges Camilo's entertainment; and, a vacillating servant, Feliciano, who first betrays Celia's trust and later, that of Camilo. Two factors prompt a major amplification of the text: the narrative limitations of the source mater-

---

[32] See note 8, above.
[33] See Ernest H. Templin, *The Exculpation*, p. 20.

ial and the need to establish the bases for the husband's removal. The expansion, of necessity, centers on what in Boccaccio had been merely background; the lady's marriage relationship. As a result, a good portion of Act I and all of Act II are devoted to a multifaceted examination of Celia's marriage; her fears and jealousy; Camilo's sense of frustration and need to escape the bonds of matrimony which, in so doing, leads to the discovery of Federico's love for Celia.

Were this a late honor play, there would be little doubt as to the outcome. Yet Lope has no desire, at this point in his dramatic career, to create tragic works. He is determined to give primacy to love. And so he does. In a strangely concocted reversal, the husband is dispensed with and the lover eventually succeeds in winning the lady. Recognizing that the removal of the husband was not a logical outgrowth of the plot, Lope makes a vigorous effort to attribute the protagonist's dishonor to flaws in his own character. Camilo's callous treatment of Celia; the lies he tells regarding a meeting with the cortesan, Julia; his unwillingness to discuss the erroneously suspected affront with his wife; and the ease with which he jumps to false conclusions leave us with little warmth of feeling for his plight. On the other hand, Camilo's preference for madness and death is decidedly unconvincing. He emerges as an hysterical fool who, buffeted by a paranoic concern for honor and the concomittant inability to act, allows his suspicions to grow into madness. To what degree Lope's audience accepted the choice is impossible to ascertain. At best we may speculate that a character torn between equal and opposite and continually oscillating emotions, especially where honor is concerned, is not unusual. That he would choose madness, given the tenor of the times, is just barely credible.

Lope's opening lines tell us that Federico has passed the *fenhedor* stage. His actions are now that of the *precador* who has not yet received the *bel acceuil*. The lines play on a basic tenet of courtly love: the amorous passion characterized as ever-unsatisfied, ever-increasing desire. Federico views the prize he receives not as a testament to his prowess but, rather, as witness to the interminable yearning for Celia. In this, he insists, he is greater than his peers:[34]

> Podré decir que al deseo,
> Fabio, ese premio le dan;
>   Que como yo no lo estoy,
> Y tanto deseo ser
> quien pueda bien parecer
> A los ojos de quien soy,
>   Quien de galán me ha premiado
> Por donde aquel angel veo,
> Me ha visto, Fabio, el deseo
> De aguardar á quien no agrado; . . .
>
>   (443a)

In truly courtly fashion, Federico is a bond-slave of love. The feather of diamonds awarded to him comes to represent the sum of his hopes and the constancy of his love; the patient suffering and the heroic committment to an impossible suit which thus far has been met only with cold disdain:

> Que en plumas y diamantes dieron
> De todo mi mal la suma.
>   Pluma son mis esperanzas,
> Que lleva el viento inconstante,
> Y mis firmezas, diamante
> Al rigor de sus mudanzas.
>   Pluma son mis prevenciones,
> Que vuelan sin galardón,
> Y diamante el corazón
> Que sufre tantas pasiones.
>   Plumas son mis diligencias
> Contra un ingrato desdén,
> Y diamante el pecho en quien
> Caben tan largas paciencias.
>   Pluma es el loco volar
> De aquesta imposible empresa,
> y diamante lo que pesa
> El peso de mi pesar.
>
>   (443b)

It has been said that courtly love ennobles; that it makes a

---

[34] In relation to these lines and the courtly love syndrome as expressed in Sonnet CXXXIII of the *Rimas humanas* see O. H. Green, p. 234.

man generous, kind, brave, and above all, wise. If we are to judge, however, by Fabio's response to his master's plaint, Federico embodies few of these qualities. True, he performs the requisite services but, as Fabio speaks on, it becomes increasingly apparent that Federico follows the letter of the law, but not the spirit. In condemning the excesses of Federico, Fabio comes to represent the voice of the rigorist who notes the truancy and pleads for emendation. Reason, we are told, has escaped Federico; Will is in control. In his love-madness Federico has not only squandered his fortune; he has also made public, much in the manner of Macías, the pursuit of a married lady.[35]

Federico's subsequent praises to Celia's beauty offer another clue to the superficiality of his courtly demeanor. The commonplace metaphors dealing with physical attributes— *cabeza, frente, ojos, boca, dientes*—center on jewels, gold and silver. Notably absent is reference to her virtue, wisdom and prudence. As the conversation with Fabio progresses, Federico's courtly halo dims perceptibly. In the verses which follow we are regaled with a strange admixture of the courtly love tenets of Andreas Cappellanus[36] and the cynicism of Ovid's *Ars amandi*. Celia is depicted as the forbidden fruit which tastes all the sweeter if it is furtively possessed. If desire is the essence of love, and precisely why courtly love endures, then marriage is the ultimate boredom:

> La estimación de una cosa,
> El conquistarla ha de ser;
> que la fruta y la mujer,
> La hurtada es la más sabrosa.
> Si el oro que te he contado
> De Celia, tuviera yo,
> Del bien que nunca me dió,
> Fabio, estuviera cansado.
> (444b)

While I do not wish to exaggerate the importance of this

---

[35] June Hall Martin, *Love's Fools: Aucassin, Troilus, Calisto and the Parody of the Courtly Lover* (London: Tamesis, 1972), pp. 7–8.
[36] Andreas Capellanus, *The Art of Courtly Love*, trans. John Jay Parry (New York: Columbia University Press, 1941).

last point regarding marriage as synonymous with boredom, it is striking that the notion is repeated twice more in the play by characters other than Federico. Ludovico explains Camilo's lack of patience with Celia's possessiveness as deriving from the fact that "gustos casados / Son hoy lo mismo que ayer" (450a). That Camilo, too, views marriage as a series of routine, tiring demands is made clear as the two men approach the house of Julia, a cortesan:

> Vamos donde sin prisiones
> Una hora tengamos buena;
> Que me cansa la cadena
> De tantas obligaciones.
> (451a)

Is Lope trying to establish the primacy of adulterous love by focusing on unexciting repetition as a characteristic of the married state? To what degree is this a personal bias on the part of the author? I note that only the male characters find marriage boring. Celia loves and respects her husband; there is not a single utterance by her of dissatisfaction. If the dates of the play are correct (1601-1605), I suspect we may be dealing again with extratextual implications. Lope married a second time in 1598 and shortly thereafter (1599-1600) began his liaison with Micaela de Luján.[37] While Lope's first marriage was one based on love, the second marriage is generally considered to have been based primarily on financial expediency, or so we are led to believe by the comments of Lope's contemporaries.[38] While I am aware of the temptation to see biographical reference everywhere in Lope's work owing to the dramatist's penchant for airing his private life on the stage, a second comment by Ludovico would seem to support this allegation. When Julia refuses to see Camilo because he is married, Ludovico argues cynically:

> Escucha, advierte . . .
> Amor tiene dos maneras

---

[37] See note 17, above.
[38] See Castro y Rennert, Vida, pp. 110–11, n. 83, for the comments of Lope's contemporaries.

De gozarse: una el gusto
Y otra el interés . . .
    Haz Julia como discreta,
Uno mande y otro elija;
Que amor es estrella fija,
Y el interés es cometa.
    Párate con el amor
Que podrás gozar después,
Porque imite el interés
De la cometa el furor.
(454b)

Why, one wonders, does Lope argue for two kinds of love, for *gusto* and *interés*? Is this an attempt at self justification for his own extramarital affairs? While these questions are slated to remain unanswered, the multiple references to marriage as boring and the cynical advice to separate private needs from social benefits suggest more than a casual interest in the matter.

It must be noted that Lope's depiction of Federico is not intended as a rejection of the courtly mode. Rather, he recognizes that there is operative in every lover a conflict between the upper and lower man, between rational and sensible love, between good and evil. The lover in the *comedia*, I noted earlier, hardly qualifies as a rational lover, one in whom Will is subordinate to Reason. Certainly not Federico, despite the initial courtly phrases. He prefers to glory in his irrational love and the suffering it brings since the lady is not only married, but also chaste. Moreover, Lope is obliged to underscore this dualism, to stress the dominance of the sensible appetite, if Federico's "conversion" at the end of the play is to have the desired impact. An uncommitted lover would not have captured the audience's favor. Although the vocabulary remains ostensibly courtly, Lope continues to underline the flaws in Federico's character, now blatantly revealed in his conversation with Julia, a former love. Julia's declaration of continued affection meets with cruel disdain: "Ni me puede agradar nada, Julia, de ti," (445a). The very cruelty of which Federico accuses Celia, he does not hesitate to inflict upon Julia. Federico claims to burn all the more with love for Celia, though she rejects him: "Porque por eso merece / Que la quiera con más veras," (445a). Yet Julia's parallel circumstances stir no warmth in Federico's unfeeling heart. Rather, they are dismissed callously as "celos / Y envidia."

Lope stresses the height of Federico's insensitivity, his total lack of *cor gentile* in the latter's reaction to the threats made by Julia. We may argue that it is only natural for Federico to react with anger, and justly so. But this is a gentleman talking to a woman who has given him her love freely, yet there is no measure of understanding, no gesture of appeasement, only a challenge to make good her threats. In response to Julia's second threat to " . . . Decir / Á Celia que eres traidor," Federico delivers the ultimate insult. He would be perversely delighted to have the offended woman serve as go-between:

> ¡Ojalá que á Celia hermosa
> Le dijeses que la quiero,
> Porque no hay tan buen tercero
> Como una mujer celosa!
> (446a)

Lope may well have intended Julia's final retort, "Yo lo haré de modo; / Que . . . / Te pinte un bajo escudero / De vil pensamiento en todo," to sum up for the spectator the shabbiness of Federico's comportment and to suggest that not only is chastisement not far off, but that it is also richly deserved.

Should the audience have any doubts concerning Federico's obsessive love, the sonnet which brings this portion of the exposition to a close dispels all reservations. Lope examines the opposing forces which plague the lover, with one exception. Here the love/hate relationship, rather than center on the object of Federico's affection, is divided between the two women; love toward she who disdains him and abhorrence for the woman who loves him. Federico remains obstinate in his service to Celia, fully recognizing his truancy, "Que cuando amor lo que es razón pretende / Ya no es amor . . . ", which he excuses by reminding us that "Amor es niño y ciego . . . ," (446a). Like a child he pays no heed to reason; in his blindness he can see no error.

The juxtaposition of this scene of love-madness to Celia's measured reaction to the feather of diamonds delivered by Fabio accentuates, once more, the foolish extravagance of Federico's suit. That the lady, too, knows the rules of courtesy is apparent: "Por ser precio de torneo, / A quien debo cortesía, / La tomo . . . ." In the next breath, however, she rejects Federico's suit, gently but firmly. Like Doña Clara in *Porfiar hasta morir*[39] Celia is shocked by his daring " . . . de la porfía / Me espanto de su deseo." Recurring to the *diamante* imagery used earlier to signify Federico's constancy, Celia employs the metaphor to symbolize her own resistance to his overtures:

> Así podrá mi dureza
> Ablandarse á su porfía,
> Porque esta dureza es mía
> Si es suya aquella firmeza.
> (448b)

She is a loving wife aware of her marital duties and determined to fulfill them. Lope, however, is not creating a play about hopeless love as in *Porfiar hasta morir*. The lady will eventually marry Federico. Thus, while Celia firmly rejects Federico at this point, Lope so structures the response that the lady's subsequent change of heart is credible:

> No porque le quiero mal,
> Esto se lo confieso,
> Mas porque siento en exceso
> Que tenga esperanza igual.
> Que soy noble, estoy casada
> Con quien sabes; no he de hacer

---

[39] Lope de Vega, *Porfiar hasta morir*, in *Obras de Lope de Vega* (Nueva edición), ed. Emilio Cotarelo y Mori et al. (Madrid: Real Academia Española, 1916–1930), X, 425a-b. Doña Clara's lines are:

> ¿Qué he hecho á aqueste mozuelo
> que contra la ley del cielo
> me sirve y me quiere agora?
> Yo soy casada, y soy noble;
> será dar pasos atrás,
> que mientras me siga más
> pienso resistirme al doble.

Cosa en que pueda ofender,
Junto de quien soy, en nada.
(448b)

The dignity of the lines, however, slips appreciably in the final portion. The passage closes with a pedestrian reference to Petrarch and his love for Laura which deteriorates to coarseness as Celia equates *galardón* with *gozar*:

Dile que á otro mundo espere
Deste su amor galardón;
    Que allá me podrá gozar,
Como el Petrarca decía
De Laura.
(449a)

This is hardly the delicate Monna Giovanna of Boccaccio's tale, we are prompted to comment. That Lope intended to strike a humorous note becomes clear as Fabio brings the conversation to a close, comparing Federico's lovesickness to a contagious malady infecting the barn animals as well as all of the neighbors. The sheer foolishness of the parallel is designed to move the spectator to laughter as is Celia's consoling rejoinder:

Vete con Dios y dirás
Que cuando el loco de casa
(Ya le conoces, pues pasa
Siempre por la vuestra y mía)
    Cobre seso, podrá ser
Que él me ablande y yo le quiera.
(449a)

From this point on, any return to the language and imagery of courtly love would be ludicrous. The chivalric tone of the opening lines has been systematically eroded by all too human frailties. Federico's protestations of gallantry are belittled by his indelicate behavior toward Julia and the cynical comments regarding marriage. Celia's failings are apparent in her unladylike responses. The *coup de grace* to the courtly mode is administered by Fabio who echoes, most appropriately, words reminiscent of Andreas Cappellanus' *Reprobatio*:[40]

---

[40] See Andreas Capellanus, "The Rejection of Love," Book III of *The Art of Courtly Love*, pp. 187–212.

"¡Oh, amor, y qué cuerdos son / Los que huyen de ti, y son pocos!", (449a).

It is not Lope's intention, however, to discredit courtly love as a convention but rather, to recognize its limitations and abuses. Federico is a courtly lover in words only; his deeds remain seriously deficient. His persistence in loving Celia, in rendering service to her in tourneys and jousts and presenting her with the rewards is, in itself, not wrong. Celia is a lovely woman of a similar social class. Unfortunately, she is also married. In this light, Federico's excesses and impertinences, in the face of the lady's rejection, are questionable. They are more properly indicative of inordinate pride and self-love and therefore worthy of chastisement.

Federico, however, unlike Macías, does not meet death at the hands of the lady's husband. Instead he is punished for his extravagance by having to live in poverty; a penance which serves to temper his ardor with the element of *mesura*[41] derived from the daily struggle for survival. Thus it is a sober, judicious man whom we meet again in Act III, one who earns the right to Celia's love by the sacrifice of his beloved falcon, a sacrifice willingly made, without thought of recompense. Only in the selfless renunciation of his most prized possession, a gesture all the more powerful in the light of Federico's extreme poverty, does he achieve the status of an exemplary courtly lover.

La boda entre dos maridos

On the Tenth Day Boccaccio brings together the three major forces of the *Decameron* under the banner "si ragiona di chi liberalmente ovvero magnificamente alcuna cosa operasse intorno a fatti d'amore o d'altra cosa."[42] Magnificence in love, as concerns the story of Tito and Gisippo (X, 8) centers on

---

[41] Consult June Hall Martin, *Love's Fools*, p. 78. Ms. Martin cites Maurice Valency, *In Praise of Love* (New York: Macmillan, 1961) p. 176, who points out that the true lover's special virtue was "the quality called *mezura*, measure, that inner restraint which governs the appetites and keeps them subject to the intellect."

[42] Boccaccio, *Decameron*, p. 1097.

generosity in the name of friendship beyond the demands of that bond. Fortune and Wit also play their part. The former causes Tito to fall hopelessly in love with his best friend's intended wife. Wit enables Gisippo to marry off Sofronia, without her knowledge, to Tito. The magnanimous gesture, however, is not without repercussions. Tito is obliged to return to Rome upon the death of his father, while Gisippo is left to face the anger and vengeance of Sofronia's family. The second portion of the story centers on Tito's confession to murder in order to protect Gisippo who, having arrived penniless in Rome, is mistakenly accused of the crime.

Boccaccio's plot, despite its Byzantine character, is not sufficiently dynamic to meet the demands of Lope's theater. The result is an increase in characters and in plot episodes. Lope is constrained to introduce, and weave into the main action, a subplot involving Andronio, a rejected suitor, who subsequently falls in love with Dorena, over whom he fights a duel and kills Guido. The murder is in turn charged to Gisippo's Spanish counterpart, Lauro. Humor is provided principally by the latter's garrulous servant, Pinabel.

While friendship and the sacrifices made for its sake was a popular theme in Spanish Golden Age prose[43] the dramatization of such a friendship presented a number of difficulties. The chief episode, in which Gisippo (a Greek) allows his friend Tito, who was moreover a foreigner (Roman), to substitute for him on his wedding night, had to be rendered plausible to an audience bound by the honor code and by established social limits. Lope was able to accomplish the task by presenting the hero, now a Spaniard, with an unavoidable choice: the death of his friend Febo, a Frenchman, over the latter's love for Fabia, or the sacrifice of his future bride.

---

[43] See Louis Sorieri, *Boccaccios' Story of Tito and Gisippo in European Literature* (New York: Institute of French Studies, 1937), pp. 232–268. On the trajectory of the story of the two friends from the *Disciplina clericalis* through José Zorilla, see Juan B. Avalle-Arce, "Una tradición literaria: El cuento de los dos amigos," *NRPH*, 11 (1957): 1–35. On the story in Castilian letters see Bourland, "Boccaccio and the *Decameron*," pp. 152–159. For the sources of this tale in Antiquity, see Vittore Branca, ed. Boccaccio, *Decameron*, p. 1164, n. 1.

In the source story the magnitude of the gesture is colored by the fact that Gisippo had seen the lady only once, briefly, after their families had arranged the marriage. Gisippo himself establishes the primacy of Tito's passion in accordance with the precepts of love at the heart of the *Decameron*: "Egli e vero che Sofronia e mia sposa[44] e che io l'amava molto e con gran feste le sue nozze aspettava; ma per cio che tu, si come molto piu intendente[45] di me, con piu fervor desideri cosi cara cosa come ella e, vivi sicuro che non mia ma tua moglie verra nella mia camera," (p. 1171).

Lope's protagonist, Lauro, on the other hand, had been courting Fabia for three years and she returns his love. The motivation for Lauro's sacrifice therefore, had to be strong, forceful and immediate. Nothing less than the threat of his friend's death would have sufficed. Lauro's gesture thereby takes on the character of a noble deed. As for a possible offense to the honor code, Lope was able to circumvent the issue through the ingenious plan arranged by Lauro. The papers which grant Febo the power to stand in for Lauro at the wedding are so worded that the lady becomes, in fact, Febo's bride. Thus morality is safeguarded and censure is avoided.

Beyond the elements of plot, Boccaccio's story of exemplary friendship was a tacit elevation of Greeek culture over Latin culture. Tito is sent to Greece to study, implying that Roman schools were no match for their Hellenic predecessors.[46] Moreover, it is the Greek youth who makes the major sacrifice with stoic calmness, while Tito, the Roman, is unable to dominate his passions.[47] Although in the latter part of the tale Tito repays Gisippo for his kindness by sharing his wealth

---

[44] Vittore Branca, ed., Boccaccio, *Decameron*, p. 1170, n. 8, indicates that *sposa* is to be interpreted as meaning *betrothed*.

[45] Branca, ed. *Decameron*, p. 1171, n. 6, interprets *intendente* to mean *innamorato, amante*.

[46] Bourland, "Boccaccio and the *Decameron*," p. 155, points out that "When Boccaccio wrote the *Decameron* the study of Greek philosophy was a subject of deep interest in Italy, and Boccaccio's insistence in this *novella* upon its importance added a charm to the story in the eyes of his contemporaries."

[47] In his speech to Sofronia's family when the exchange of husbands is discovered, Tito fares poorly. Boccaccio's narrator por- *(continued on page 94)*

with the now impoverished Greek and by marrying Gisippo to his sister, the recompense discharges an obligation but in no way may be equated with the gesture of the Greek citizen.

Lope's shift in locale raises several issues. The Greek and Roman origins of the protagonists could easily have been retained since Spanish audiences were no strangers to plays with these settings. Extratextual realities, however, may have influenced the choice of nationalities. While it does not seem unnatural that national pride should have stirred Lope to make the Greek hero a Spaniard, the shift of the Roman friend to a Frenchman invites speculation. Does the change suggest the same high regard for the French which characterized the portrayal of Rugero in *El servir con mala estrella*? Or is Lope, in so doing, implying the superiority of Spanish culture over that of France, as Boccaccio had done with Greece and Rome? To answer this question I believe we need consider the source story in relation to the tale which immediately precedes it in the *Decameron*. The seventh story of Day X recounts the magnificent gesture of Peter of Aragon toward a young lady of humble birth who had fallen ill for love of him. A visit from King Peter restores her health. Promising to wear her colors in all tourneys, Peter marries her to a young but poor gentleman and bestows a handsome dowry upon her, sealing their agreement with a chaste kiss. Boccaccio's narrator for the next tale (that of Tito and Gisippo), in reaction to the praises sung to the magnificence of kings who, after all, can afford to be generous, offers the story of "una laudevole opera e magnifica usata tra due cittadini amici," (p. 1165). Morever, story seven glorifies an Aragonese king who arrived and was warmly received as a ruler by the Sicilians in August of 1282,[48] a few months after the French has been expelled from Sicily. Is it not possible that the popularity of the Spanish over the French in this tale might have spilled over and colored Lope's approach to the next

_____

(continued from page 93) trays him as haughty and contentious, even to threatening his indignant in-laws with reprisals. See Boccaccio, *Decameron*, pp. 1179–1181.

[48] See Branca, ed., *Decameron*, p. 1153, n. 6 for further details concerning the Aragonese king and his magnanimous gesture.

story? I am inclined toward the latter hypothesis on the basis of Febo's characterization throughout the play. While he bears Lauro a genuine affection, he possesses to a lesser degree those qualities which Lauro comes to represent: devotion, fidelity, constancy in friendship and a cool, reasoned approach to human relations. Although Febo willingly confesses to a crime he did not commit in order to save the life of a friend, the gesture never achieves that level of generosity as exemplified by Lauro. This is partially due to the fact that we hardly expect a man of Lauro's dignity to take advantage of such a confession. Nor is there any indication that the provost, a relative of Febo, would easily accept a confession which was not legally sound. In this light, Febo's false admission of guilt, though motivated by genuine love for his friend, emerges as a grand but useless gesture, one that is not likely to be taken seriously. The confession, however, suffices to reestablish the friendship between the Frenchman and the Spaniard on equal footing at the end of the play. Yet the portrayal of Febo throughout the work lingers to mitigate the Frenchman's glory.

Despite the selection of a contemporary setting to provoke a specific audience reaction, Lope returns to the classical world for character names which would accurately depict the loving commitment of the protagonists. In choosing the names Lauro and Febo, Lope exploited fully the spectator's recognition of the myth of Daphne and Phoebus Apollo and the inseparability of the sun god and the laurel tree. The intensity of a companionship such as that of Boccaccio's Tito and Gisippo, easily put forth in a prose work set in Antiquity, presented a challenge when offered dramatically for an audience which felt keenly the demands of a rigid behavioral code. Flickers of homosexuality in Antiquity might not have offended Boccaccio's reader; Lope's public would have found the insinuations intolerable, especially as concerns a Spaniard. Although he must repeatedly focus on the mutual devotion of Lauro and Febo in order to make the point of the story, Lope avoids the pitfall by accentuating the youth of the protagonists. They are university students; reckless, daring and prone to excess in gesture and speech. The stress on their young years and the lack of *mesura* which characterizes that age makes their intense emotional attachment comprehensible. By focusing on the extremes to which they go in the name of friendship, Lope paves the way for Febo's melancholy as well as for Lauro's sacrifice.

In the opening scene, Lope underscores immediately the young men's propensity for hasty action and passionate attachment. Lauro, having set out to visit Fabia secretly, without sword or dagger to protect himself, is forced to send his servant, Pinabel, to retrieve them. The unexpected arrival of Febo, his offer to accompany Lauro, the latter's gentle negation, and Febo's intense reaction, enable Lope to center on the depth of the friendship with imagery which recalls the indivisible nature of their classical counterparts. Lauro's tactful rejection also fixes the origin of the companionship as that of their respective fathers:

> Febo, de mi alma Apolo,
> Luz de mi vida y honor,
>   Nuestros padres son amigos,
> Este amor es heredado,
> Con la sangre nos le han dado,
> Las obras son los testigos.
>   Quédate en casa y descansa;
> Que este negocio es seguro,
> Pues llevarte no procuro.
>   (571a)

The classical metaphors are repeated as Lauro tries to assuage Febo's anger at being excluded from the rendezvous and to assure him of his devotion: "Mira, Febo, que eres Febo, / Y que es Lauro tu laurel." Febo retorts with like imagery: "Si eres ingrato como él, / Lauro, los nombres repruebo," (571a). As the exchange becomes increasingly argumentative, Febo's reaction, like that of Apollo, emerges as that of rejected suitor at the mercy of his passion. While the conceits, commonly associated with altercations between members of the opposite sex seem unnatural under the circumstances, they serve Lope well. Febo appears clearly as one given to emotional extremes in matters of love:

96

Bastan los agravios hechos,
No me digas que me quieres
Más que yo á ti, Lauro, si eres
El alma de nuestros pechos;
    Que si porque amor se arguya
Entre dos, que no han der ser,
Un alma sola ha de haber,
¡Por Dios, Lauro, que es la tuya!
    Yo sólo soy cuerpo aquí;
Tú eres la razón, la ley;
Tú la voluntad y el rey,
Que vive y manda en mí.
    La estrella con que naciste
Tiene imperio en mí, y la estoy
Tan sujeto, que no soy
Más ser que el ser que me diste;
    Que á no conocer los dos,
Que hay Dios, para más ejemplo
Te hiciera labrar un templo
Y te adorara por Dios.

(571b)

Lope underlines Febo's propensity for irrational behavior through Lauro's response: "Tente que el amor te lleva / Á ser loco." The *amor/locura* parallel is repeated in Febo's insistence, "y aún es poco; / Que amor, sólo con ser loco, / Sus ejecutorias prueba," (571b).

Having established those character traits which render Febo's subsequent behavior a natural outgrowth, Lope strategically reaffirms the friends' mutual devotion as they move toward the rendezvous with Fabia:

Lauro.   … Y está seguro de mí,
            Que esta sangre, este alma, es tuya.
Febo.   La mía, Lauro, ¿no es tuya?
            Tú sabes que vive en ti.

A final query and response points to the primacy of their attachment over any that might exist between Fabia and Lauro:

Febo.   ¿Tanto la quieres?…
Lauro.   Pues Febo, después de ti,
            Es la cosa que más quiero.

(572a–b)

97

Beyond its long-range implications, the comment bears directly on Lauro's comportment in the scene which follows. The episode is marked by Lauro's restlessness and distraction until Febo is admitted and, contrastively, by the levity of Fabia and Celia who are unable to comprehend the nature of such a friendship. Hence the puns on Fabia's part:

Fabia. ¿Febo dices que está allí?
Pues así me guarde Dios,
Que pensé que érades vos,
Según alumbráis en mí,
· · ·   · · ·   · · · (537a)
Gran prisa tenéis por Febo
· · ·   · · ·   · · ·
Antes de mi compañía
Tan cansado, Lauro, estáis,
Que si á Febo deseáis,
Es para que traiga el día.
                              (573a)

Celia, too, injects a barb, as she makes ready to leave, "Porque no me siento / Para esperar el calor / De tanto sol," (573b).

In the midst of the humor we are reminded again by the dramatist of the bond between the two men:

Febo.   Veisme, señoras aquí;
La mitad de Lauro soy.
Lauro. Es verdad; entero estoy
Después, que dentro te ví;
Y así os ofrezco en los dos
Uno sólo: yo soy Febo,
Febo es yo.
                              (574a)

I suspect that Lope, fully conscious of what the audience might infer if the dialogue between Lauro and Febo were to continue in this vein, preferred to diffuse the tension by anticipating the spectator's thoughts. Fabia's retort, which at first glance seems flippant and tinged with jealousy, is deliberately intended to prevent the emotional compenetration of the two young men from suggesting aberrant behavior. The lines, moreover, provide the necessary measure of levity to hold the play to the comedic mode:

98

> Ni yo me atrevo
> Á hablar con él, ni con vos.
> Basta, Celia, que se dicen
> Los amores que pudieran
> Á nosotras.
>
> (574b)

Lope's play, however, centers on the bond of friendship. He must, therefore, continue to affirm the immutability of that bond if Lauro's sacrifice is to be convincing. Lope offers a hint of what is to come in Lauro's continued preoccupation with Febo as he courts Fabia. Anxious for her to know and appreciate his friend, Lauro suggests that he and Febo change places, "Que son sus merecimientos / Dignos desta cortesía." If Fabia's earlier repartee had been playful, the tone is now one of shocked disbelief: "De vuestra afición me espanto," (574b). Lope's recourse to the word *espanto* is deliberate. The lady's perception of a frightening level of intensity in the relationship between the two men alerts the audience to extraordinary happenings. The episode is brought to a sudden halt by a noise from within, but not before Febo has been struck by Cupid's dart. The apprehension of Pinabel by the lady's male relatives brings the affair into the open and a marriage is hastily arranged. Lope, in a few scenes, has set before his public all the factors which will condition Febo's melancholy as well as Lauro's response to it.

I noted earlier that in order to make Lauro's sacrifice credible, Lope had to create an equally credible motivation: Febo's madness and death wish. The dramatist carefully establishes Febo's *locura* both directly and indirectly. As Act I comes to a close Febo exhibits a childish petulance and persistent unwillingness to accept reality. Despite protestations by Lauro to the contrary, Febo complains repeatedly:

> Hoy te perdí...
> Querrás luego a tu mujer,
> Estarás siempre con ella,...
> ¡Ah, Lauro, hoy te pierde Febo!...
> (580a-b)

Febo's reluctant "Un siglo os gocéis," followed by an aside,

"¡Ojos, mirad como veis, / Que he de callar y morir!", sets the stage for the near-fatal melancholy which will alter the direction of the play's action.

Lope continues in this vein as he moves into Act II. Aurelio's reference to the strangeness of Febo's malady and the failure of all medication to alleviate it are corroborated by the sudden advent of Febo, screaming, in pursuit of Pinabel and Leonido. Lope offers a young man obsessed by death who begs:

> Llévenme luego a enterrar,
> Que tener es desconcierto
> En la cama un cuerpo muerto
> De sufrir y de callar.
>
> (582b)

The playwright's desire, however, is to create a comedy. While the prolonged consideration of Febo's *locura* is essential in terms of Lauro's subsequent gesture, some comic business is necessary to keep the play from degenerating into melodrama. The humorous respite is provided by Leonido, whom Febo insists should die with him since a good servant must always follow his master. Leonido's verbal extrication from the predicament serves a dual function. It reaffirms Febo's love madness through jest and by its lighter nature contrasts sharply with the tension-laden scene which follows. It should be noted that beyond this point there are few humorous episodes. Once the change of husbands is effected, the threat and the eventual discovery of the ruse, with its ensuing complications, dominate the play's action. If Lope found it necessary to occasionally view with levity the excesses of the two young men's devotion, from here on, with the exception of some comic fillers between Pinabel and other servants, the play holds to a very sober mood.

Lope concentrates once more on the mutual affection of the two men as they move toward the decision which will turn the tables on convention. Given Febo's illness, the tone of the exchange is a far cry from the easy bantering of earlier scenes. Lope's sensitivity for character portrayal enables us to feel the torment of each man: Lauro's frustration and desolation at being unable to pry from Febo the reason for his anguish; Febo's desire not to offend Lauro and thereby end a friendship which is dearer than life. Lauro likens their friendship to a mirror in which each could see the other clearly, a mirror not darkened by deception and secrecy until this moment. Febo equates himself to the wall which sustains the mirror. It would be better for the wall to crumble than to crack the mirror with the truth:

> Pared del espejo fuí;
> Hazme Lauro, una merced,
> que se caiga esta pared,
> Y se caiga sobre mí.
>
> (585a)

Lope, in one final exchange, brings alive the tension between Lauro's ever angrier insistence that his friend speak out and Febo's equally obstinate refusal to do so. It is now Lauro, in desperation, who would die:

> . . . si mi alma
> Era luz de tu cristal,
> Y por encubrir tu mal
> Vive tu salud en calma,
>   Este pecho, que la encubre,
> Romperé con esta daga,
> Para que lugar le haga;
>   Que si el alma se descubre,
>   Todo su luz dará en ti,
> Y tú en mí entonces verás,
> Que ni puedo alumbrar más,
> Ni hay mayor verdad en mí.
>
> (585a)

The gesture provokes a passionate response which underscores strongly the intensity of the bond:

> Por el inmortal amor
> Que en nuestras almas se engendra,
> . . . .
> Por la santa fe jurada
> En justa correspondencia
> De la deuda de la amistad,
> Que es la más estrecha deuda,
> Te pido, Lauro, que al punto
> Que mi traición se refiera,
> Acabes mi vida infame,
> Que es la más justa respuesta.
>
> (585b)

101

The dramatist has made an eloquent case for Lauro's sacrifice. No further defense is necessary. By focusing on the depth and strength of the friendship—each would rather die than betray that bond—Lope has rendered Lauro's magnanimity not only credible but almost a natural consequence of that attachment. I would venture that we are not so moved by the sacrifice as we are by the friendship which prompted it. The playwright may well have intended it to be so if we consider Lauro's response when Febo hesitatingly mentions Fabia: "Aún no es mi esposa; / Di lo que quisieres della," (585b). In contrast to Febo's impassioned confession and plea for death, Lauro's demeanor evidences the equilibrium and calm of a reasonable man who sees clearly the path he must follow. The reaction of Lauro is almost one of relief in light of the simple nature of the problem. In this Lope takes his cue from Boccaccio's protagonist who, after only a moment of silence ". . . senza indugio deliberò la vita dello amico più che Sofronia dovergli esser cara," (p. 1170). The dramatist reaffirms Lauro's uncompromising devotion in the face of Febo's disbelief:

> No soy amigo de agora,
> Si en estas cosas me pruebas;
> No hay honra, Febo; no hay vida,
> No hay padres, duedos, ni deudas,
> Que no te ponga en las manos.
> (586a)

The passage is especially pertinent in that it allows the playwright to anticipate and assuage the potential disease of the spectator as concerns the question of *honra*. Lope reminds us, through the utterances of the protagonist, that honor has not been offended, ". . . pues no es mi prenda / De la honra, . . ,"; that Lauro understands what is at stake for, had they been married, ". . . el amigo / No es bien que al honor se atreva, . . ." (586b). Although he places himself squarely in the camp of the upholders of *honra*, the dramatist feels constrained to reassert Lauro's lack of choice in the matter: "Febo, tu estás á la muerte / De amores desta doncella, / Y yo no me muero agora; . . ." (586b). Lope offers us, then, a protagonist whose gener-

102

osity in the name of friendship is unparalleled. Through his sensitive handling of characterization we are made to share Lauro's anguish as he stands guard outside the bridal chamber. Despite the flashes of remorse which rise up to plague him, Lauro is steadfast in his allegiance:

> ¡Muerto soy! Mas ¿qué digo?
> No me neguéis que supe ser amigo.
> . . .   .
> Aunque me veis perdido,
> ¡Vive Dios que no estoy arrepentido!
>
> (591a)

Although the pivotal issue of *La boda entre dos maridos* has been resolved, Lope, like Boccaccio, must continue to affirm Lauro's uncompromising friendship for Febo if audience interest is to be sustained as fortunes are reversed. Thus, the same unflinching devotion exemplifies Lauro's demeanor when he is forced to flee Madrid. He will brook no criticism from Pinabel for his magnanimity:

> Calla, loco Pinabel;
> No me digas nada dél,
> Que pondré á la espada mano,
> . . .   .
> Febo es el rey de los hombres,
> No hay más bien que Febo en mí;
> Cuando dél me hablas á mí,
> Así quiero que le nombres.
>   Dejo lo que debo á Dios
> Que Dios sobre todo es rey;
> Pero si amistad es ley,
> Esta ley vive en los dos.
>
> (603b)

Nor does he regret his kindness when he is robbed of clothes and weapons. Pinabel's "Mucho te cuesta Febo," is met by a crisp retort: "Todo es nada." The remainder of the play, with the exception of the episodes generated by the subplot, follows Boccaccio's arrangement: Febo's failure to recognize his friend when the latter begs for alms outside Febo's home; the courtroom recognition and subsequent confession by Febo to save Lauro; the confession of the real killer motivated by the exemplary devotion of the two friends; and, finally, the reconciliation of all parties.

In creating *La boda entre dos maridos*, Lope takes Boccaccio's tale of magnanimity in friendship, set in Antiquity, and recasts it in a modern ambience so that the hero now embodies the traditional values of a Spanish gentleman: devotion, fidelity, constancy and discretion. Plot elaboration and characterization are sensitively handled so that the honor code is not offended. The depiction of Fabia is particularly effective and natural. Although she does not understand the intensity of the relationship between Lauro and Febo and expresses anger when she learns she has been duped, Fabia accepts the spouse which fate has given her.

Love triumphs roundly in each of the plays discussed above. It transcends parental objection, financial security and social strictures. Each comedy is a testament to love's ability to cast aside all man-made barriers to that passion and to circumvent them in the fulfillment of natural desires. Yet while Lope espouses the cause of love with all the zest and vigor of the Italian source, he never loses sight of the exemplary function of his theater. Love does not have its way in defiance of society's norms. Rather, love turns the tables on convention only in the manner in which the protagonists approach their legitimate goal—marriage.

IV. *Ingegno*

The first fifty *novelle* of Boccaccio's human comedy define man in terms of his capacity for dealing with the two major forces which determine his existence: *Fortuna* and *Amore*. The first, external to man, continually tempers him; the second, bestowed by Nature, demands that man acknowledge and govern those appetites within him. The bawdy, raucous tales of Days VI, VII and VIII, on the other hand, celebrate man's ability to meet life's challenges successfully through the use of operative intelligence, *Ingegno*, and its correlatives *senno*, *sapere*, *saviezza*, *discrezione* and *avvedimento*. The stories extol human intelligence in all its manifestations, be it in the ability to recapture one's dignity with a clever retort or to escape danger through perspicacity (Day VI);[1] by the use of one's wits in the satisfaction of natural instincts (Day VII);[2] or, by the wily

---

[1] Boccaccio, *Decameron*, p. 697. The introduction to the Sixth Day reads, ". . . incomincia la sesta, nella quale, sotto il reggimento d'Elissa, si ragiona di chi con alcuno leggiadro motto, tentato, si riscosse, o con pronta risposta o avvedimento fuggì perdita o pericolo o scorno."

[2] Boccaccio, *Decameron*, p. 771. The stories of Day VII, told under the guidance of Dioneo, center on "le beffe, le quali, o per amore o per salvamento di loro, le donne hanno già fatto a' lor mariti, senza essersene avveduti o no."

tricks which men and women play on one another (Day VIII).[3]
In each case, man either stands or succumbs. He is either *astuto*
or *sciocco, beffatore* or *beffato*. Even when his efforts are fruitful
there remains an element of uncertainty which demands that
he be constantly on guard lest the tables be turned. Such is the
fate, for example, of Madonna Jancofiore, the professional
trickster who is undone by one more astute than she (VIII, 10).
The protagonists of Days VI, VII and VIII, then, must confront
a formidable array of obstacles using only wit and determination as a corrective force. That the methods encompass trickery
and deceit matters little; all manifestations of astuteness and
mental agility which enable one to prevail against the odds
appear to command Boccaccio's instinctive respect.

The Italian *novelliere*'s indulgent attitude toward the
clever rascal, however, is not to be taken as the condoning of
unscrupulous deception and trickery for its own sake. Rather,
as R. Hastings maintains, the celebration of intelligence turns
on the notion that virtue itself cannot exist without it. For
while intelligence enables man to secure the satisfaction of his
desire, though it be by less than honorable means, it is that
same intelligence which renders him capable of a rational
control of human passions and the "refinement of instinct and
impulse which are at the basis of all virtuous and responsible
conduct."[4] Though the antisocial behavior of the criminal is
reprehensible, in the very intelligence which he exercises in
the perpetration of deceits, lies the potential for good—if that
intelligence could be redirected to right goals. The stupid man,
on the other hand, has little chance of becoming virtuous for
he lacks the necessary acumen to make right choices.

Boccaccio inherited much of his liberal attitude and secular outlook from the sound common sense and practical spirit
that characterized the merchant world, of which he had been a

---

[3] Boccaccio, *Decameron*, p. 873. The Eighth Day is presented thus: ". . .
comincia l'ottava, nella quale, sotto il reggimento di Lauretta, si ragiona di
quelle beffe che tutto il giorno o donna ad uomo o uomo a donna o l'uno uomo
all'altro si fanno."

[4] R. Hastings, *Nature and Reason*, p. 76.

106

part in his youth.[5] No single tale better reveals Boccaccio's first-hand familiarity with that world than the tenth story of Day VIII.[6] The prologue abounds in mercantile vocabulary concerning docks and warrants, brokers and monetary exchange. The lengthy introduction serves to point up the uncertainties of the merchant trade and the need for constant vigilance, especially against those "femine del corpo bellissime ma nimiche della onestá,"[7] who ply their trade at the port. Madonna Jancofiore the cortesan and Salabaetto, her unwary victim, represent two rival but complimentary worlds: inimical in that one preys upon the other; similar in their common preoccupation with profit and gain. The dynamism of the tale derives from the tension between the *beffa* and the *contrabeffa*, between the wiles with which Madonna Jancofiore seduces the merchant and relieves him of his money and the parallel scheme by which Salabaetto subsequently takes his revenge.

Despite the fact that the subtle trickster is artfully deceived by an opponent equally sharp-witted, we are left with the unmistakable feeling that Boccaccio harbors a sneaking admiration for this clever lady. Calculated authorial distance notwithstanding, Boccaccio tips his hand repeatedly. We see it in the adverb "maestrevolmente," used to describe the efficiency with which she fleeces her victims. Boccaccio's narrator, Dioneo, labels her a "sottile artefice," implying that she is remarkably good at her trade. Moreover, Dioneo takes great pride in narrating the *beffa* to surpass all *beffe* because it was perpetrated against she who was "maggior maestra di beffare altrui. . . ."[8]

[5] See Vittore Branca, *Boccaccio, The Man and His Works*, trans. R. Monges (New York: New York University Press, 1976), pp. 18–23.

[6] Boccaccio, *Decameron*, p. 995. The introductory caption reads: "Una ciciliana maestrevolmente toglie ad un mercatante ciò che in Palermo ha portato; il quale sembiante faccendo d'esservi tornato con molta più mercatantia che prima, da lei accattati denari, le lascia acqua e capecchio." For the folkloric antecedents see Stith Thompson, *Motif-Index of Folk Literature*, IV, 418, K 1667, and V. Branca, ed., Boccaccio, *Decameron*, p. 995, n. 1.

[7] Boccaccio, *Decameron*, p. 996.

[8] Ibid. pp. 995–996.

One may argue that in spite of the flattering comments, Madonna Jancofiore is outwitted in the end and that, in fact, Salabaetto is the sharper of the two, except for one small detail. The plan by which Salabaetto leads her to advance him a large sum of money on a huge store of dummy packages, is ideated by a character external to the story proper. He is Pietro dello Canigiano, Salabaetto's mentor in Naples, and a personal friend of Boccaccio in real life. In this light, the Florentine merchant's astuteness is diminished somewhat since in the first part of the tale he falls prey to the lady's tricks and in the second half he executes a plan invented by a friend. Thus Madonna Jancofiore, despite her discomfiture at the end of the tale, remains the undisputed protagonist.

Although the cortesan falls victim to her own greed, it is not Boccaccio's purpose to offer an exemplary tale. There is no intent to moralize. The narrator simply tells the story as it happened. Qualitative comments are limited to those already noted. There is no attempt at psychological penetration, no effort to explain the motivation behind the lady's actions. We must go to Lope's play for this. The *Decameron* celebrates intelligence, not its goals, purposes or direction. The deed and *how* it is perpetrated lies at the center of these tales. The *why* of it is left for the moralists or psychologists to ascertain.

El anzuelo de Fenisa

In creating *El anzuelo de Fenisa* Lope retains all the essential particulars of Boccaccio's rowdy, picaresque ambience so as to give full rein to the craft and guile of the cortesan. The world of the port and its customary inhabitants permits the inclusion of a character like Osorio, a Spanish captain and procurer for Fenisa. The shift of the Florentine merchant to one from Valencia may have been prompted by several factors, not least among them Lope's personal fondness for that port city.[9] Morever, the reputation of the Valencians for relaxed social

---

[9] On Lope's residence in Valencia see Castro y Rennert, *Vida*, pp. 59–83.

and moral postures, commonly alluded to as "la molicie valenciana,"[10] gives credence to the merchant's facile seduction. The adventures of a merchant and a cortesan, however, motivated primarily by profit and gain, and each a victim of weakness of character, are hardly the stuff of which seventeenth-century *comedias* are made. Therefore, to the scenario of the docks Lope counterposes a subplot involving Spanish nobles and the indispensable questions of love and honor. The expansion allows for the introduction of another clever lady, the Sevillian maiden Dinarda, who successfully outwits the cortesan at her own game. She not only wins back the love of Albano, temporarily infatuated with Fenisa, but Dinarda's impersonation as Don Juan de Lara stirs the cortesan's amorous passions.

By focusing on the marked social distance between the members of the subplot who are concerned with honor and the characters of the central intrigue who are preoccupied with *ganancia*, Lope is able to transpose the tension inherent in the narrative rhythm of Boccaccio's *beffa* and *contrabeffa* to one between two opposing world views which, given the structure of seventeenth-century Spanish society, are mutually exclusive. Beyond the points of contact occasioned by Fenisa who links both segments, interraction between the two levels is held to a minimum. While the honor question and the social values of the upper class eventually dominate the latter portion of the play, the title and all of the action point to Fenisa and Lucindo as the principal characters. They are the personages most carefully and lovingly delineated, for whose shrewdness Lope evinces the same covert admiration as Boccaccio. It is into the presentation of the world of the docks that Lope throws all of his creative energies, a world of cozenage and trickery at the center of which is Fenisa, *anzuelo* poised and waiting.

---

[10] For the attitude of Spaniards in general towards the Valencians see, Miguel Herrero-García, *Ideas de los españoles del Siglo XVII* (Madrid: Editorial Voluntad, 1929), p. 429.

In fashioning the title for his play,[11] Lope takes the substantive *anzuelo*[12] which, in its multiform varieties symbolizes the activities of the port, and uses it to résumé, figuratively, the wit, talent and beauty of the cortesan as she plies her trade on the docks. That same practical intelligence which Lucindo exercises in bringing his goods safely to port and in unloading and securing them, characterizes Fenisa as she sets out to steal the worth of that cargo. She knows exactly the quality and proportion of bait required, the degree of pull and slack necessary to secure the catch and the mode of disposition once the fish has been landed:

Tiendo la red en el mar,
Que es la estrella en que nací.
Ojos y lengua son cebo
Del anzuelo deste amor;
Si pica y es bobo y nuevo,
Doyle cuerda y del favor
Asido un año le llevo.
Si es ladino y está diestro,
Aunque caiga, vuelve al mar,
Porque ofendida me muestro
Que, si no ha de aprovechar,
Ocupe el anzuelo nuestro.
(485b)

The focus on *anzuelo*, however, is not merely conditioned by its appropriateness to the world of docks and customs houses.

---

[11] Lope Félix de Vega Carpio, *El anzuelo de Fenisa*, in *Obras*,XIV, 481–526. On Lope's adaptation of *Decameron* VIII, 10 for this play see C. Bourland, "Boccaccio and the Decameron," pp. 136–141; Charles Dejob, "La 10ª Novella dell'ottava Giornata del *Decameron* ed *El anzuelo de Fenisa* di Lope de Vega," *Rassegna bibliografica della letteratura italiana*, Anno I, num. 5, 149–152 and J. C. J. Metford, "Lope de Vega and Boccaccio's Decameron," *BHS*, 29 (1952): 85–86.
[12] Sebastián de Covarrubias Orozco, *Tesoro de la lengua castellana*, f. 68v–69r. The definition reads as follows: "1. ançuelo, Lat. Hamus de aquí hamuelo, y corruptamente, ançuelo, o del nombre diminutivo unculus; garfio pequeño, de uncus, que sinifica el garfio, uncuelo, unçuelo, y ançuelo. Tragar el ançuelo se dize del que con codicia del cebo, que le han representado se arroja a aceptar alguna cosa que después ha de escotar con setenas . . . . Picar en el ançuelo, acudir al cebo peligroso, por cuya codicia se quedan . . . se aplica a los moços, que engolosinados con la hermosura y gracia de alguna muger, vienen a perder su libertad, y a perderse absolutamente."

Lope exploits fully the etymological association of its root *hamus* with *amicus* and, by extension, with *amor*.[13] By calling into play the extended linguistic aspect of *anzuelo*, Lope is able to bring together and to counterpoise the disparate worlds of the plot and subplot. In both, Fenisa's attractiveness is the common denominator, the "... cebo / Del anzuelo deste amor," which enthralls the prey.

There is a second point of juncture between the two social spheres that could not have escaped Lope's audience. I refer to the autobiographical reverberations associated with the names Albano and Lucindo, pseudonyms often employed by the dramatist, but rarely, to my knowledge, in the same play.[14] Albano is generally linked to Lope's love for Belisa, the literary disguise of Isabel de Urbina, his first wife, although he continued to use the name long after her death. Lucindo is clearly attached to Lope's liaison with Camila Lucinda (Micaela de Luján).[15]

I suggest that in *El anzuelo de Fenisa*, both Albano and Lucindo are aspects of Lope. The inclusion of a verse from a sonnet to Camila Lucinda[16] as the opening line of the play, and

---

[13] On the use of fishing imagery in connection with love, see Isidore of Seville, *Etimologías*, ed. and trans. Luis Cortez y Góngora (Madrid: Biblioteca de autores cristianos, 1951), p. 241. The text reads: "amicus viene de hamo, gancho, esto es, anillo de la cadena de caridad y de ahi hami, anzuelo, porque prende." The imagery is repeated in Andreas Capellanus' *Art of Courtly Love*: "Love gets its name from the word for hook (amus), which means 'to capture' or 'to be captured' for he who is in love is captured in the chains of desire and wishes to capture someone else with his hook. Just as the skillful fisherman tries to attract fishes by his bait and to capture them on his crooked hook, so that the man who is a captive of love tries to attract another person by allurement. . . ." (p. 31).

[14] On Albano and Lucindo as literary disguises for Lope de Vega consult S. Griswold Morley, *Pseudonyms*, pp. 425 and 463, respectively.

[15] For bibliographical data related to Lope and Micaela de Luján see Chapter III, n. 19 of my text.

[16] See Lope de Vega, *Rimas*, ed. Gerardo Diego (Madrid: Palabra y Tiempo, 1963), p. 86. The sonnet to Micaela/Lucinda reads as follows:

> Así en las olas de la mar feroces,
> Betis, mil siglos tu cristal escondas,
> y otra tanta ciudad sobre tus ondas
> de mil navales edificios goces.

(continued on page 112)

the implicit suggestion that the audience was familiar with that work can hardly be considered a haphazard occurrence. The dramatist was dependent on that recognition to give greater impact to the initial dialogue from which Albano emerges as a jealous, unsuccessful lover, obstinate in the pursuit of his passion:

Camilo.	"Que estoy celoso y voy leyendo en ellas"
	Acaba aquel soneto castellano.
Albano.	¿Dónde vais a matarme plantas bellas?
Camila.	¿En la arena del mar miras, Albano,
	Las estampas que deja tu Fenisa?
Albano.	Por ellas sigo su desdén en vano,
	Por besar el arena donde pisa
	. . . .
Camilo.	¿Letras escribe con los pies?
Albano.	Y tales,
	Que leyendo la historia de mis celos,
	Aprendo penas á la causa iguales.
	No han hecho furia ni rigor los cielos,
	Para castigo de la humana vida,
	Que sufran compararse a sus desvelos.

(483a)

Albano's emotionally charged responses parallel those in a number of sonnets to Camila Lucinda; sonnets written at a time when Lope had not yet won the lady's love.[17] Moreover, the first stirrings of passion for Camila Lucinda occurred while Lope was married to his second wife, Juana de Guardo. This

---

(continued from page 111)
> Así tus cuevas no interrumpen voces,
>   ni quillas toquen, ni permitan sondas;
>   y en tus campos tan fértil correspondas,
>   que rompa el trigo las agudas hoces.
> Así en tu arena el indio margen rinda,
>   y al avariento corazón descubras
>   más barras que en ti mira el cielo estrellas.
> Que si pusiere en ti sus pies Lucinda,
>   no por besallo sus estampas cubras
>   que estoy celoso, y voy leyendo en ellas.

[17] See Castro y Rennert, *Vida*, p. 403, n. 13, for a listing of those sonnets which "manifiestamente pertenecen a la época en que aún no habiá logrado Lope ser favorecido por Micaela."

emotional conflict may well underlie the strong disagreement with Camilo over whom one should love. Albano insists that love transcends all barriers, spiritual and concrete: "Amor no es calidad, gusto ni fuero; / Amor no es honra, ni es mercadería;" and that it is a natural coming together: "Amor es consonancia y armonía / Que hacen el deseo y la hermosura, . . ." (484a). Camilo's insistence on "virtudes . . . y calidades" meets with a violent denunciation which coalesces into a single concept: "Si amor es gusto, el que yo tengo es justo," (484a). Considering the allusion to Micaela in the opening lines and Albano's rejection of the limitations placed on love, the passages may well be read as a justification by Lope for that illicit passion. The autobiographical reminiscences, however, diminish as the plot evolves. Albano emerges cured of his infatuation. Lope's liaison with Micaela lasted for almost a decade. I suggest that in portraying Albano as a lover driven by *celos*, Lope drew on his own feelings under similar circumstances, a period not far removed from that of the play's writing, if not actually coinciding with it.

That Lope attached a special significance to the name Lucindo, closely associated with his love for Micaela, has been amply demonstrated by scholars.[18] As concerns *El anzuelo de Fenisa*, J. H. Arjona,[19] in an effort to establish the date of the play, calls attention not only to the opening line but also to Fenisa's response when Lucindo tells her that he is from Valencia. "Si fuérades de Toledo," the lady responds, "tenía que preguntaros." The latter, Arjona maintains, suggests that Lope was writing the play at a time of divided emotional loyalties and alludes to Lope's residence in Toledo with his wife, Juana. Beyond this oft-cited relationship, I would propose still another for the characterization of Lucindo, one not visible from the text of the play. I refer to Lope's account of his adventures with a cortesan of Lisbon related in a letter of September, 1611, to the Duke of Sessa:

---

[18] S. Griswold Morley, *Pseudonyms*, p. 462.
[19] J. H. Arjona, "Un dato sobre la fecha de *El anzuelo de Fenisa* de Lope de Vega," *MLN*, 53 (1938): 190–192.

> Llegando yo mozuelo a Lisboa, cuando la jornada de Inglaterra, se apasionó una cortesana de mis partes, y yo la visité lo menos honestamente que pude; dile unos escudillos (reliquios tristes de los que había sacado de Madrid) a una vieja madre que tenía, la cual con un melindre entre puto y grave me dijo así: "No me pago cuando me huelgo."[20]

Is it not possible that the youthful episode in Lisbon might be at the heart of Lope's attraction to the Boccaccian tale; that he fused to the source and transferred to the stage the recollection of that account? The speculation may be venturesome but certainly not without precedent in much of Lope's creation. I would posit that in *El anzuelo de Fenisa* both Albano and Lucindo are Lope; the former only in the initial portions of the comedy, the latter as the literary projection of a youthful adventure. Just as the two levels of the play are joined by the double *vertiente* of *anzuelo*, so the two characters, Albano and Lucindo, are joined by a common referent: Micaela de Luján. While the reminiscences function clearly to captivate the spectator's attention and to act as a literary *anzuelo* in the pursuit of approbation, they also serve the interest of the play textually by setting *honra* against *mercadería*, and dynamically by calling forth the picaresque world of the port.

It is to this world that we are immediately transported as the play begins. The opening scene, for all its deliberate appeal to that special author-public relationship, offers, simultaneously, a candid portrait of the wily cortesan. In Camilo's eyes, she is entirely without scruples: ". . . una mujer famosa / En engañar y en no querer ninguno, / Supuesto que confieso que es hermosa. / . . ." (483b). Albano, on the other hand, finds the lady's inconstancy a stimulus to love:

---

[20] Reference to the letter of September 1611 appears in Cayetano A. de la Barrera's *Nueva biografía de Lope de Vega*, I, 44, n. 1: "En carta que Lope escribió al Duque de Sessa por septiembre de 1611, que forma parte de la colección que tengo copiada y anotada, se lee el siguiente párrafo . . . (as reproduced in my text). The citation from de la Barrera is repeated by Rennert and Castro, *Vida*, p. 59, n. 1. On Lope's presence in Lisbon see R. Schevill, "Lope de Vega and the Year 1588," *HR*, 9 (1941): 65–78. See also J. Millé, "Lope de Vega en la Armada Invencible," *RH*, 56 (1922): 380–385.

Aquella libertad me rinde y mata,
y el ver que deje amor e interés siga
. . .   .
Que amor ha de ser fina picardía,
Poca seguridad, menos contentos.
(483b)

Unlike his predecessor, however, Lope allows the lady to speak for herself, perhaps in an effort to blunt adverse criticism arising from the lady's profession or even to wrest a measure of understanding from his audience for Fenisa's actions:

Desde el primero que amé,
y que á olvidar me enseñó,
Tan diestra en no amar quedé,
Que de uno que me burló,
En los demás me vengué.
. . .   .
Según corre entre los hombres
Esto de amar con engaño,
De mi desdén no te asombres:
Basta al cuerdo un desengaño.
¿Qué es amor? No me lo nombres.
No porque yo no perciba
Sus regalos y su bien;
Pero no es razón que viva
Quien nació libre también
De un hombre libre cautiva.
Yo he dado en esta flaqueza
De burlar cuantos engaña
Esto que llaman belleza.
(484b)

These introductory remarks direct the spectator to the central problem of the cortesan. Denied recourse to satisfaction against the man who betrayed her, Fenisa's anger and desire for vengeance is displaced toward all subsequent men who fall prey to her beauty. Contrary to her initial love encounter, the man is now the hapless victim, while Fenisa assumes the role of the faithless seducer, and relishes the power which the turnabout affords. However, beneath the resentment, Lope suggests, there is a heart that yearns for love and its blessings. Yet, here too, there is resistance, for how can

115

one who is born free, Fenisa argues, live in the captivity of another? In the context of the play, however, despite the logic of her remarks, Fenisa is doomed to failure, for in denying submission to the bonds of love and marriage, she alienates herself from society and the role which it prescribes for women.

Lope recognized the potential theatricality and sheer fun of the Boccaccian material and capitalized on it by giving the cortesan an equally wary opponent in Lucindo. The Valencian merchant, in the spirit of Boccaccio's prologue, is fully cognizant of the hazards of trading, especially as concerns women:

> Ni el fiar ni el porfiar,
> Ni el alzarse, ni el quebrar,
> Ni el no pagar los señores
> Ni el morirse los deudores,
> Ni la inclemencia del mar,
>   Igualan a que se arroje
> Un mercader á querer,
> Ni hay pirata que despoje
> Como una hermosa mujer
> Que entre los brazos le coge.
>   (486b)

Tristán's reaction, however, "¡Plega el cielo que te dure / Tan alto conocimiento!", immediately suggests that Lucindo's confidence and resolve are hardly the product of experience and that they may soon be undermined.

If Lucindo's limitations are his inexperience, Fenisa's shortcomings derive precisely from the reverse. The unchallenged success which she has enjoyed in satisfying her overriding covetousness will, in the end, make her an easy victim to Lucindo's scheme of revenge. For the moment, however, Lucindo's guarded behavior serves only to sharpen her wits:

> Engañar, Celia, un cuitado
> Barbitonto, boquinecio,
> No fuera hazaña de precio
> Ni digna de humor taimado;
>   Pasmar un ingenio agudo
> Es lo que se ha de estimar.
>   (492b)

In this battle of wits Fenisa is as shrewd as Boccaccio's *barbiera*.[21] Throughout two masterfully orchestrated episodes (in the first she softens Lucindo's resolve; in the second she loosens his purse), the cortesan baits her hook and plays the catch, ever careful to let the prey run free when necessary, only to pull the line taut in the next exchange. For example, in the interim between the initial meeting on the docks and Lucindo's visit to Fenisa's shortly thereafter, the merchant, as a precaution, divests himself of all valuables, a gesture which does not escape the cortesan. To dispel Lucindo's distrust and his emotional distance, Fenisa pretends to be smitten by the Valencian but disappointed in his lukewarm reaction: "No, español, yo no te agrado, / O tú quieres bien allá, / . . . / Oye, estás enarmorado?" (493b). Insinuating that the gold chain she had seen earlier was a gift from another woman, Fenisa pries from Lucindo the fact that he had given the chain to Tristán, to which the latter quickly adds: "Yo la llevé / en casa de un caballero / . . . No estaba en casa y dejela," (494a). Lope's protagonist, quick to grasp that she has an enemy in Tristán— "El pícaro me desvela; / Pero destos pesco yo,"—shrewdly turns the ploy to her advantage. Lacking funds, Lucindo cannot refuse the gifts which Fenisa now lavishes upon him: gloves, *pastillas*, stockings and a purse containing one hundred *escudos*. Nor does she forget to regale Tristán. A well placed aside by the merchant, "Perdido vamos, Tristán,"

---

[21] The *Vocabolario degli Accademici della Crusca* offers this definition: "Barbiera dicesi di femmina disonesta che attende a pelare chi le da tra le mani, . . ." 5th ed. (Firenze: Cellini, 1866) II, 67. The association of "barbiera" with "prostitute" to suggest someone who shaves her victim clean of all he possesses, appears to have its Spanish counterpart in the word "afeitadilla". The meaning is apparent from the following passage found in Lope's *La ingratitud vengada* (Ac. N. VI, 474a):

Porque en una casa entró,
que vergüenza he de decirla,
de una cierta afeitadilla
que en Nápoles conoció . . .

In *El anzuelo de Fenisa*, however, Lope prefers the word "dama", the meaning of which is quite clear in Tristán's retort: "Dama es oficio, y no ser," (487b).

points to Lucindo's quickly fading resolve. Lope underscores the Valencian's losing battle by flashing to comments from Fenisa's servants:

Liseo.   Ganando va por la mano.
Celia.   Perderáse por el pie.
Estacio.   Pues que Fenisa le fía,
              Hipotecado tendrá.

(495b)

For the moment, however, the dramatist holds to the sense of unresolved conflict through Tristán's suspicious assessment: "Notable modos . . . / De amor o de engaños . . ."(495b).

Although Lucindo and the cortesan are at odds with one another they are part of the same world, one in which material gains are the yardstick against which each man's ingenuity is measured. It is most appropriate, then, for Lucindo, a merchant, to declare his affection in terms of precious cargo. It is a language both protagonists understand and a code by which each operates:

> Pienso que sabré pagarte
> Aunque si esta nave fuera
> De oro puro, no pudiera
> Deste bien mínima parte.
>   ¡Ojalá fueran sus jarcias
> Cuerdas de perlas de oriente,[22]
>   El corredor de su popa
> Fuera de diamantes hecho.
> De historias varias el techo,
> Del pincel mejor de Europa;
>   Y para arrastrar en faldas
> De tu ropa ricas telas,
> Fueran brocado sus velas,
> Sus árboles de esmeraldas.
>   La jarela de cadenas,
> Los trinquetes y mesanas
> De rubíes como granas,
> Y de coral las antenas!

(496a)

---

[22] Ac. XIV, 496, n. 1, mentions that these are two "versos sueltos" but offers no explanation for their presence in this text.

Having established the unity of the world of custom-houses and *mercadería*, Lope is now free to introduce, contrast-ively, the world of nobles and *honra*. If Fenisa's *ingegno* domi-nates the former, that supremacy will now be challenged by the resourcefulness of Dinarda, posing as Don Juan de Lara. To this end Lope brings the protagonists together, briefly, at the end of Act I. The encounter functions to remind the specta-tor of Fenisa's single weakness: her secret yearning for the joys of love suddenly rekindled by the presence of this "¡Gentil mozuelo!" Dinarda's words, which bring the First Act to a close, suggest that Fenisa's customary astuteness is about to be subverted: "Picada está ya . . . / Aunque sin alfiler," (497b).

As the play unfolds, Fenisa and Dinarda come to em-body, respectively, the two opposing aspects of intelligence. While both possess *ingegno* it is the application of that gift to the surrounding ambience which distinguishes and separates the two women. Fenisa uses her wits to escape her dilemma as a woman seduced and abandoned. She assuages the injury by creating little fictions in which each subsequent seduction is the reenactment of the unhappy love-affair of old. Only now it is Fenisa who seduces and dispatches the lovers with disdain.

Dinarda's intelligence, on the other hand, is at the ser-vice of social conformity. In Dinarda's world one can neither buy nor barter honor and virtue. These are first, inherent, and second, acknowledged by the rest of society in the degree to which one conforms to a preestablished code. Dinarda, unlike Fenisa, uses her wits to create a different kind of fiction, one through which she is eventually reunited with Albano. Al-though she temporarily defies the rules set by society, the infraction will be overlooked provided she returns, properly married, to assume the role Nature and society have ordained. Ironically, once married, Dinarda will come to represent that same prosaic reality against which Albano railed in the open-ing scene. Fenisa, consequently, in the zealous desire to pre-serve her freedom and individuality, emerges as the more exciting and warmly human of the two women, perhaps pre-cisely because her plight is hopeless. In the satisfaction she derives from momentary conquests we perceive the useless

119

flaying of one's arms against the vicissitudes of life. In her present state, Fenisa can never be reintegrated into the harmonious world system which Dinarda represents.

Although the values of Dinarda's world will prevail, the dramatist, for the moment, continues to focus on the genius of the Italian cortesan, for in the ability to defeat so astute an opponent lies the test of true ingenuity. And Fenisa, Lope would have us know, is indeed a clever trickster. To tantalize her victim as she readies him to be plucked, Fenisa softens Lucindo's resolve with more gifts, plays on his sense of virility with erotic suggestions—Celia is sent to check his bed linens for the scent of another woman—and feigns a despondent jealousy which can be relieved only by a visit from Lucindo. Lope has set the scene for Fenisa's master coup. The episode exudes a vitality which derives as much from the dialogue as from the affective prejudice of the man who penned it. Although the dramatist must chastise Fenisa resoundingly at the end of the play, he is not prevented from indulging his admiration for the lady and the slick efficiency with which she relieves Lucindo of his money. Relying on the efficacy of surprise to disorient her victim, Fenisa appears unexpectedly dressed in black and consumed by tears. Never relinquishing control for a moment, the cortesan methodically transforms Lucindo's solicitousness into concrete assistance—two thousand ducats worth. She is quick to allay all qualms with an offer of jewels and *hacienda* as security, knowing full well that Lucindo's sense of indebtedness will never permit him to accept.

Fenisa plays, finally, on Lucindo's pride as a Spaniard "De tierra, ejemplo en el mundo / En hacer bien . . ." (506b). The degree to which Lucindo has been duped by the flattery is apparent in his response to Tristán's admonitions. The merchant insists, "Déjame ser noble un poco, / Y no ingrato a tanto amor; . . ." (506b). Disillusionment will come later. For the moment, Lucindo fancies himself a generous Spanish nobleman. A touch of picaresque realism, however, brings the episode back down to earth as Fenisa and Tristán using colorful jargon sum up the day's events to their respective partners.

120

Fenisa gloats, "Mamóla su senoría, / . . . / No se ha de olvidar jamás / Del anzuelo de Fenisa," while Tristán mutters uneasily, "Este ratón al revés / Nos ha cogido el gato . . ." (507a-b).

Except for Lucindo's revenge which occupies a small portion of Act III, the Boccaccian source has been exhausted. Lope is now free to engage his talents in developing the subplot. The dynamics of the play, however, still depend on Fenisa, now frustrated progressively in her pursuit of Don Juan de Lara. Dinarda, on the other hand, remains largely a catalyst owing to the nature of her role. She initiates no new action. Her presence as Don Juan de Lara, however, provokes a stream of lively episodes which sustain the comicity established from the play's inception. Dinarda is obliged to fend off the cortesan's advances which become increasingly explicit. In order to protect her disguise and hold Osorio's trust, Dinarda must pretend that she does not wish to encroach upon his relationship with Fenisa. Lastly, she is barely able to keep her servants, by now suspicious of the masquerade, from forcing themselves upon her. These scenes, however, are intended largely as a staying device until Lope can bring together the two levels of the play for the climax.

As he approaches the final portion of the work, Lope seems to feel keenly the need to reaffirm a hierarchy of values, one which clearly establishes those of the Sevillian nobles as the greater good. Lope's recognition of the obvious warmth with which he portrays Fenisa and Lucindo, and the consequent desire to clarify his position in the eyes of the spectator and the censor, may be at the heart of the scene which follows. I can see no other reason for its inclusion. In an exchange between Don Félix and Lucindo, as they approach Palermo on the latter's ship (Act III), Lope underlines the polarity of the value systems which guide each man. Don Félix and Lucindo belong to two distinct social orders, one subordinate to the other, with the tacit acceptance of that superiority by the lower-ranking group. Lucindo's words could not be more explicit in this regard:

Lucindo.	Habéisme honrado
	Que siendo don Félix vos,
	Caballero sevillano,
	Yo mercader valenciano,
	Tan desiguales los dos,
	Debo estimar con razón
	Que me tratáis como amigo
	. . . .
	Yo vengo á tomar venganza
	De una mujer . . .
D. Félix.	Así mi dicha fuera;
	Que como hacienda perdiera,
	Ella y yo fuéramos mudos.
Lucindo.	¿Es honra?
D. Félix.	No es menos prenda.
Lucindo:	Sí; pero habéis de saber
	Que en cualquier mercader
	Es honra también la hacienda.
	Tras el caudal, si se pierde,
	Va el crédito, pues perdido . . .

(516a)

In this final portion, Lope seems to venture, although he does not insist upon it, that while the principles which govern the lives of the two men derive from different motivations, those of Lucindo's class may be no less valid. For Lucindo, *hacienda* is equal to *honra*. His is a world of hard-headed self sufficiency, dependent for affirmation on financial success rather than peer approbation. Unfortunately, he harbors no preoccupation of a transcendent nature. Hence the need, as the play nears its end, to subordinate the main plot, verbally and dramatically, to the secondary intrigue concerned with honor. In Lope's scheme of things and, most importantly, in that of his audience, these are the values which must prevail, even if their sudden rise to prominence seems forced. As a consequence, Lucindo's counterscheme is quickly enacted. Fenisa, her customary acumen dulled by success and the promises of Dinarda, is unable to devise the ruse. Once Lucindo has retrieved his money Lope removes him from the play, leaving the stage to Don Félix and the resolution of the honor conflict.

The latter is brought to a happy conclusion through the quick thinking of Dinarda. Still disguised as Don Juan de Lara, she extracts from Don Félix an oath of forgiveness for herself and for Albano before revealing her true identity, much to the chagrin of Fenisa. The latter, having regaled everyone handsomely in expectation of her marriage to Don Juan de Lara, is reduced to a laughing-stock as she attempts to recuperate her gifts and her dignity.

It is in the meting out of justice to Fenisa that the superb adaptation loses some of its power. It follows naturally that Fenisa should, at some point, be tripped up by her own greed. It does not follow that this clever, intelligent, freedom-loving woman should be so easily enslaved by the appearance of Don Juan de Lara. We are prompted to question why, after giving the lady's antisocial behavior credibility, does Lope reduce her to behaving so foolishly? Similarly, while Fenisa's discomfiture at Lucindo's hands is richly deserved, the cruel humor with which Dinarda, the servants, and Osorio respond to her requests seems unduly harsh. I suspect that Lope, caught between admiring the calculating wiles of the subtle trickster and the need to ridicule her so that the world and traditional values of the Spaniards might occupy center stage, opted to stress the latter at the expense of fidelity in character portrayal. Despite the apparent concession to extraliterary pressure, however, Lope offers us a vibrant, unscrupulous cortesan, not easily forgotten and, at times, even capable of arousing our sympathy.

V. Theatrical Innovations

The Role of the Commedia dell'Arte

Beyond the skills with which Lope adapted the *Decameron* themes to seventeenth-century concepts of Fortune, love and wit, the success he experienced as a playwright can be attributed to the uniquely personal stamp which he brought to each theatrical work. At the heart of that talent was the fact that he possessed both a poet's heart and an actor's mind. Despite protestations to the contrary, Lope was a man of the theater, flesh and bone of the very medium for which he wrote abundantly. Although never a performing artist, his intimate ties, both private and professional, with Spanish actors and actresses, led him to a full appreciation and understanding of their craft. As such he could not remain aloof, as he cast the Boccaccian plays, from the innovative theatrical techniques brought to the peninsula by the *Commedia dell'Arte* troupes.[1]

---

[1] On the origins and development of the *Commedia dell'Arte* and its masks see Alessandro D'Ancona, *Origini del teatro Italiano* (Torino: E. Loescher, 1891) II, 443–534; Pierre Duchartre, *The Italian Comedy*, 3rd ed. rev., trans. R. Weaver (New York: John Day, 1929); Allardyce Nicoll, *Masks, Mimes and Miracles* (New

Performing in Spain between 1574 and 1597,[2] the traveling players have been credited, and justly so, with contributing directly to the founding of permanent theaters, the formation of the first Spanish professional companies,[3] the development of the comedy of intrigue, the official presence of women on

York: Harcourt, 1931); Katherine M. Lea, *Italian Popular Comedy*, 2 ed. (New York: Russell and Russell, 1934); Mario Apollonio, *Storia del teatro Italiano* (Firenze: Sansoni, 1951); Vito Pandolfi, *La Commedia dell'Arte. Storia e testo* (Firenze: Sansoni, 1957–60); Winifred Smith, *The Commedia dell'Arte* (New York: Benjamin Bloom, 1964); Giacomo Oreglia, *La Commedia dell'Arte*, trans. L. F. Edwards (New York: Hill and Wang, 1968); and "La Commedia dell' Arte," *Enciclopedia dello Spettacolo* (Roma: Sansoni, 1956), III, 1185–1226.

  [2] For data corroborating the performances of Italian players in Spain see Casiano Pellicer, *Tratado histórico sobre el origen y progresos de la comedia y del histrionismo en España* (Madrid: Real Arbitrio de Beneficiencia, 1804); J. Sánchez Arjona, *El teatro en Sevilla en los siglos XVI y XVII* (Madrid: A. Alonso, 1887); Cristóbal Pérez Pastor, *Nuevos datos acerca del histrionismo español en los siglos XVI y XVII* (Madrid: Imprenta de la Revista Española, 1901); Hugo A. Rennert, *The Spanish Stage in the Time of Lope de Vega* (New York: Hispanic Society of America, 1901); N. Díaz de Escovar, "Anales del teatro español correspondiente a los años 1581–1599," *La Ciudad de Dios*, 82 (1910): 432–40; 789–96; 83 (1911): 146–56; 290–94; and John V. Falconieri, "Historia de la *Commedia dell' Arte* en España," *RLit*, 11 (1957): 3–37; 12 (1957): 69–90.

  For the influence of the Italian masked comedy on Spanish drama of the Golden Age see N. D. Shergold, "Ganassa and the *Commedia dell'Arte* in Sixteenth Century Spain," *MLR*, 51 (1956): 359–68; John V. Falconieri, "Historia," *RLit*, 12 (1957): 78–90; Othón Arróniz, *La influencia italiana en el nacimiento de la comedia española* (Madrid: Gredos, 1969), pp. 208–309; Randall W. Listerman, "Some Material Contributions of the *Commedia dell'Arte* to the Spanish Theatre," *RN*, 17 (1976): 194–98 and "*La Commedia dell'Arte*: Fuente técnica y artística en la dramaturgia de Lope de Rueda," *Actas del Sexto Congreso Internacional de Hispanistas* (Toronto: Univ. of Toronto Press, 1980), pp. 464–66; N. L. D'Antuono, "Lope de Vega y la *Commedia dell'Arte*: Temas y figuras," *Cuadernos de Filología*, Universidad de Valencia, 3 (1981): 261–78.

  [3] According to John V. Falconieri, "Historia," p. 81, a comparison of the earliest Italian theatrical contract on record (1545) and a Spanish contract of 1614 reveals striking parallels as to the payment of regular salaries regardless of illness; the levy of fines for negligence or absence from rehearsals, to be subtracted from the actor's salary for the day; the holding of fines in escrow to be distributed according to the will of the company to charities or pious works; and the same detail as concerns a deposit chest with three keys. For the Italian contract see also E. Cocco, "Una compagnia comica nella prima metà del secolo XVI," *GSLI*, 65 (1915): 56–57. The Spanish contract is reproduced by Cristóbal Pérez Pastor, *Nuevos datos*, pp. 145–48.

stage,[4] and the evolution of the *gracioso*, as perfected by Lope from the comic servant or *zanni*.[5]

Characterized by the recurrence of masked personages, the *Commedia dell'Arte* was an actor's theater made up of professionals bound together by a legal contract with a *capocomico* at the head who functioned as director, manager, actor, and often as author of the evening's comedy.[6] Their performances were imbued with a vital theatrical spirit which they were able to communicate with great success to a wide and multiform audience. It was not the substance of their theater, however, which marked the *Commedia* as innovative but, rather, its elusive flavor which imparted to their performances a dramatic energy as unmistakable as it was hard to define. The *comici* were masters at improvisation, working with *scenari* or *soggetti*, three-act skeleton plots enriched at the moment of execution by the *lazzi*,[7] or comic business which each actor took from his book of commonplaces. It is an aliterary art form in

---

[4] Although it is known that Mariana, the first wife of Lope de Rueda appeared with his acting troupe, it is generally assumed that her role was that of a singer and dancer and not that of an actress. Permission for the offical presence of women on stage as actresses was first granted to Italian actors of the *Confidenti* troupe in 1587. Spanish companies subsequently requested and were granted the same privilege. For details see C. Pérez Pastor, *Nuevos datos*, pp. 19–22.

[5] For a discussion of the evolution of the *gracioso* from the *zanni* and specifically from Harlequin see Edwin B. Place, "Does Lope de Vega's *gracioso* Stem in Part from Harlequin?" *Hispania*, 17 (1934): 257–70; Othón Arróniz, *La influencia italiana*, pp. 285–90. For possible derivation of the name Harlequin and the development of the mask see Otto Driesen, *Der Ursprung des Harlekin* (Berlin: Duncker, 1904) and Giovanni Jaffei, "Note critiche su le maschere in genere e su Arlecchino in ispecie," *Revista d'Italia*, 13 (1910): 771–825.

[6] On the *Commedia dell'Arte* players as the earliest professionals who made of the stage their trade, see John Falconieri, "The *Commedia dell'Arte*, The Actor's Theatre," *The Theatre Annual*, 12 (1954): 37–47.

[7] Katherine Lea, *Italian Popular Comedy*, I, 68, considers the most satisfying definition of the *lazzi* to be that of Luigi Riccoboni: "Nous appellons 'Lazzi' ce que l'Arlequin ou les autres masqués font au milieu d'une scène qu'ils interrompent par des épouvants ou par des badineries étrangères au sujet de la matière que l'on traite et à laquelle on est pourtant toujours obligé de revenir: or ce sont ces inutilités, qui ne consistent que dans le jeu que l'acteur invente suivant son génie, que les comediens italiens nomment 'lazzi," [*Histoire de l'ancien theâtre italien* (Paris, 1728)].

126

which gesture prevails over word, the mask over the individuality of the artist and whose action turns on the basis of schemes and deceptions. The plots, characterized by a pattern of balance and duplication and a rapid forward thrust, are variations on a simple theme: the anguish of young lovers who, after much travail, despite the obstacles posed by avaricious and ever vigilant elders, and with the help of astute servants, succeed in marrying. Not only are the lovers united, but the collective nuptials of all couples on hand is imprescindible. What is Lope's *comedia*, if not a Spanish version of these ingredients?[8]

The *Commedia dell'Arte* masks[9] are subordinate to the intrigue, each assuming a sterotyped name and mode of behavior which came to have greater significance than the actor who played the role. (We remember Harlequin and Punch, but rarely the actors who made them famous.) The masks caricature those personal qualities attributed by Italians to people from the different regions. The old Venetian merchant, Pantalone, is the symbol of an ambitious bourgeois, obdurate in the pursuit of money and foolishly susceptible to love; in short, the requisite figure for burlesquing middle-class social rigidity. Dr. Gratiano, a second father figure and friend or rival of Pantalone, serves to ridicule the pedantry of the Bolognese in his penchant for exaggerated speech saturated with faulty Greek and Latin. The lovers (unmasked), who in the name of youth are permitted all sorts of antics, speak a refined and elegant Tuscan liberally laced with Petrarchan and Neoplatonic conceits. The *zanni*, a lazy, cowardly, uncouth servant,

---

8 Karl Vossler suggests that the Spanish *comedia* in general had almost as little regard for literary perfection as did the Italian traveling players: "Podrían añadirse testimonios sin fin . . . que niegan alto valor artístico a la comedia española. La más contundente prueba del desdén que para ella se guardaba es el apresuramiento que se ponía en su composición, el hecho de que no se tenía el menor reparo en copiar, plagiar, malbaratar, alterar los textos, remendarlos y recurrir al pegote y a la improvisación," [*Lope de Vega y su tiempo*, 2 ed. (Madrid: Revista de Occidente, 1940), p. 257].

9 For a discussion of the masks and their origins by a contemporary, see Pier Maria Cecchini, *Frutti delle moderne commedie e avisi a chi le recita* (Padova: G. Guareschi, 1628).

127

concerned primarily with the pleasures of bed and table, recites in a coarse *patois*, usually the dialect of the Bergamask porters.[10] This mask would eventually evolve into two: an astute, clever *zanni* to attend to the plot and to function as a worldly, cynical servant whose greatest joy is deceiving others; and his complement, the dumb, good-natured fool who is not without an occasional flash of ingenuity. With the advent of women to the stage during the latter half of the sixteenth century, a female counterpart was added. The coquettish serving maid, speaking either in Tuscan or in dialect as the circumstances required, functions as go-between for the *prima donna*, accompanying her to nightly assignations, only to create her own scene as she and the *zanni* parody the high-blown conceits of the lovers.

The mask of the braggart captain is unusual largely because of the circumstances of its conception. As the target of Italian hatred for Spanish domination, the captain comes to represent, in dress as well as in speech, "la soberbia española convertida en fanfarronería y vana jactancia."[11] Not all *Commedia dell'Arte* captains are Spanish, of course. There are also famous French and Italian captains. However, if a Spaniard is on stage, he is always a captain. The captain is sometimes a second lover, always unsuccessful; sometimes a servant, gravitating toward one nucleus or the other at the whim of the *capocomico*. Regardless of the role he assumes, the captain remains the figure most mercilessly ridiculed, especially by the leading lady.

Once women are admitted to the stage, the female roles change radically. Recognizing the drawing power of a lady's

---

[10] The prototypes of the *zanni* were the porters (*facchini*) of Bergamo who made their living in Venice and other cities of northern Italy fetching and carrying merchandise. Katherine Lea, *Italian Popular Comedy*, I. 59, n. 2 suggests consultation of E. Zerbini, *Notizie storiche sul dialetto bergamasco*, 1886) for specific data concerning the stage dialects of the *zanni*. See also B. Belotti, *Storia di Bergamo e dei Bergamaschi* (Milano, n. d.), II, 331 as cited by N. D. Shergold, "Ganassa and the *Commedia dell'Arte*," p. 360.

[11] On the reputation of the Spanish military abroad see Miguel Herrero-García, *Ideas de los españoles*, pp. 59–66.

presence, the *capocomico* and subsequently the *siglo de oro* dramatists, invent excuses for keeping the actresses on stage as much as possible. As a result, we find women immediately accessible at a window or on a doorstep and ready to allay the suspicions of parents or servants with the ploy of an escaped hen or a dropped handkerchief as does Fenisa, in *La discreta enamorada*. The desire for prolonged exposure led quite naturally to the assumption of disguises as slaves, pages (Lisarda as Pedro in *El ruiseñor de Sevilla*), pilgrims or soldiers (Dinarda as Don Juan de Lara in *El anzuelo de Fenisa*). Playwrights begin to make optimum use of the dramatic possibilities inherent in the scenes between the girl/page and the unfaithful lover as Lope does with Albano and Dinarda in *El anzuelo de Fenisa*; and between the willful daughter and the avarcious father or mother, as in the case of *La discreta enamorada*. In short, the female begins to control the action and to exhibit more daring than the young man. The latter consults his servants regarding tricks or deceptions; the lady invents new schemes at a moment's notice. Outwardly modest, the *prima donna* could be as brazen as the practiced cortesan when the need arose. Underlying her often outrageous behavior was the fact that conventional marriage was based on financial expediency and not on emotional affinity. So love became the pivot of every intrigue with the young heroine struggling to exercise what little prerogative she had in the matter.

Lope's familiarity with the Italian players and their masks has been well documented. His repeated attendance at their performances,[12] the innumerable references in his plays to Alberto Naseli, alias Zan Ganassa, to Drusiano Martinelli,

[12] The deposition of Amaro Benítez, in conjunction with the suit for libel against Lope de Vega, confirms the latter's presence at the *Commedia dell'Arte* performances. The testimony reads in part, ". . . y conoce a Lope de Vega . . . y lo que más sabe es que habrá como diez días . . . que estando este testigo en el corral de las comedias en la calle del Príncipe oyendo a los italianos, . . ." and later, ". . . estando este testigo en la comedia del dicho Arlequín entró el dicho Lope de Vega, y haciéndole este testigo lugar, porque entró tarde . . . ," A. Tomillo y C. Pérez Pastor, *Proceso de Lope de Vega por libelos contra unos cómicos* (Madrid: Fortanet, Impresor de la Real Academia de la Historia, 1901), pp. 41–42.

the Trastullo or Arlecchino of the *Confidenti* troupe,[13] and the imitation of their speech in several plays[14] all clearly establishes Lope's intimacy with the new art form. While the servant masks are those most often recalled in his plays, Lope seems to have had a personal predilection for that of Pantalone. The latter mask, made famous in Spain by Stefanello Bottarga,[15] holds so much appeal for the dramatist that during the Carnival festivities in Valencia in 1599 Lope appears costumed allegorically as *Carnaval*, ". . . vestido de botarga, ábito italiano que hera todo de colorado con calzas y ropillas seguidas y ropa larga de levantar de chomelote negro . . ."[16]—in sum, wearing the traditional red and black garb of the classic Pantalone. By the beginning of the seventeenth century, the word *botarga*,[17] a fusion of the actor's name and his costume,

---

[13] References to the Italian comic masks of Ganassa, Trastullo and Arlecchino in Lope's theater have been compiled by Ricardo del Arco y Garay, *La sociedad española*, pp. 721–22. The success of Ganassa and his troupe of players is corroborated by contemporary Spaniards who were, in general, resentful of the attention and earnings he commanded. Othón Arróniz, *La influencia italiana*, p. 216, cites the following statement by Luis Zapata: ". . . había ganado veinte mil ducados . . . en encerrar asnos en un corral," [*Miscelanea*, in *Memorial Histórico Español*, tomo XI, p. 405], and by Rodrigo Fernández de Ribera: "Y de encerrar en un corral Ganassa / asnos (qual otros con mas toldo agora) / ganó para fundar familia y casa," [*Asinaria* (Sevilla: Bibliófilos Sevillanos, 1947)]. In Ricardo del Turia's *Apologetico de las comedias españolas*, written while recollections of the famous Bergamask comic were fresh in his mind we encounter: ". . . como lo vieron los que se acuerdan en España del famoso cómico Ganasa, que en la primera entrada que hizo en ella robó igualmente el aplauso y dinero de todos," *Dramáticos contemporáneos de Lope de Vega* (Madrid: Atlas, 1951, *BAE* XLIII), p. xxiv. For further details regarding Ganassa's life and career see Emilio Cotarelo y Mori, "Noticias biográficas de Alberto Ganassa," *RABM*, 3ª época, 19 (1908): 42–61 and J. V. Falconieri, "Más noticias biográficas de Alberto Ganassa," *RABM*, 60 (1954): 219–222.

[14] Joaquín Arce, "Italiano e italianismi," p. 14.

[15] On Stefanello Bottarga in Spain see N. D. Shergold, *A History of the Spanish Stage* (Oxford: Clarendon Press, 1967), pp. 187–188 and 244–45, and the appropriate portions of works cited in note 1, above.

[16] See F. De Gauna, *Libro . . . del Casamiento y bodas de . . . Phelipe tercero . . .* , ed. Carreres y Zacarés (Valencia, 1926), fol. 142 and Eduardo Juliá Martínez, "Lope de Vega en Valencia en 1599," *BRAE*, 3 (1916): 541–59.

[17] For the popularity of *ganasas* and *botargas* in festivals, processions and tourneys to the present day, see N. D. Shergold, "Ganassa and the *Commedia dell'Arte*," pp. 364–65 and Othón Arróniz, *La influencia italiana*, pp. 246–47.

had become so common that when in *La boda entre dos maridos* Pinabel, a lackey, is stripped down to his underwear by two servants whom he had earlier duped, the stage annotation reads: "Quítenle la sotana y queda en un *botarga* gracioso" (571b). Nor was Lope's audience less familiar with the female roles, especially that of the second servant girl, the coquettish Franceschina.[18] In *El anzuelo de Fenisa*, the cortesan's servant, Celia, is twice referred to as a *Francisquiña*, the name by now a substantive equivalent of a flirtatious maid.

At this point it bears repeating that the *scenari* of the *Commedia dell'Arte* are not literary but theatrical documents.[19] They are bare outlines which describe with varying adequacy each turn in the plot as it is to be presented on stage. As such, they offer, with rare exceptions, no basis for textual comparison. However, if we look to the broad contours of the action and the characterization rather than to the details of conception, the parallel techniques can easily be recognized. For it was not so much the content of the Italian pieces but, rather, the actors' skill in presentation, their creative expressiveness, which held the audiences enthralled.[20] It is this representational capacity absorbed from the *comici* which gives Lope's theater its special coloring, its theatricality, so to speak. While one may argue that many of the masks and techniques find their ultimate source in the Greco-Roman comedy of Plautus and Terence, their immediate accessibility to Lope must be laid

---

[18] The role of the coquettish servant, *la Franceschina*, associated with the *Confidenti*, is responsible for bringing about the official permission for women to play on stage since the lady who assumed the role was unmarried and could not have otherwise fulfilled her obligations to the troupe. See Hugo A. Rennert, *The Spanish Stage*, pp. 142–43 and p. 143, n. 2. In addition to the references in *El anzuelo de Fenisa*, Lope alludes to fickle servant girls as "Francisquiñas traditoras" in *Los amantes sin amor*, Ac. N., III, 152b.

[19] For the extant *scenari* and their locations see K. Lea's "Handlist of Scenari," in *Italian Popular Comedy*, II, 506–54. Plot résumés of the extant *scenari* are provided in Volume V of Vito Pandolfi's *Commedia dell'Arte*.

[20] The traveling players did not only perform comedy, they were excellent tragedians as well. Their dramatic expressiveness won them the respect and admiration of most Europeans. For the reaction of French, Dutch and English critics see John V. Falconieri, "Historia," pp. 3–37.

131

at the door of the *Commedia dell'Arte*. To call attention to this debt is not to impugn the originality of Lope's theater. Rather, it gives testimony to a heightened theatrical intuition which enabled Lope to see in the style of the Italians the myriad possibilities for enriching the nascent Spanish *comedia*. To ignore this relationship would be an injustice as much to the contribution of the *comici dell'Arte* as to the capacity for innovation which characterized Lope's theater and distinguished it from that of his successors.

Lope's captivation with the tripartite structure of the *scenari* is clearly visible in the Boccaccian plays. The symmetry in the disposition of content, inherent in the *novella* and apparent in the Italian performances is successfully transposed to their Spanish counterparts. In *El llegar en ocasión*, for example, the Marquis calls on Laura three times, once in each Act. Otavio, the young lover, appears with the same frequency: in Act I as himself; in Act II disguised as a shepherd; and in Act III pretending to be a *primo casamentero*. Lope adheres to the threefold division in four additional plays. Fenisa, *la discreta enamorada*, sends three messages to her beloved, one in each Act. In *El servir con mala estrella*, there are three instances in which Rugero anticipates a reward and receives none. Laurencia of *El ejemplo de casadas* is subjected to three *pruebas*: the loss of her daughter, the loss of her son, and, finally, rejection by her husband, ostensibly in favor of a younger woman. The lovers of *El ruiseñor de Sevilla* meet on three occasions, once in each of the *jornadas*. *El anzuelo de Fenisa* and *La boda entre dos maridos*, on the other hand, hold to the double pattern inherited from their respective *Decameron* sources.

Beyond the obvious structural parallels, we sense Lope's grasp of the spirit of the *Commedia dell'Arte* in the constituent comic elements and in the delineation of characters strongly reminiscent of Pantalone and the braggart captain. It follows naturally that the personages and episodes which recall the masks and bufoonery of the Italian players should be found in the more lighthearted comedies and, not by coincidence, in those plays where at least one female character is at the center of the action: *El llegar en ocasión* (Laura); *El anzuelo de Fenisa*

(Fenisa, Dinarda); *El ruiseñor de Sevilla* (Lucinda); and, *La discreta enamorada* (Fenisa, Gerarda). This is not to suggest that the remaining plays contain no humorous episodes. It is not, however, the prolonged, rollicking good fun which characterizes the female-dominated plays. For example, although Laurencia is the pivotal figure in *El ejemplo de casadas*, the exemplary nature of the work leaves little avenue for the broad humor and playfulness of the *commedia all'improvviso*. Levity is provided instead by the *loa* and *baile* which precede the work and by one or two brief instances of rustic banter within the play. *El servir con mala estrella* is similarly restricted since all the available dramatic space is taken up with the complexities of a double plot. The only respite is provided by an occasional pithy remark by Turín, Rugero's manservant. While *La boda entre dos maridos* also turns on a double plot, the intrigues do not evolve simultaneously. Consequently, there is some room for trickery among the servants. Comic moments in *El halcón de Federico*, on the other hand, center around Perote, the town fool, who is more appropriately treated in the next section as a uniquely Lopean adjunct.

The narrative core of the *scenari*, limited as it was to the plight of young lovers striving to free themselves from parental restraints, required considerable fleshing-out in order to provide an evening's entertainment. It is here that the talent of the actors, particularly the *zanni* (and later the *gracioso*), is put to the test. Whenever the plot flagged the *zanni* was expected to contrive a *burla* with which to molest a fellow servant or his master. If the time frame were brief, then a *lazzo* would suffice. Depending on the circumstances, this *lazzo* might be a riddle, an anecdote, some funny stage business to delay the action momentarily, or an episode centering on a dramatic knot which had to be unraveled before the play could move forward. In either instance, the purpose was to offer a pause from the intensity of the main line of action before sweeping the spectator along in a new burst of dramatic energy.

The *lazzo* might be no more than the verbal dexterity of a servant as he attempts to escape being throttled by an irate father such as we find in *La boda entre dos maridos*. In this case,

Pinabel concocts a lame excuse in clumsy Latin in an effort to befuddle his captors:

> Señor, ego sum pauper scolasticus:
> Ad prata et fontes veni anime gracia,
> Utinam nunquam me tentaset demon,
> Sedebam illic, quando magnas fames
> Me provocavit as quoerendum fructos;
> Vidi prunas pendentes ex arboribus,
> Ascendo por parietes modo, et intro
> In domum tuam: ¡nunquam ego intrassem!
> Captus sum, sicut paser laqueo istius.
> Misericordia, cordia, cordia, domine.
>
> (576b)

Once the old gentleman storms off, Pinabel is left to fill in the time lapse with a *burla* of his own. Pinabel's facility with Latin enables him to ward off a beating by pretending to be a necromancer as he offers Prudencio's angry servants two magic formulas: "Dos cédulas que valen mil escudos," (578a). One insures success in love; the other at cards. Pinabel now exits hastily, leaving the comic business to the two foolish lackeys who pour over the nonsense syllables only to conclude that they must be Greek. The unresolved efficacy of the *cédulas* and the servants' reactions to their consequences allow for a humorous respite in the next act.

El llegar en ocasión offers a lively variant of the *scena* or *lazzo-in-terzo*.[21] Here the servant usually plays peacemaker between two of the protagonists and hurries to and fro across the stage misinterpreting one party to the other. Lope gives the episode a delightful twist as he offers an enterprising female servant (Fenisa) who translates into piquant language the awkward phrases of a would-be lover (the Marquis of Ferrara) too embarrassed to plead his own suit directly and a reluctant widow who, ostensibly concerned for her honor, appears unable to grasp the nobleman's utterances. The scene is a masterpiece of racy dialogue as the Marquis is reduced to a

---

[21] See K. Lea, *Italian Popular Comedy*, I, 65.

bumbling, inept suitor at the mercy of his feelings and Fenisa presses him to be more specific about his desires:

Fenisa.   Dile que verla querías
           . . .   .
           Y quiere de ti saber
           Que cómo verla pretendes.
Marqués.   ¿Cómo? Pues, ¿tú no lo entiendes?
Fenisa.   Ella lo quiere entender.
           Que, cuanto á mí, bien sé yo,
           Por muy tonta que nací,
           Que la verás y ella á ti,
           De la manera que vió
             Mi padre á mi madre el día
           Que á nueve meses de aquél
           Nació mi hermano Miguel.
Marqués.   Pues dile que eso querría.
Fenisa.   Decláralo un poco más.
Marqués.   Verla en mis brazos
           . . .   .
           Sólo la quiero ofrecer
           Los ojos con que la veo.
Fenisa.   Cierto que es gran devoción;
           ¿Hacéisla Santa Lucía?
Marqués.   Tras los ojos, la querría
           Ofrecer el corazón.
Fenisa.   Eso no es tan santo ya;
           Aguárdame un poco aquí. (354b)

The widow's acceptance, however, does not bring the scene to an end. Lope now reverts to the familiar delay tactic to keep characters and audience alike dangling. Fenisa plays on the Marquis' discomfort, keeping him on tenterhooks with false reports of the lady's obstinacy. Only when he begins to lose all patience does she announce that Laura will see him at ten o'clock that evening.

The *lazzo* of delay may be extended by the telling of anecdotes which, while entertaining, also allow for the passage of dramatic time and the fulfillment of off-stage plot episodes. To account for the assassination attempt which will divert the Marquis from the assignation and result in Otavio's timely arrival, the robbery episode is extended to include two

135

ribald stories about cuckolded husbands. The tales in themselves point again to Lope's acute awareness of Italian materials since they are, in fact, two stories from the *Novellino*.[22] However, they are neither haphazard nor gratuitous additions included merely to provoke laughter. The presence of a cuckolded husband in each case points to a wayward wife and may be seen as an allusion to the easy virtue of the widow who will become Otavio's lover only hours after he arrives at her door. The remainder of *El llegar en ocasión* turns on the reverse of an old *Commedia dell'Arte* ploy. Instead of the lady hiding her lover from a father or husband, we have a widow who must protect her spouse (by promise of marriage) from a higher ranking nobleman who would make her his mistress. The Marquis' persistent efforts to gain the widow's favors provokes the highly comical *rabiar* scene noted earlier in conjunction with the notion of *ocasión*. I call attention to it here for the variation it offers as a staying device. In contrast to the customary Italian pattern, Lope's comic pause is spontaneously engendered by the disguised lover, rather than by a servant, in order to prevent the lady's forced departure. The unbridled hilarity of the scene, however—a gentleman running about, raving, claiming to have been bitten by a rabid dog, a feigned bite to the lady who then pretends to be similarly afflicted and the confusion of the servants who feel obligated to help but tremble at the thought of contamination—are pure and unmistakable *Commedia dell'Arte* farce. The comic gimmickry of the play is so outrageous that Lope himself cannot resist mocking it through one of the servants:

> Después de que éste en casa entró
> Hay mil difuntos, mil cuentos,
> Hablan por los aposentos,
> Y aún he visto sombras yo;
>   Hay brujas, hay mil traiciones,
> Hay primos, y es muy sin duda
> Que en casa de una viuda

---

[22] See Cesare Segre, "Due racconti," pp. 483–87.

Son las más malas visiones.
¡Ya sólo rabiar faltaba!

(386a)

While disguises have always been part of comic theater,
the major contribution of the Italian comedians to Spanish
dramaturgy and especially to that of Lope de Vega is the *disfraz
varonil*. It is, by Lope's own admission, a winning combination, provided the dramatist:

> . . . siempre guarde
> El debido decoro á las mujeres.
> Las damas no desdigan de su nombre;
> y si mudaran traje, sea de modo
> que pueda perdonarse, porque suele
> el disfraz varonil agradar mucho.[23]

Despite its success as a vital feature of Lope's *comedia*, however, the presence of a disguised female inevitably lends itself
to erotic suggestiveness and the implication of a certain loose-
ness of morals which drew the fire of contemporary dramatists
and clergymen.[24] While there were no objections to the artistic
aspects of the technique, a lovely young woman encased in
silk hose, critics insisted, could not fail to stir the libidinous
passions of the spectator. J. Homero Arjona posits that Lope,
ever anxious to please the plebian clientele of the *corrales*,
consciously and repeatedly exploited the erotic potential of the
technique. How else, Arjona argues, does one explain the use

---

[23] Lope de Vega, *El arte nuevo*, p. 296. For studies on the *disfraz varonil* in
Golden Age comedy see M. Romero Navarro, "Las disfrazadas de varón en la
comedia," *HR*, 2 (1934): 269–86; Carmen Bravo-Villasante, *La mujer vestida de
hombre en el teatro español. Siglos XVI-XVII* (Madrid: Revista de Occidente, 1955)
and B. B. Ashcomb, "Concerning *la mujer en hábito de hombre en la comedia*," *HR*,
28 (1960): 43–62. For Lope's use of the technique see J. Homero Arjona, "El
disfraz varonil en Lope de Vega," *BH*, 39 (937): 120–45.
[24] On the censure incurred by Lope's excessive use of the device see J.
Homero Arjona, "El disfraz varonil," pp. 135–45. On censure of the *comedia* in
general (the behavior of actresses was no small part of the condemnation) see
Emilio Cotarelo y Mori, *Bibliografía de las controversias sobre la licitud del teatro en
España* (Madrid. Est. de la Revista de Bibliotecas, Archivos y Museos, 1904), J.
C. J. Metford, "The Enemies of the Theatre in the Golden Age," *BHS*, 28
(1951): 76–92.

of the device in roughly one-fourth of Lope's dramatic production and the steady stream of censure which that usage provoked?[25]

We need only look at *El anzuelo de Fenisa* to find exactly the kind of entertainment which titillated the audience and incensed the moralists. Dinarda's pose as Don Juan de Lara, the amorous inclinations which the disguise arouses in Fenisa and the latter's blatant pursuit of the girl/soldier could hardly have gone unnoticed. Conversely, in the context of the play's setting—the picaresque realm of Palermo's docks—Lope's approach is entirely in keeping with the earthy sensuality of the ambience.

Dinarda has barely appeared on stage when the dramatist calls attention to her overall beauty, and to her legs in particular, through Fenisa's reaction:

> Fenisa.   Fuera de la cara hermosa,
>   Me matan piernas y pies.
> Celia.   Tienes lindo gusto.
> Fenisa.   El mío
>   Este despejo procura;
>   Que del hombre la hermosura
>   Consiste en piernas y brío.
>
>   (497b)

A monologue by Albano, whose memory is jarred by the resemblance of Don Juan de Lara to Dinarda, his former love, alerts the spectator to the disguise. The audience may now view the subsequent encounter between Dinarda and Fenisa with delicious *a priori* irony. Dinarda's natural reticence coupled with feigned *requiebros* to maintain the disguise in the face of Fenisa's ardor are doubly charged, ultimately centering attention on Dinarda's femininity through its opposite manifestation.

Lope holds to the erotic orientation in yet a third sequence, a lively example of banter and by-play in the manner of the Italian *comici*. The scene is twofold: a preliminary ex-

---

[25] For a list of the one hundred thirteen plays in which Lope uses the *disfraz varonil* see J. Homero Arjona, "El disfraz varonil," pp. 121–22, n. 3.

change between Albano and Dinarda's servants which plants seeds of doubt in the latter's minds as to their master's sex and a second portion in which the servants set out to ascertain the truth. As for Albano's inquiries, the episode lends itself to great farce as the astute *criados* put him off by pretending to be Italian servants, a common reality of the times. What makes their comments especially good theater is their round denunciation and ridicule of all Spaniards, a natural reaction given the historical circumstances, but particularly humorous (and also much safer) when placed in the mouths of Spaniards:[26]

Fabio.   ¡Guarda! ¿Spagnuolo marrano?[27]
         ¡Cáncaro che venga a tutti
         Li traditori spagnuoli,
         Furfanti, ladri, mariuoli,
         Assassini per tre scuti!

                                    (501b)

Lope keeps the tirade going, even to the inclusion of a Sicilian song no doubt well-known to soldiers serving on the island:[28]

         Se tutta la Sicilia
         Fosse macarrone,
         Il faro di Messina
         Vino moscatello,
         Il Monte Mongibello
         Formaggio grattato,
         E tutto lo spagnuolo
         Fossino ammazzato,
         ¡Come trionfaria
         Lo siciliano!
                 (502 a-b)

---

[26] The Spaniards were not very tolerant of defamation by Italian actors. Benedetto Croce recalls an episode in which a Pulcinella, performing in Pesaro, "fu bastonato a morte da alcuni ufficiali spagnuoli per certi suoi frizzi contro la loro nazione," [*Saggi sulla letteratura italiana del Seicento*, 3ª ed. (Bari: Laterza e Figli, 1948), pp. 225–226].

[27] On "marrano" as a national insult to Spaniards see: Benedetto Croce, "Ricerche Ispano-Italiane: Appunti sulla letteratura spagnuola in Italia" *Atti della Accademia Pontaniana*, 28 (1898): 1–27; Arturo Farinelli, *Marrano. Storia di un vituperio* (Geneve: L. Olschki, 1925) and Arturo Farinelli, *Italia e Spagna* (Torino: Fratelli Bocca, 1929), II, 212.

[28] See Eugenio Mele, "Una canzone popolare siciliana in una commedia di Lope de Vega," *BH*, 35 (1933) 454–456.

139

The rambunctious humor carries over into the next portion as Fabio and Bernardo set out to certify their suspicions. Bernardo, feigning illness, initiates a series of tactile overtures which become progressively more suggestive as Dinarda, unaware of the ploy, responds to each demand. Lope takes us from "Tócame este pulso," to "Ponme la mano en la frente," to the more personal "Tócame el rostro" until finally Bernardo insists: "Saltos me da el corazón /. . . / Ponme la mano, así vivas, / Sobre el corazón." The rapid movement from temple to forehead to face now gives way to the prolonged holding of Dinarda's hand to Bernardo's breast as the latter challenges, "¿No te dice nada? / . . . / ¿Ni que eres tú quien le mueve?" Before Dinarda can recover, Fabio enters with a more direct confrontation, charging that he already knows the truth, not from what he has discerned but from "Lo que no he visto" (512 a-b). How better to stimulate the spectator's imagination than by reference to unseen private portions? There can be no doubt that Lope is catering to the vicarious enjoyment of his public. Unlike the Italian players, however, whose antics under similar circumstances often degenerated into outright grossness, Lope knows instinctively when to halt the erotic overtures, just short of bawdiness.

In *El anzuelo de Finsa*, Dinarda's disguise, aside from its sensual playfulness, had functioned as a catalyst for dramatic action. The *disfraz varonil* in *El ruiseñor de Sevilla*, on the other hand, remains purely accesorial. Lisarda's pose as a former cabin boy and then as one of Don Félix's staff makes her the perfect candidate for the role of second *zanni* to Riselo, Don Félix's valet. The pair engage in typical *Commedia dell'Arte* buffoonery with Lisarda/Pedro as the trickster and Riselo as the witless fool in these encounters. In the context of the play, however, it is Riselo who undertakes the development of the intrigue, carrying messages back and forth between the lovers. Lisarda/Pedro, with a genius for practical jokes, manages the intervals with her deceptions. The *burlas* serve no purpose other than to augment the sheer exuberance of the play. The disguised maiden's sole dramatic contribution comes at the end of the play when the revelation of her identity prevents a tragic outcome. That Lope intended the Lisarda/Pedro *disfraz* to be primarily one of comic relief is established early in the play by Riselo. When the girl/cabin boy presents herself to Don Félix, Riselo brushes her aside with "No me sirvo de siervos / Que trepan como arlequín." While the use of the verb *trepar* may well allude to the lively manner in which one kept one's balance aboard ship, the designation as *arlequín* recalls immediately the humorous acrobatics of the Italian mask and alerts the audience to the merry romps it may expect from this newcomer. The spectator is not disappointed.

Having barely come upon the scene, Lisarda deceives Riselo with the ploy of the buried gold. Motivated by the greed typical of the comic servant, Riselo anxiously follows Lisarda to the river's edge and sheds his clothes as he searches for the hidden treasure only to discover that there is no gold and that Lisarda has run off with his clothing. Lope keeps the *burla* going as Riselo is forced to run home nude, shouting to passers-by all the while that he is doing this on a bet, only to be greeted by a locked door and Lisarda's shouts from a balcony that Riselo is a ghost. For reasons of propriety the episode is never presented on stage. However, Riselo gives a detailed recollection of it as he attempts to lay hands on Lisarda when next they meet.

Riselo is not above an occasional jest of his own, if only to tease his master with the *lazzo* of the delayed message. While Don Félix paces anxiously about waiting for news that Lucinda's marriage to Don Juan has been foiled, Riselo proffers a note the contents of which, he insists, bring only bad news. It is only when Don Félix can endure no more that Riselo delivers the love note.

The more vigorous *burlas*, however, are still Lisarda's domain. Toward the end of Act II, as Don Félix nervously anticipates the evening's rendezvous, Lisarda indulges in one of the oldest *Commedia dell'Arte* tricks, that of the double disguise. Dressed as a woman, Lisarda lures the gullible Riselo to a nearby house with promises of love, only to extract from him a ruby worth one-hundred *reales*. On the pretext of checking to see that the way is clear, Lisarda slips into the house and

141

emerges minutes later as Pedro, much to the chagrin of the amorous Riselo who now races around frantically in search of a secret door. The jokes go no further, however. The arrival of Adrián, whom Lisarda loves, early in Act II forces the lady to reveal her identity and to ask Don Félix's protection.

Beyond the buffoonery of the servants, additional comicity is provided by the characterization of Justo, Lucinda's father. Although he is a nobleman and a *veinticuatro*, he bears a striking resemblance to Pantalone, the profit-oriented Venetian merchant. The *veinticuatro*, like Pantalone before him, believes that money and gifts will dispel all gloom. Blind to Lucinda's need for love, he offers instead *galas* and *regalos*. Like his Italian counterpart, his credulity knows no bounds. Rather than see his daughter unhappy he readily accedes to the *ruiseñor* ploy, even to the extent of quieting the servants so as not to disturb the "nightingale's" song. Again, however, it is not the simple mimicry of a *Commedia dell'Arte* prototype. Lope's characterization is entirely in keeping with the play's socio-historic reality. Throughout the work we find numerous references to commerce, shipping, lands owned, and goods received. We sense the bustle of a port city in which all citizens regardless of rank engage in trade. The seeming incompatability of nobility and commerce is explained by the common acceptance that Sevillian gentlemen, unlike Castilian *hidalgos*, saw no dishonor in wresting a profit from overseas enterprises.[29] Thus, while Lope ostensibly offers us a traditional father figure of noble lineage, the gentleman's mercantile con-

---

[29] In Justo's consideration of potential husbands for Lucinda from among Sevillian nobility, we find two of Genoese extraction. For the presence of the Genoese in Seville and their contribution to commercial enterprise with the Americas, see Ruth Pike, *Enterprise and Adventure: The Genoese in Seville and the Opening of the New World* (Ithaca: Cornell University Press, 1966). On the commercial interests of the Sevillian nobility, see Ruth Pike, *Aristocrats and Traders. Sevillian Society in the Sixteenth Century* (Ithaca: Cornell University Press, 1972). For Lope's familiarity and possible friendship with Genoese nobles see my study on "Genoese History and Lope's *El genovés liberal*: Sources and Implications," *AION-SR*, (1976): 9–13.

cerns and the taste for opulence point to a relaxed perception of values not dissimilar to those of Boccaccio's Messer Lizio. In *Justo*, Lope succeeds once more in bowing to convention while simultaneously undercutting it.

The play in which we feel the strongest residue of the *Commedia dell'Arte* techniques, however, is *La discreta enamorada*. Here, Lope's indebtedness goes well beyond the occasional use of Italian by a servant or references to a specific role. In its comic liveliness, sparkling dialogue and swift forward movement, the work corresponds exactly to the kind of intrigues for which the Italian players were famous. The plot advances almost entirely on the basis of deceptions, tricks and jokes perpetrated by the characters on one another. Despite the Spanish setting (Madrid), the social conduct and aspirations of the characters have a decidedly Italian flavor. Except for brief references in Act I and in the final sequence of the play, there appears to be little concern for honor. The question of the protagonist's nobility, usually an inseparable adjunct in matters of honor, is also absent. If anything, the characters— with the exception of the lovers—seem more inclined toward the accumulation of wealth than the pursuit of transcendent principles. Their behavior imparts to the work a bourgeois orientation attributable as much to its Boccaccian source as to the spirit of the *Commedia dell'Arte*. Moreover, the personages, though nominally Spanish, are patent calques of Italian prototypes. In addition to the obvious parallels of *zanni/gracioso* and *innamorati/enamorados*, Lope's Captain Bernardo is a brilliant fusion of the Italian braggart captain and Pantalone. The transposition and subsequent melding of these two roles in *La discreta enamorada* warrants comment as it serves to underscore Lope's debt to the *comici* as well as his particular affinity for the masks. Although the mask of the captain had functioned primarily as a vehicle for expressing Italian anger at the Spanish military presence, once the corresponding historic reality was altered, bombastic rhetoric and exaggerated dress could no longer guarantee the role continued vitality. The captain became of necessity a satellite character playing an unsuccessful suitor, a foolish old man, or even a servant. In each and every circumstance, nevertheless, he remains the mask "maggiormente bersagliata . . . senza pietà."[30]

That Lope, too, intended to burlesque the military may be gleaned from the stage directions for the character's first appearance: "Sale Bernardo [viejo] muy galan, con su gorra de plumas, espada daga [en fin] como capitan a lo antiguo."[31] The description, if not in itself humorous, thrusts into relief a figure long since passed from vogue and consequently risible. The captain's initial swaggering posture as well as his presumptuous comportment throughout the work render him as fatuous as his outlandish garb. When he calls on the ladies, Bernardo's audacious entrance and the tenor of his speech sets the tone for the caricature. His return from Flanders, Bernardo insists, has stirred him to great deeds. And forge ahead he does. Neither humble nor reticent, he embarks on a lengthy discourse regarding his age, birth, illustrious godparents and even the state of his health. Anxious to appear young and virile, Bernardo refers to his grown son as "ese hijuelo" and ends with a play on words concerning his ". . . cansada edad . . . que no es cansada" (401b).

In his desire to please the young girl he believes to be in love with him, Bernardo suffers all sorts of tribulations, much in the fashion of Pantalone, "il vecchio scioccamente innamorato, oppure padre destinato alla burla."[32] Like his Italian counterpart, Bernardo relies for his success on the power of gifts and gold:

> Y si esta nieve no trata
> Bien el juvenil decoro
> Juntando á tus hebras de oro
> Estos cabellos de plata,

---

[30] Vito Pandolfi, *La Commedia dell'Arte*, I, 328.

[31] Lope de Vega, *La discreta enamorada, in Comedias escogidas de los mejores ingenios de España* (1652–1705), III, 62v. The words in brackets are omitted in the Royal Spanish Academy's edition, XV, 401b, and in that of the *Biblioteca de Autores Españoles*, XXIV, 158b.

[32] For a fuller description of the mask of Pantalone see V. Pandolfi, *La Commedia dell'Arte*, I, 297–99.

Suplir en regalos y galas
Los defectos de la edad . . .
(403b)

Were this not enough, Captain Bernardo's congratulations to Belisa, the girl's mother, when he learns that his son Lucindo wishes to marry her (a ploy intended to throw the mother off guard) underscores not only his inability to capture the prevailing circumstances but also the degree to which he has been duped. As for the Captain's assumption of a servant's role, the three messages which Fenisa tricks him into delivering to her beloved offer ample testimony.

The intimate relationship between the role of Captain Bernardo and that of Fenisa, who once having accepted his proposal of marriage orchestrates the Captain's every move, prompts the recollection of a well-known sixteenth-century *Commedia dell'Arte* captain and first lady. I refer to Francesco Andreini, *capocomico,* famous for the mask of the braggart *Capitano Spavento della Val Inferno,*[33] and his wife, the *prima donna* Isabella Andreini, whose performances were hailed throughout Europe.[34] Could not the Italian acting couple and the roles they immortalized have suggested the characterization of the corresponding roles in *La discreta enamorada*? I believe so. My assumption is encouraged by several pieces of data. According to Morley and Bruerton, Lope's play was written between 1606 and 1608. Isabella Andreini died in

---

[33] Francesco Andreini, *Le bravure del Capitano Spavento* (Venetia, 1615), reproduced in V. Pandolfi, *La Commedia dell'Arte,* I.

[34] There is no record of the Andreini's having performed in Spain. However, the following commentary suggests otherwise. Concerning the role of Flaminio, Allessandro D'Ancona notes that G. Fabri, the actor who was the most celebrated Flaminio (lover), had traveled to Spain, with the Andreini's. Unfortunately, D'Ancona does not give the source of his information, [*Lettere di comici Italiani del Secolo XVII* (Pisa: Nistri, 1893), p. 19, n. 1]. John V. Falconieri, "Historia," p. 85, n. 16, mentions a document in the Archives of Seville which refers to a popular Spanish company of actors playing under the name of *Los Celosos,* clearly in imitation of the Andreini's world famous troupe, *I Gelosi*. The question remains, however, did the Spaniards model themselves after a group with which they had had direct contact or one which they knew by reputation?

France on June 11, 1605.[35] Shortly thereafter her husband, Francesco, retired from the stage. Had Lope intended to honor their memory in *La discreta enamorada*? While the lack of an autograph manuscript of the play precludes a definitive answer, there is no doubt that Lope had been strongly impressed by the acting talents of the Andreini. He pays unmistakable tribute to the fame of the Italian couple in an early scene from *El castigo sin venganza*, composed almost three decades later. In this episode, the Duke of Ferrara, anxious for a night of revelry, sets out with his servants to find an appropriate place:

Ricardo.	Si quieres desenfadarte
	Pon á estas puertas el oído
Duque.	¿Cantan?
Ricardo.	¿No lo ves?
Duque.	¿Pues quién
	vive aquí?
Febo.	Vive un autor
	de comedias.
Ricardo.	Y el mejor
	de Italia.
	. . . .
Duque.	¿Ensayan?
Ricardo.	Y habla una dama.
Duque.	Si es Andrelina, es de fama;
	¡Qué acción! ¡Qué afectos! ¡Qué estremos!

(239b–240a)

If we consider that the play takes place in Ferrara, domain of the Este family,[36] who, with the Gonzagas of Mantua[37] were the patrons of the Andreini, then "la Andrelina," despite the slight shift in spelling, can be none other than Isabella An-

---

[35] For details concerning the funerary honors to Isabella Andreini see Armand Baschet, *Les Comédiens Italiens á la cour de France* (Paris: E. Plon, 1882), pp. 146–48.

[36] On the friendship of the Andreini's with the Este family see Winifred Smith, *The Commedia dell'Arte*, p. 151.

[37] The relationship of the Spanish court with the Gonzaga family is treated by Othón Arróniz, *La influencia italiana*, pp. 192–99. See also Gerald E. Wade and Jaime José González, "Tirso de Molina and the Gonzagas," *Hispania*, 55 (1972): 264–77.

dreini and the "autor de comedias" her husband Francesco. That Lope should, thirty years after the lady's demise, pay homage to her talent and that of her spouse implies a high regard stemming from the possible direct contact with the acting couple during the latter half of the sixteenth century. Certainly, the vitality of *La discreta enamorada* which derives from the superb manner in which Fenisa tricks and manipulates an elderly betrothed, a foolish, avaricious mother and Gerarda, rival for Lucindo's affection prompts us to echo: ¡Qué accion! ¡Qué afectos! ¡Qué estremos!

The possibility of homage to the Andreini's notwithstanding, *La discreta enamorada* remains the Boccaccian play which best exemplifies the degree to which the *Commedia dell'Arte* masks and techniques were incorporated into Lope's dramaturgy. While there is no *disfraz varonil*, the play abounds in disguises, all of which lend an air of constant upheaval to the work. The humorous misconceptions resulting from the disguises send the play hurtling in unexpected directions from which the dramatist must retrieve it with yet another scheme or timely clarification by the all-knowing *gracioso*. Hernando's pose as "Estefanía," a ploy designed by Lucindo to make Gerarda jealous, is rollicking good fun in the truest *Commedia dell'Arte* spirit, to the point of ending in the on-stage beating of Hernando by the furious cortesan. "Estefanía" acquires a life of her own and begins to make her presence felt in the complications of the second and third acts. Gerarda's subsequent reference to the incident and to the lady's name send Doristeo in pursuit of Lucindo with drawn sword, for Estefanía is also the name of Doristeo's carefully guarded and recently widowed sister. Bloodshed is avoided only by Lucindo's rejoinder that Fenisa is his intended bride. The latter information, once relayed to Gerarda, results in the introduction of yet another "Estefanía," the role Gerarda assumes in an effort to stay the elopement of Lucindo and Fenisa. Who would not be moved to uproarous laughter at the sight of "Estefanía" running to Fenisa's home steps ahead of a knife-wielding "husband"? Only the *gracioso's* revelation of the truth of the disguise restores the action to its original course—but not without a last-ditch effort by Gerarda, this time disguised as a man. The commotion she creates outside Fenisa's home, while too late to prevent the marriage, brings the play to a quick and happy resolution.

Any reservation we may have as to the *Commedia dell'Arte* orientation of Lope's *mise en scène* is quickly dispelled by the notation of the reverse of the pattern—the Spanish playwright's contribution to the Italian comic repertory of the seventeenth and eighteenth centuries.[38] Lope's dramatic power, along with the technical and theatrical innovations absorbed so thoroughly from the Italian traveling players, made him the single most imitated playwright, with nineteen *scenari* clearly traceable to his theater. It is not surprising then that from among the Boccaccian plays, *La discreta enamorada* emerges once again as the most cogent expression of that compenetration. We find it recast in 1734 as a *scenario* entitled *L'innamorata scaltra* by the amateur actor/priest, D. Placido Adriani.[39]

---

[38] An examination of the "Handlist of Extant *Scenari*," as published by K. Lea (II, 506–54), reveals a total of thirty–eight *scenari* deriving in the following manner from among Spanish playwrights: Lope, 18; Calderón, 9; Tirso, 2; Moreto, 3; Pérez de Montalván, 2; Mira de Amescua, 2; Guillén de Castro, 1; and Ruiz de Alarcón, 1. Three others are labeled as Spanish in origin but no precise source is indicated. Lea considers an additional thirty *scenari*, on the basis of content, to also be taken from Spanish materials. In light of the seven hundred scenari which Lea examined, the Spanish-based plots constitute then, approximately ten percent of the total production. I would conjecture, as a result of my own investigations, that we may find many more *scenari* to be based on Spanish models. For the nineteenth *scenario* of Lopean origin see N. L. D'Antuono, "The *comedia* in Italy: Lope's *La discreta enamorada* and its *Commedia dell'Arte* Counterpart," *La Chispa '81. Selected Proceedings* (New Orleans: Tulane University Press, 1981) pp. 69–82.

[39] *Selva overo Zibaldone di concetti comici raccolti dal P. D. P. Adriani di Lucca.* MDCCXXXIIII. Biblioteca Comunale, Perugia, Codex A. 20. The miscellany contains a carefully indexed collection of plots, *lazzi*, songs, sonnets, prologues, salutations, soliloquies, tirades, dialogues, riddles and musical or comical *intermezzi*. A substantial portion of the material is written in the Neapolitan dialect, especially that which concerns the masks of Pulcinella and Coviello. These masks appear in *L'innamorata scaltra* as well as in a large number of other pieces. Don Placido's religious calling—he was a priest of Lucca—did not apparently interfere with his favorite pastime, amateur acting. He is also the author of four plays, one of which, *La commedia in commedia*, he readily labels as being "trasportata dallo spagnolo."

148

In bringing the *Decameron* tales to the Spanish stage, Lope took from the Italian players all that would give impetus and vitality to his theater. As the preceding pages indicate, his was not a servile imitation but, rather, a selective adaptation of those components which would prove most fruitful for Lope's new conception of the *arte de hacer comedias*: "Lope de Vega ha encontrado lo que buscaba. Se levanta entonces, de su asiento del Corral del Príncipe y abandona el sitio."[40]

The Lopean Imprint

The intelligent manipulation of Boccaccio's narrative content and the representational skills of the Italians, however, is not sufficient to account for the vigor of these plays and the popularity they enjoyed. Their dramatic energy stems from Lope's ability to codify the novellistic and theatrical formulations available to him and to fuse these to the social and ideological mandates of his age in such a way that the emerging comedies are cohesive units which speak to the minds and hearts of seventeenth-century Spaniards.[41] When we consider the physical limitations of the Golden Age *mise en scène*—performances by daylight, primitive scenographic elaboration and a restless and demanding audience—Lope's accomplishments loom all the more spectacular.

The blending of these disparate ingredients was no simple matter, for while Lope found much to imitate in both

---

[40] See Othón Arróniz, *La influencia italiana*, p. 290.

[41] Rinaldo Froldi delineates clearly the shortcomings of the Italian comic mode and the adjustments necessary for the elaboration of a theater which spoke to the esthetic and moral exigencies of seventeenth-century Spanish drama: "En este clima se explica como en España, ante el éxito de la nueva forma de arte que amenazaba con deslizarse hacia una burda reproducción de la realidad o a esquematizarse en fórmulas, tipos y gestos fijos, con una finalidad meramente edonista, los literatos advirtiesen, por una parte las inmensas posibilidades del teatro dentro de estas mismas exigencias éticas y estéticas, y, por otra, la necesidad de una disposición del nuevo género en formas de arte más coherentes con vistas a un orden, a una disciplina y a principios teóricos, que no fuesen, sin embargo, abstracción doctrinal, sino que se organizasen en contacto con la misma experiencia," [*Lope de Vega y la formación de la comedia* (Salamanca: Anaya, 1968), p. 93].

Italian sources, the production of a play in the immediate esthetic climate demanded a continuing compromise between Lope the poet and Lope the man of the theater, between the claims of literature and those of the stage. Total separation of the two aspects is impossible, since neither can function alone and both demand their due.[42] Witness the eventual dissipation of the *Commedia dell'Arte*. Entertainment was their primary concern. They made no claim to literary significance. Experience taught the actors *what* would please their audience; *how* they did so was the task of their art. A theater that functions on the basis of a written text, on the other hand, requires that the dramatist resolve the differences between literature and performance by adroitly counterbalancing both interests. The playwright's capacity for dealing with the tension generated by the polarity is invariably reflected in his plays. In Lope's case the pull between literature and theater spurred him to greater inventiveness as the challenge was converted into a life-giving force which is happily transfered to the Boccaccian plays.

This is not to suggest that there are no occasions when Lope's efforts fall short of the mark. Precisely because the balance was not always easy to sustain we find in the comedies under discussion some moments when the delicacy of the Boccaccian source is awkwardly adjusted to the demands of acting and others when Lope augments the joyful spirit of the *Decameron* with humorous inventions for which there is no justification other than to satisfy the cravings of a popular audience. We are less apt to be offended by the latter since they are extraneous to plot development. The former, however, affect the very fiber of the play.

A case in point is Boccaccio's falcon story, recast as *El halcón de Federico*. Here the chivalric mode falls apart for it is far too lyrical and not sufficiently theatrical. In his attempt to vitalize the static human dimension of the source, Lope destroys the spiritual aspect of the chivalric exercise as much for

---

[42] K. M. Lea, *Italian Popular Comedy*, II, 339–342.

Federico as for the Spanish counterpart of Monna Giovanna. The result is a pedestrian love story in which the gentility of the Italian *novella* has been sacrificed to the exigencies of the stage. A similar fate might have befallen *El ejemplo de casadas*, whose source is equally undynamic, except for the fact that the figure of an exemplary Christian wife continued to have meaning for Lope's spectator. The rarified world of chivalry, on the other hand, had long been enervated.

As Lope's *comedia* began to make its presence felt on the boards, an additional set of circumstances heightened the tension between the literary text and stagecraft. By the late 1580's, Spanish men of letters were obliged to respond to the pressure of a new direction as literature became, in addition to a medium of entertainment, a vehicle for the propagation of Post-Tridentine reforms. The spirit of Counter-Reformation morality, based as it was on an inordinate fear of corruption equated with Protestantism, so infused Spanish society that both public and author acceded to a self-imposed censorship. What limitations the dramatist failed to accept were willingly handed down in the form of ecclesiastical restrictions: the censorship of plays and performances, the prohibition of low-ranking clergy—a goodly portion of the literate audience—to attend the plays, and the refusal to grant communion and even burial to actors.[43] In sum, Lope was constrained to create from the tensions between theory and practice a new dramatic expression, one within the confines of Church and Monarchy. This does not mean that each and every Lopean comedy is primarily a ritualistic celebration of national ideals. Had it been so, the audience would have soon abandoned the theater. Rather, Lope offers a make-believe world into which to escape as a relief from the pressures of Counter-Reformation strictures; a fantasy world in which Lope simultaneously, though never heavy-handedly, reaffirms, or at least appears to reaffirm, those very precepts.

---

[43] For a résumé of ecclesiastic restrictions see John V. Falconieri, "Historia," pp. 76–78. See also Emilio Cotarelo y Mori, *Bibliografía*, cited in note 24, above.

Compliance with the expurgation of material deemed morally offensive was easily accomplished. Objectionable episodes were placed, wherever possible, in an acceptable context or eliminated altogether. The love motif, present in the source material or invented by Lope, was made to conform to contemporary standards of morality. The code of honor, an inseparable aspect of the configuration, demanded that love matches end in marriage or death, preferably the former. The treatment of ruling sovereigns as men in love, however, called for a most particular sensitivity since the women they loved were rarely their wives. How would one satisfy, then, the requisites of the honor code and the dramatic convention of poetic justice when one is dealing with a king who, by virtue of derived power, was answerable only to God? Not without a great deal of forethought and imagination. The subplot of *El servir con mala estrella* offers an excellent example of Lope's capacity for an accommodation which satisfies all moral, social and theatrical exigencies. When Tello, brother to Doña Sancha, accidentally comes upon the king in Sancha's quarters, he is prevented by feudal law from taking revenge. Yet he cannot remain silent and thus give tacit consent to dishonor. To free Tello from his obligation to act, Lope resorts to the motionless-figure device whereby in the imagined darkness the king may be taken to be a life-size portrait of himself. Tello thus is able both to vent his displeasure and ironically to reprimand the intruder, without openly criticizing his sovereign:

> ¿Hay más notable pintura (aparte)
> De la majestad de un rey?
> Divina y humana ley
> De mi espada le asegura.
> . . .   .
>   ¿Quién trajo a casa el retrato,
> Hermana, del senor Rey?
> . . .   .
>   Pero yo, Sancha, quisiera
> Que el pintor que lo ha pintado,
> Como está en la guerra armado,
> En el lienzo lo pusiera;

Que son lustrosas y bellas
Las armas reales y adorno,
Y otra vez a decir torno
Que parece mal sin ellas.
  Los que le vieran galán
En casa de una mujer
Por casar, que el lo ha de ser,
Ó que lo ha sido, dirán.
  Con el bastón y la espada,
Como está ahora en la guerra,
Que entra el moro por su tierra,
Será pintura extremada;
  No en nuestra casa, no así . . . .
                                    (536a)

Sancha and the king become lovers, however, and an illegitimate child is born to them, but not before Tello is poisoned by his sister in order to protect the child and herself. Yet no punishment is meted out to either character in the course of the play. Lope placates the audience's moral indignation through the auguries of Zelima, Sancha's Moorish servant, that both Alfonso VII and Sancha will pay for their transgressions in the horrible end which awaits their daughter Estefanía.[44] Castigation is left to Divine Providence and offense to the monarchal ideal is averted.

---

[44] Marcelino Menéndez y Pelayo offers two possible sources for Lope's data concerning Estefanía, the illegitimate daughter of Alfonso VII: *Crónica del emperador D. Alonso VII* of Fray Prudencio de Sandoval (1600) and the *Tragedias de amor* of Juan de Arce Solórzano (1604). Menéndez y Pelayo cites Sandoval's version as one which must have been known to Lope's audience. A servant of Doña Estefanía, when the lady was asleep, would make her way to the garden, wearing her mistress' cloak, to meet her lover. She was seen on several occasions by two squires. The latter, believing her to be Lady Estefanía, report this to her husband, Fernando, who has just returned from a long journey. Fernando and the squires observe the same scene the next night. Fernando interrupts the meeting and kills the man. The woman escapes and hides under Estefanía's bed. Fernando bursts into the room and kills his wife as she is asleep with her son. When lights are brought, Fernando discovers that his wife is wearing only a nightshirt. He then finds the maid who confesses all. She is publicly burned at the stake. Fernando gives himself up to his wife's family for punishment but is absolved, (*Obras de Lope de Vega*, VIII, lxviii–lxix).

Underlying Lope's talent for accommodating the content of his plays to Counter-Reformation dictates was an instinctive sense of theater and a consummate understanding of human weaknesses, his own as well as those of the spectator. Lope recognized the need to grasp and sustain the spectator's attention, never allowing the dynamism to wane and using every device conceivable, so that the spectator remains ever attentive to the fiction before him. Although Lope makes full use of the external contrivances suggested by the *Commedia dell'Arte*, the totality of his art makes exclusive dependence on them unnecessary. With a fixed text, the playwright can avail himself of a number of internal techniques to rivet the public's gaze and ear. Given the multifaceted audience which by Lope's time included a healthy number of the working classes, a faultless exposition of plot becomes essential to audience control.

Within a few scenes the dramatist offers his audience all the major threads which he will systematically weave and interweave. Moreover, the exposition is so structured so that the material in the succeeding acts is a logical outgrowth of elements already present in Act I. Occasionally, however, the nature of the content or the complexity of the intrigue requires a more protracted introduction. For example, the exposition in *El servir con mala estrella* cannot be hurried since Lope is creating a hero in the image of the Cid. Time is needed to bring out Rugero's valor, his eagerness to serve the king well, the envy that those qualities provoke among other nobles and the king's lack of recognition. Similarly, the exposition of plot for *El ejemplo de casadas* and *La boda entre dos maridos* moves slowly owing to the fact that both plays involve sacrifices of an extraordinary nature; one out of love and fidelity to her husband; the other out of love for a friend. Given the unusual behavior of the protagonist in each instance, the extensive introduction does not appear unnatural; ample background is necessary to render the sacrifices comprehensible.

Although Laurencia is the protagonist of *El ejemplo de casadas*, her Job-like patience and humility can only have meaning in comparison to the tests to which she is subjected.

The major portion of Lope's exposition, therefore, is devoted to clarifying for the spectator the psychological motivations which prompt Enrico to test his wife in such a drastic manner. The nature of his fears is evident in conversations with his vassals and in his violent reaction as town judge to the cases of marital discord brought before him. Insights into Laurencia's character are brought forth in the talks with her companions, with Enrico on how to choose a good wife, and, later, with her father when he announces that Enrico has come to marry her. Laurencia's words which bring Act I to a close, ". . . aquí se burla la fortuna: / Yo seré ejemplo extraño," give only a slight hint as to what may happen. The main thrust of the play is stated in the opening scene of Act II although, oddly enough, it does not refer to Laurencia. It is uttered by Danteo, a shepherd who also loves Laurencia: "Yo vengo, Belardo, á ver / La prueba de la paciencia / Mayor que pudo tener," (23b). The recitation of a portion of the title is sufficient to point the way for the spectator.

In *La boda entre dos maridos*, Lope devotes a considerable part of Act I to the close relationship between the two protagonists, especially Febo's excessively strong attachment to Lauro. The latter's immoderate degree of emotion gives credibility both to the melancholy into which he sinks out of love for Lauro's fiancée and in turn to the sacrifice made by Lauro. The inseparable nature of friendship is underscored repeatedly in Act I. The full inference is clarified early in Act II when Andronio, Fabio's rejected suitor, in anger, foreshadows the outcome of the play:

> ¡Plega á los cielos que ni á Lauro goces
> Ni en tus brazos jamás á Lauro veas,
> Que vengas á gozar quien no conoces,
> Y que te goce á ti quien no deseas!
> (587a)

Once the play is set in motion Lope is obliged to develop, heighten, and sustain the tension engendered by the exposition until the conflict can be brought to a satisfactory resolution. This is accomplished in several ways. All incidents are prepared well in advance so that they are a natural consequence of a previous hint, references or suggestion. Audience satisfaction is ensured as the complications they had been led to expect come to pass. The flow of the drama is enhanced by a clever concatenation of events and the playwright's ability to shift tone quickly to avoid monotony. Serious, tense moments are generally of short duration, and are followed by lighter episodes or humorous commentary. Lope knows instinctively when to halt the rapid flow of the play, insert a pause scene, and then gather up the audience in a new burst of excitement.

Unlike the farcical moments of the *Commedia dell'Arte*, Lope's pauses, though momentarily refreshing, are well-integrated, logical interludes dictated by the needs of the script. They may be a comment on the principal action from the point of view of a servant or a minor figure. For example, the musician's ballad in Act III of *El servir con mala estrella* while treating of the Cid and the envy at court which prevented his just reward, is clearly intended as a résumé of Rugero's faithful and unrecompensed service to Alfonso VII.

Pause scenes often appear at the beginning of Act II as part of the technique of recapitulation when considerable time has elapsed between acts. In *El halcón de Federico*, a lengthy conversation between the protagonist and Riselo, a servant whom he has not seen in years, tells the audience about Celia's continued disdain, despite her widowhood. Don Íñigo's absence from court serves as an opportunity for Ramiro of *El servir con mala estrella* to tell us that Rugero is still unrewarded, and that the king has kept his former mistress and child at court, much to the chagrin of the lady.

Pause scenes may function to heighten dramatic tension by contrasting sharply with what has preceded as well as what will follow. Act II, Scene 5 of *El ejemplo de casadas* concerns the visit of several *villanos*, former companions to Laurencia, on the occasion of her new-born son's christening. The happy moment, replete with songs by the villagers, thrusts into distinct focus Laurencia's unexpressed anguish over her daughter who minutes before had been taken from her, on Enrico's orders. Enrico's unreasonableness is all the more striking as he chases the villagers disparagingly and, once they have gone, announces that he intends to deprive Laurencia of her new son.

Lope often inserts a pause just prior to the dénouement. Contrived momentarily to confuse the spectator, this scene usually introduces a new element which threatens to alter the projected course of the resolution, thereby enhancing the impact of the dénouement when it is finally brought about. The reader will recall Otavio's accidental stumbling over Federico (the escaped assassin of *El llegar en ocasión*), the subsequent misinterpretation of the latter's presence, and Otavio's violent denunciation of Laura. In *El halcón de Federico* Celia finally calls on Federico after ten years, not to dine with him as he erroneously assumes, but only to buy his falcon for her ailing son. Before she can make her request, however, Federico goes out and kills the bird, planning to serve it for dinner. The dramatic irony is intensified by the fact that the sacrifice is unnecessary.

The use of pause scenes to ease dramatic tension and the resultant balanced dispersement of serious and happy moments, along with the transposition to the stage of the symmetry characteristic to the *novella* and the Italian *scenari* are but one aspect of Lope's theatrical architecture. To the highly contrived plots and preordained conclusions Lope brings an intense humanity deriving from the presence of the author in his own works, the ability of the comedia to laugh at itself without breaking the illusion, and the vitality of character portrayal. In no other Golden Age dramatist do we find such a willingness to pour forth one's creative energies and to divulge without reservation personal anguishes as well as stock contrivances until author, actor and spectator are no longer separate entities but co-creators of a new theatrical reality. Mutually stimulating yet independent, each makes demands on the other as Lope educates his public while simultaneously catering to their whims and pleasures. It may be termed an *engañar-con-la-verdad* pattern between author and spectator in which Lope teases the audience with parody-like summaries of theatrical ploys, then proceeds to develop them right under the spectator's very nose. The public, though conscious of the tricks, was not ready to cast aside the time-honored formulas. Rather, they looked to Lope for their reinforcement. Lope never disappointed them.

One of the most stylized aspects of the seventeenth-century *comedia* is the relationship between the sexes. Marriage, within the theater and without, was most often a matter of parental decision governed by financial expediency. As a consequence, social intercourse between men and women was possible only under the most controlled circumstances. Rigid codes, however, make poor theater, unless they can be circumvented, or at least bent slightly, in the name of love. The more inflexible the code, the more inventive and numerous the subterfuges by which the *galán* hopes to reach the carefully guarded maiden, or she to escape the vigilance of a wily parent. And who better than Lope to enumerate the most common deceptions of frustrated lovers? The following lines from Act I of *La discreta enamorada* underscore the game-like nature of the courtship pattern. The verses are doubly delightful in that they are recited by the young lady herself in defense against her mother's accusations:

> ¿Qué mancebo me pasea
> Déstos que van dando el talle?
> ¿Qué guijas desde la calle
> Me arroja, porque le vea?
>   ¿Qué seña me has visto hacer
> En la iglesia? ¿Quién me sigue?
> ¿Qué á estar celosa te obligue?
> ¿Qué vieja me vino a ver?
>   ¿Qué billetes me has hallado
> Con palabras deshonestas?
> ¿Qué pluma para respuestas,
> Qué tintero me has quebrado?
>   ¿Qué cinta, que no sea tuya
> O comprada por tu mano?
> ¿Qué chapín, qué toca?
>   (400b)

Lope addresses the artificial yet indispensable character of the courtship formula through a second Boccaccian heroine, the widow of *El llegar en ocasión*. Here, the lady berates her lover for his presumptuousness while listing the requisite gestures for winning and holding a woman's love:

> ¿Qué años te cuesto de pena?
> ¿Qué papeles, qué paseos
> Debo á tus locos deseos?
> ¿Qué noche de nieve llena?
> ¿Qué torneos en Ferrara
> Has hecho, Otavio, por mí?
> Dime, ¿qué lágrimas vi
> Que te bañasen la cara?
> ¿Qué hacienda tienes perdida?
> ¿Qué mercader te ha fiado
> Los vestidos que me has dado?
> ¿Qué sortijas, qué vajillas,
> Cintura, coral, manillas,
> Y cadenas al platero?
> ¿En qué enfermedad primero
> Me has servido de rodillas?
> Di, ¿qué diamantes al tope
> Me cuelgan de las orejas,
> Para formar tantas quejas
> Tu amor, de que un hombre tope?
> ¿Qué lacayos has sacado,
> Vestidos de mi color?
> ¿Qué bravo competidor
> Has muerto ó acuchillado?
> ¿En qué plaza, con rejones,
> De mi ventana delante,
> Hiciste suerte importante,
> Que á darme quejas te pones?
> (371b)

Ironically, Otavio has already won the lady's love with only the promise of marriage while the Marquis, who complies with all the appropriate gestures, fails miserably.

As for the oft-criticized rapidity with which the *galán* falls in love, Lope both defends and spoofs the technique in *La boda entre dos maridos*, as Teodoro reacts to Andronio's suddenly-conceived passion for Dorena. Teodoro's reference to his own presence at *comedia* performances in Madrid, as if the latter were theater and the present stage fiction "real life", serves to remind the spectator of the illusory nature of art:

> Cuando yo en España oía
> Comedias, ví que cansaba
> Si el galán se enamoraba
> Luego de aquello que vía;
> Que con saber que en dos horas
> La historia era fuerza acabar,
> Un mes quisiera esperar
> El punto en que te enamoras.
> Contigo disculpo aquí
> Lo que en las comedias veo; . . .
> (601a)

The same complicity between Lope and his audience which allowed for the satirization of stock techniques while simultaneously deploying them often gives rise to incidental reference to other Lopean compositions in the play being presented. I noted in Chapter IV that the opening line of *El anzuelo de Fenisa* is a direct quotation from an earlier sonnet written for Micaela de Luján. Lope apparently enjoyed some fame as a writer of song lyrics, at least those to be used in his plays. The musician in *El ruiseñor de Sevilla* "Canta apacible-mente á lo moderno / Con tonos de Juan Blas, letras de Lope," (70b). In the Prado scene of *La discreta enamorada*, the cortesan, Gerarda, asks the musicians to play "la de Lope," (410a).

The latter play allows Lope to indulge in yet another form of satire: the burlesquing of his own poetry written years earlier and no doubt familiar to the spectator. In Act III, as part of a ruse which enables the young lovers to plot their elopement, Hernando poses as his master and pretends to court the future bride's mother. Initial Neoplatonic conceits quickly deteriorate into equestrian imagery as Hernando compares Belisa to a large draught horse. The hilarity is accented threefold: by the contrast between the elegant discourse and the baseness of the material, by Belisa's ecstatic attention to every word, and by the fact that the lines are a parody of the technique used by Lope in an earlier sonnet.[45] Who could resist the

---

[45] Hernando's speech to Belisa, especially the accumulation of nouns at the end of the discourse, appears to be a burlesque of a sonnet from Lope's *Arcadia* (1598), cited by Dámaso Alonso for its extravagant use of color and

raucous humor of these verses as Hernando moves upward from Belisa's thick-soled shoes, which provoke thoughts of a newly-shod horse, to her large red nose:

Ese chapín[46] enlutado
Que del pie los puntos sabe,
Que pisa el suelo, más grave
Que un frisón recién herrado;
Esa bien compuesta voz,
Ese olor, de amor espuela,
Que es azúcar y canela
De aquestas tocas de arroz;
. . .   .
Esa encarnada nariz
Donde amor destila y saca
Ambar, mirra y tacamaca
Más que el Arabia feliz;
En fin, tocas, pies, frisón,
Nariz, monjil, manto, antojos,
Voz, chapín, son á mis ojos
Selvas de varia lición.
(425b-426a)

A modern reader is prompted to ask why all this gimmickry worked so well when it was so obviously fake. We can only aver that it was exactly what Lope's audience wanted: the world as it should be or could be, not the colorless reality it was. The public came to be entertained, to be shown the myriad ways in which the monotony of a hum-drum existence might be surpassed by the imaginative machinations of their favorite playwright. Small wonder, then, that Lope unabashedly employed to maximum advantage every contrivance at his disposal. He had the spectator's blessing.

The assumption of a recognized pseudonym or posture enabled Lope to become part of his own creations and to

---

texture, [*Poesía española: Ensayo de métodos y límites estilísticos* (Madrid: Aguilar, 1966), p. 433]. On Lope's use of a servant to ridicule his own poetry see Lucile K. Delano, "Lope de Vega's *gracioso* Ridicules the Sonnet," *Hispania*, 17 (1934): 19–34.

[46] See Victor Dixon, ed., *El perro del hortelano* by Lope de Vega (London: Tamesis, 1981), p. 188, n. 422, for further details regarding "chapines."

comment on his own life and art. The technique also allowed Lope, when the spirit moved him, to indulge in more than a little deprecation of the art of others, especially of those detractors who would condemn his talents as a poet. Lope's commitment to poetry without artifice is humoristically though no less forcefully expressed by Perote, the town fool of *El halcón de Federico*. Perote classifies poets as "locos" in their concern for what others write. He reminds us that few write well and that even these are mad, "Si les falta el natural"[47] (452b). Perote is the perfect mouthpiece for Lope as he berates the poet's craft and, no doubt, that of Lope's literary enemies:

> Para ser poeta, hermano
> Muy poco habréis menester,
> Porque no es más que leer
> Al poeta mas cercano,
>   Y hurtalle hasta las razones;
> LLamar al agua cristal,
> A los madroños coral,
> Concetos á las razones:
>   Para decir que amanece,
> Contar que el alba salía,
> Y que al sol un cuello hacía
> De círculos doce ó trece,
>   Y otros cien mil disparates,
> Y alabar una mujer,
> Haciéndola mercader
> De joyas y de alpargatas;
>   Y haciendo, si os inquieta
> Envidia, un soneto ó dos
> Á quien no sabe si Dios
> Os hizo bestia ó poeta
>   Que tanto lo seréis
> Entre amigos y vecinos
> Laureado con pepinos
> Hasta que el mundo canséis,
>   Y en la última partida
> Restituyáis con verdad
> Á la misma necedad
> Lo que hurtastes en vida.
>   (452b)

_____

[47] See Chapter III, note 8.

Lope's disdain for poetasters, especially those of a *cultista* bent, emerges again, in *El anzuelo de Fenisa*. Here, a soldier named Orozco, claiming to be a poet, is questioned by a comrade: "Y ¿érades vos de aquellos impecables / Cuyos versos destila en alambique / La culta musa?" Orozco (or is it Lope?) is quick to reply, "Fuí de los palpables, / Imitador de Laso y de Manrique" (508b).

While the lines strike one more blow at Lope's detractor's, in the context of the surrounding episode they stand out sharply as a momentarily flattering comment in an otherwise wholly unfavorable view of Spanish military men. As for Lope's assumption of the role of social critic, we can only deduce that as part of the unique bond between the dramatist and his public, it represents a selective response to a stress felt keenly by both. Lope's examination of the behavior of Spanish officers and their disservice to national ideals enables him to explore, with the spectator, the basic conflictive aspects of Spain's overseas expansion. In this regard the retention of Boccaccio's Italian setting (Palermo) is of primary importance. It precludes any correspondence between a member of the audience and the officers and allows for the critical distance necessary for a thoughtful assessment of the nature and consequences of Spanish imperialism.[48]

Central to Lope's denunciation is the figure of Captain Osorio, an example of the degeneracy into which idle and unprincipled officers often fell. Osorio is not only procurer for Fenisa the cortesan but also her partner in fleecing unwary foreigners, including his fellow countrymen. Among these are Orozco and his companions. Their initial appearance allows for the ridicule of often-bizarre Spanish military dress, left to the individual gentleman to provide. A few well-chosen words, in the mouths of Celia and Fenisa, paint a picture of ostentatious vestments and equally exaggerated gestures, excessive pride and bellicosity:

---

[48] On the removal of the play's action to a distant time and place see Bruce W. Wardropper, *La comedia española en el Siglo de Oro* (together with Elder Olson, *Teoría de la comedia*), (Barcelona: Editorial Ariel, 1978), pp. 195–96.

Celia.	¿Qué chusma es ésta? ¿Es gente de provecho?
Fenisa.	Soldados y españoles, plumas y galas,
	Palabras, remoquetes, bernardinas,
	Arrogancias, bravatas y obras malas.

(508b)

Osorio's solicitous attention to the officer's needs permits Lope to add a few more strokes to the portrait. The soldiers emerge as being given to every excess: gambling, drinking, eating, and womanizing. Osorio is more than willing to indulge the familiar vices. "Como entables / Juego en tu casa, y español se pique / Habrá día que valga cien ducados," he reminds Fenisa. To flatter his prey, Osorio orders lavishly,". . .cuatro capones, / Seis perdices, tres conejos . . . / . . . cuatro pellejos (of wine) . . . / Peras y melones . . . ," (509b). The venality of the ambience is underscored by Campuzano's request, only moments after he arrives, that he be permitted to spend the night with Celia, and Orozco with Fenisa. It is at this point that Lope mitigates the negative characterization with comments regarding Orozco's poetizing.

Despite the kind words, undoubtedly intended to distract Inquisitorial censors, the tenor of the episode points to a continued uneasiness on the part of the dramatist concerning Spain's political and economic reality. Lope's discomfort surfaces again, several scenes later, as Fenisa gloats over having duped the Valencian merchant a second time, or so she believes: "¿Hay hombre tan mentecato? ¿Estas bestias cría España?" Celia's response enables Lope to call into judgment Spain's prodigality and the nation's resultant impoverishment:

Es toda España montaña
Bárbara en ingenio y trato.
　¡Mira tú qué policía
Pues de plata que le ofrece
La India, á Italia enriquece,
A Francia y á Berbería!
　¿Qué nación sustenta el mundo
Donde no corre por ley
Plata y armas de su rey?

(523b)

Lope, however, is no *arbitrista*. He proposes no radical solution for Spain's economic woes. Rather, the expressed concern for costly wars and unprincipled soldiers who demean Spanish military grandeur functions to strengthen social cohesion through the delineation of a common problem.[49] Moreover, the final verses, when taken alone, invite multiple interpretations. In their allusion to Spain's world-wide presence they are as much an exultation of the nation's prowess as they are a condemnation of her imperialism. Are the lines, we are prompted to ask, a ringing endorsement of national policy or is Lope in fact ridiculing the state of affairs by assigning the verses to an antagonistic Italian maid who shares her mistess' abhorrence for Spaniards?

A further ambiguity as to Lope's stance derives from the characterization, early in the play, of Spaniards as pretentious opportunists, both at home and abroad: "Que en saliendo de su tierra / Ó sea en paz ó en guerra / Se hacen príncipes y soles . . ." (490b). Lope bemoans the obsession with social status which results in all manner of fabrication, as evidenced by the image Bernardo and Fabio set out to create for their master:

> Añadirémosle un don,
> Diremos que es caballero,
> Y aunque con poco dinero,
> Tendrá mucha presunción.
> (490b)

Pretensions to purity of blood and nobility lead Spaniards to claim ties with celebrated old-Christian families. Here again Lope appears to ease the desultory portrayal by chastising the fault through its opposite manifestation: Dinarda's refusal to take, as part of her disguise, the names of Guzmán or Mendoza. Yet the very rejection of the former on grounds that

---

[49] See Charlotte Stern, "Lope de Vega, Propagandist?," *BCOM*, 34 (1982): 1–36. Stern (p. 13) suggests Northup Frye's denomination, the "myth of concern" as perhaps a more adequate description of the function of the *comedia*. See Northup Frye, *The Critical Path. An Essay on the Social Context of Literary Criticism* (Bloomington: Indiana Univ. Press, 1971), pp. 36–38.

"Tómaselo ya quienquiere" and the latter because ". . . no hay morisco aguador / Que no se enmendoce" (491b), serves to mock what was apparently a common practice.[50] The intensity of the ridicule, though not the fact of it, is mitigated only by the knowledge that it is a dramatic ploy.

Just as Lope knows when to ease dramatic tension with a pleasant interlude, so he also recognizes the need to back away from criticism in order to ensure its effectiveness. Dinarda's affirmation as she steps forth to win back Albano's love, "Aquí / se ve la industria española," is clearly intended to flatter the spectator by suggesting that when it comes to *industria*, Spaniards are better at it than Italians, at least in this play. Dinarda's lines are a key expression for they tell us that despite Lope's desire to give theatrical formulation to a problem of general concern, the dramatist will opt for a traditional solution (as I noted in Chapter IV) which reaffirms at least on the surface, the values already ascribed to by his audience. In the successful recapturing of her wayward lover and in the outwitting of the Italian cortesan, Dinarda exemplifies the superiority of Spanish *ingenio* which Celia had been so quick to disparage. On a deeper level, however, the derision of Spanish officers abroad and of the social pretensions of Spaniards on the whole points to a reality far removed from the official myth and forcasts the disintegration of the very institutions which the outer structure proports to uphold.

Lope's innate talent for capturing and dramatizing the ideological concerns of his public is reinforced by his consummate skill in portraying human nature. Unlike character development in the *novella* which is, of necessity, dependent upon narrative content, or in the *Commedia dell'Arte* in which the function of the masks resulted in fixed patterns of comportment, the dramatic genre enabled Lope to create three-dimensional characters endowed with appetites, desires and

---

[50] On the pursuit of social mobility in the seventeenth century in Spain see José Antonio Maravall, *Teatro y literatura en la sociedad barroca* (Madrid; S y E, 1974), pp. 142–43; and José María Díez Borque, *Sociología de la comedia española del Siglo XVII* (Madrid: Ediciones Cátedra, 1976), pp. 254–59.

impulses which his audience knew and shared. Although Lope's protagonists are depicted with more profundity and psychological realism than those of the source stories, the personages rarely evidence any serious conflicts or philosophical doubts. Their actions are motivated, for the most part, by the satisfaction of basic human needs. Those desires not compatible with the moral code are frustrated or chastised. As a result there are no great archetypes or memorable characters in these plays. Unlike Elizabethan drama, Golden Age *comedia* in general had little concern for the individual soul at war with itself. The society represented by the *comedia* was of one mind and spirit, accepting without question the moral and theological teachings of the time. Under these circumstances it is difficult, if not impossible, to envision a hero plagued by a tragic dilemma.

Male protagonists emerge as "types"[51] although Lope varies each delineation significantly and avoids, wherever possible, predictable modes of behavior. Two portrayals, Enrico de Moncado (*El ejemplo de casadas*) and Camilo (*El halcón de Federico*), do broach to a limited degree questions of inner torment. In both instances, however, theatrical exigencies preclude full development of the conflict. The audience's limited interest in such portrayals, the need to maintain a rapid forward movement, and the consequent curtailment of long, introspective moments does not allow for a protracted dramatization of internal crisis. For this reason, the several scenes devoted to Enrico's deep psychological fears regarding mar-

---

[51] On the delineation of the *galán* in Golden Age comedy, Arco y Garay, *(La sociedad española)*, asserts: "La mayoría de los hombres . . . son inactivos e irresolutos. Un verdadero carácter de hombre, fuera de los labradores y aldeanos, es raro . . . Aunque tratados masculinamente, quedan todos en energía de acción y voluntad detrás de los caracteres femeninos. Le falta al hombre firmeza . . . frecuentemente es egoísta . . . ." In her study of *The Short Story in Spain in the Seventeenth Century* (Northhampton, Mass.: Smith College, 1972), Catherine Bourland draws these conclusions about the male figure in that genre which may be applied to the *galán* of Lope's theater: "He is the typical south European gallant, prone to fall in love at first sight, hot in pursuit, capable of extremes of fidelity and of fickelness . . . at the mercy of his feeling . . . easily offended in his dignity and reckless of his life," (p. 25).

riage and the choice of a wife are not sufficient to justify the cruel tests to which Laurencia is submitted. A similar shortcoming concerns the illness and death of Camilo. The hint from Julia that Federico loves Camilo's wife, Celia, but with no indication that the lady returns the affection, hardly constitutes grounds for Camilo's profound dejection, much less for his eventual insanity and death.

Bruce Wardropper has shown, however, that in Lope's theater reality is inverted and society appears to stand on its head in a make-believe world that paradoxically is placed in contemporary surroundings. Men and women exchange roles. Women come out on top. They even dress and behave like men. They are most often the aggressors. They provoke the play's action and exercise total control over a world normally dominated by men.[52] The Lopean heroines exhibit all of those qualities the *galán* often lacks—fidelity, patience, determination, moral and spiritual strength of heroic proportion, and an unfailing recognition of duty. The Boccaccian plays corroborate the charge. In all but two of them females dominate the action and give the play its vibrancy.

For example the character of Laura, the widow of *El llegar en ocasión*, is considerably more developed than that of her Italian prototype. Unlike Boccaccio's lady, who is a "merry" widow, Laura becomes sincerely attached to Otavio and having received a promise of marriage, proceeds determinedly to control the play's action until the wedding plans are realized. Similarly, in *La discreta enamorada*, Fenisa's ingenuity and determination enable her to change the course of Fortune and to marry a man of her own choosing. Boccaccio's heroine had merely sidestepped Fate by taking a lover.

Lope's Laurencia is a far cry from the colorless, submissive Griselda. While Laurencia may lack some of the fortitude and unquestioning acceptance of the torments to which her Italian progenitor is also subjected, she is decidedly more credible in her humanity. She carries out Enrico's orders, but

---

[52] Bruce W. Wardropper, *La comedia española*, p. 226.

the audience is made aware of the struggle within her. The Spanish heroine evidences an independence of spirit and a sense of personal worth not found in her Italian counterpart. Laurencia is a feminine *rústico noble*, an eloquent spokeswoman for the bucolic ideal. As part of that world of noble country folk, Laurencia's values are equal to those of Enrico and therefore she feels free to protest, if only mildly, his excessive cruelty.

Lucinda, the heroine of *El ruiseñor de Sevilla*, shows no traits that are not suggested by the Italian girl, Caterina. The complications of Lope's plot, however, require Lucinda to be considerably more astute than Boccaccio's maiden. The Spanish girl's inventiveness is given full rein as she, under the watchful eye of her father, manages a secret rendezvous with her lover and postpones signing the marriage contract with an unwelcome suitor.

The portrayal of Celia, like that of Federico (*El halcón de Federico*), does not fare well at Lope's hands. She lacks the dignity of Boccaccio's Monna Giovanna. We cannot imagine the latter sending a servant to spy on her husband or entering into a loud altercation with a woman of dubious reputation (Julia). The stature of the Spanish protagonist is decidedly reduced by these gestures which are more appropriate to a *comica* of the Italian troupes.

The most exciting characters are the cortesans and are entirely Lope's invention: Fenisa (*El anzuelo de Fenisa*), Gerarda (*La discreta enamorada*) and Julia (*El halcón de Federico*). A fourth cortesan, though she never appears on stage, is Lucrecia of *El ruiseñor de Sevilla*. Judging from the frequent appearance and importance of this character, the cortesan was obviously acceptable to Lope's audience, a convention which now seems strange, in light of the moral restrictions. Apparently there was no objection to the *galán* having an affair with a woman of easy virtue. In each of the plays the cortesan is never extraneous. Rather, the freedom of movement which the cortesan enjoys makes her a valuable asset to the development of the intrigue. While these women are destined to remain on the fringe of respectable society by the nature of their lifestyle, one senses in the depiction of each that Lope is making a plea for understanding. Although the cortesan, depending on her dramatic function, may be spiteful, petulant, or vindictive, Lope never allows the spectator to lose sight of the fact that the behavior is motivated by love, past or present, in whose name all is pardonable.[53] Fenisa's cruel treatment of men, the playwright explains, stems from the anguish of seduction and abandonment by her first love. Gerarda's misguided existence, Lope suggests, is the result of an early marriage contracted against her wishes with an elderly husband. While we know nothing of Julia's background, we sense a number of scruples in her refusal to be visited by a married man. Julia's subsequent actions are the result of the merciless rejection she suffers at Federico's hands.

Social and moral pressures, however, demand that all three women emerge as losers since anything less would constitute a tacit approval of their transgressions. Nevertheless, the humaneness and obvious sympathy with which the playwright consistently handles their presence suggests that

----

[53] On the cortesan-prostitute as a social reality and as a frequent character in Lope's plays, see Ricardo del Arco y Garay, *La sociedad española*, pp. 833–42. Margherita Morreale, in *Castiglione y Boscán: El ideal cortesano en el Renacimiento español*, Anejos del *BRAE*, 1 (1949), p. 116, no. 1, points out: "Dicho sea de paso, mientras que Castiglione usa de vez en cuando el femenino, *cortigiana*, Boscán evita esta forma, seguramente por su acepción peyorativa, prefiriendo siempre, "dama" o "dama perfeta." *Cortesana*, however, was not always synonymous with "prostitute." For a discussion of the evolution of the concept see Joseph E. Gillet, ed. *Bartolomé Torres Naharro. Propalladia and Other Works* (Bryn Mawr, Pa. 1951), III, 265, n. 243. For the Latin sources of the *cortesana* as a stock character, see Marvin T. Herrick, *Comic Theory in the Sixteenth Century* (Urbana: University of Illinois Press, 1964), p. 62. Herrick cites three types of cortesans which may be distinguished in Terentian comedy: "(1) the conventional gold-digger . . . (2) the exceptional good cortesan . . . (3) the in-between type, the gold-digger with amiable qualities . . . ." The latter type was most probably the model for Lope's Gerarda, Julia and, to a lesser degree, Fenisa, since his treatment of the characters seems to follow closely the Terentian predecessor, Thais, as described by Herrick: ". . . although she always makes sure of her reward, Thais is not solely a gold-digger. Terence has humanized her so that she is much more than just a cortesan . . . Thais is the kind of cortesan who often makes the reader forget her profession and regard her as a lively, attractive . . . young woman," (pp. 163–64).

Lope's compliance is mechanical and that despite their short-comings, he feels a strong attraction for these women and their passionate zest for life.

While the conventions of the *comedia* restricted the development of major characters, the dramatist enjoyed almost total freedom in the creation of the servant figures. Usually from the lower classes and therefore on the outer edges of the social structure, the servants were not subject to the same degree of censure as were the protagonists. Hence Lope could offer an infinite variety of servant types, from the astute *gracioso* to the most vulgar lackey, each bringing to the *comedia* an unbridled dynamism and earthiness rarely displayed by a major personage. On one level the servant figure is usually a materialist, intent upon satisfying elementary and alimentary needs and holding little regard for the lofty sentiments concerning love and honor which motivate his master. His humor is broad, sometimes obscene. The resultant contrast with the idealized world of the protagonists affords Lope a large measure of the comic counterpoise necessary to sustain audience interest. Unlike the main characters who, for the most part, have their antecedents in the Italian stories, the minor figures are the product of Lope's fertile imagination, stimulated, as I noted earlier, by the antics of the Italian *zanni*.

Lope's public, however, was unified on social and religious issues. The comic servant might freely parody the high-blown conceits or the amorous escapades of his master provided he possessed the following qualities: fidelity to master, Church and the monarchical ideal. According to Charlotte Stern, Lope's *gracioso* "follows his master unconditionally and, although he occasionally complains of erratic remuneration, he never breaks the bond of dependence and loyalty." As such he is incorporated into the dominant ethos of the *comedia* and thereby serves to neutralize "any latent hostility lurking among the servants in the audience."[54] Beyond these requisite

---

[54] See Charlotte Stern, art. cit., p. 5 and José Antonio Maravall, "Relaciones de dependencia e integración social: criados, graciosos y pícaros," *I and L*, 1 (1977): 3–32.

characteristics, the playwright was at liberty to call on the *gracioso* to perform any and all dramatic tasks.

The degree to which the *gracioso* is developed in the Boccaccian plays depends on Lope's prior conception of the protagonist. Where the character is self-possessed and independent of a confidant, the servant's role assumes minimal proportions. While the servant may offer advice, and encourage and abet the protagonist in his adventures, the main line of action is not directly dependent on the intervention of the servant. Examples of this sort of character are Fenisa, the female *gracioso* of *El llegar en ocasión*; Turín, Rugero's lackey, in *El servir con mala estrella* and Pinabel, Lauro's manservant in *La boda entre dos maridos*. The characters of Tristán, Lucindo's servant, (*El anzuelo de Fenisa*) and Fabio, valet to Federico in *El halcọn de Federico* are somewhat better developed, though here too the direct contribution to plot development is curtailed. Tristán's words of caution are heeded only briefly. Once Lucindo's passion gets the better of him, Tristán's role is reduced to providing humorous commentary as the cortesan proceeds to fleece his master. Similarly, Fabio's continued admonitions to Federico concerning the dissipation of his fortune fall on deaf ears. Only in the last act does Federico heed his valet's warnings regarding a repetition of earlier thoughtlessness. Throughout the play, however, Fabio's reprimands serve to accentuate his master's obstinacy and lack of common sense.

Where a major character is weak or indecisive, the role of the *criado gracioso* is amplified and closely linked to the development of the story. It is the latter's responsibility to take the initiative which his master is too awkward or ill-equipped to assume. In *La discreta enamorada* it is Hernando, the *galán's* manservant, who interprets the heroine's cryptic messages, distracts the lady's mother so that the lovers can speak, and reveals the true identity of "Estefanía" when Gerarda's scheming threatens to upset the wedding plans. Without the help of Riselo in *El ruiseñor de Sevilla*, Don Félix could never carry his love affair with Lucinda to a successful conclusion.

The ingenuity and creativity with which Lope peopled his *comedia* brought to the seventeenth-century theater a vitality and representational energy unmatched by his contemporaries. His sensitive portrayal of the major characters inherited from the *novella*, especially the female personages; his invention of subordinate characters from the lower classes who, though acting independently, function to underline the social and religious beliefs of the dominant minority; and his delicate handling of marginal figures such as the cortesans all point to Lope's incomparable skill in depicting human nature. This, coupled with Lope's ability to strike the proper balance between literature and performance, between the demands of the spectator and those of art, brought Lope four decades of undiminished applause in Spain and abroad.

Conclusion

In the foregoing chapters several aspects of Lope's refurbishing have been considered individually as reflections of a broader, more inclusive approach to the adaptation of the eight *Decameron* tales. The time has come to reconsider those findings in terms of the problems involved in the transposition of *novella* to drama and the playwright's creativity in meeting the challenge. The scope of Lope's undertaking is all the more impressive if we consider those elements which comprise the social and literary reality of Boccaccio's masterpiece.

Amado Alonso, in his study of Lope's theater proffers this evaluation:

> Siempre resulta el punto de partida mera materia para el nacimiento de una forma. El secreto está en el visionario corazón del poeta que penetra y traspasa con ojos de zahorí las fibras inertes de la materia para encontrar allí inesperados sentimientos; ésa es la mágica piedra filosofal que transmuta los metales en oro. [1]

---

[1] Amado Alonso, "Lope de Vega y sus fuentes," in *El teatro de Lope de Vega*, ed. F. Gatti (Buenos Aires: EUDEBA, 1962), p. 213.

No words are more appropriate to Lope's rendition of the Boccaccian stories. The dramatist's acute theatrical sensitivity enables him to capture not only some of the finest narrative moments of the *Decameron* but the very spirit, the *razón vital* at the heart of Boccaccio's masterpiece.

The *Decameron* stories exude a vigor and vitality deriving from the unique ambience of mid-fourteenth-century Italy, its ports bustling with trade from the East and the rise of a powerful mercantile class. It is a period alive with the growth of independent *comuni*, an age of personal freedom where literature in the vernacular is not yet subject to ecclesiastic censure. Boccaccio's narrators are at liberty to relate stories that run the gamut from scenes characterized by gross, bawdy humor to those episodes which exalt the highest virtues. All protagonists, virtuous or vice-ridden, find equal expression, regardless of social station. Characters are free to behave according to the logic of the world, each concerned with his own survival. As a result, the stories evolve logically, free from extraliterary pressure. There is no didactic intent, nor was one expected. The *Decameron's* only purpose is to delight the reader. Hence, Boccaccio neither moralizes nor stands in judgment. Rather, he offers us "una vasta e multiforme epopea della società italiana."[2]

Lope enjoys few of these artistic freedoms. The tales, once viewed with the indulgent spirit of the *lieta brigata*, now come under the scrutiny of Counter-Reformation censorship. Obliged by contemporary moral dictates to instruct as well as to entertain, Lope cannot remain aloof from his creation as an

---

2 Vittore Branca, ed., *Decameron*, pp. xxvi–xxviii. Branca describes the world of the *Decameron* as follows: "Il Boccaccio riesce a rappresentare nel suo capolavoro la mirabile e ideale continuità fra quell'età dei cavalieri della spada e questo mondo dei cavalieri dell'ingegno dell'industria umana; fra quelle figure principesche . . . e questi eroi esemplari della nuova civiltà, balzati dal seno della borghesia italiana, che nell'espansione mercantile dei quei decenni aveva scritto una nuova epopea . . . Il Decameron è . . . la rappresentazione, o meglio la consacrazione artistica, della realtà più quotidiana di quel mondo umanissimo. È anch'esso in certo senso una *summa*: la *summa* di quella vita faticosa, ricca di avventure e di agguati, in cui ogni giorno l'uomo misurava le sue capacità e le sue virtù, e la borghesia e la folle più umile e anonima provavano la loro energia industriosa, il loro slancio operoso in una serrata lotta per l'esistenza."

impartial observer but must act as his own censor. He is constrained to judge the actions of the protagonists, reward the good and punish (if only through frustration) all those who offend the laws of God and society. Unlike Boccaccio, Lope's literary world reveals little of the middle class. It is a world of social polarities—nobles and servants—in which the values of the dominant minority must prevail at any cost, even death.

Despite the apparent concession to the social, religious and esthetic mandates of his age, Lope's openmindedness, sympathy and tolerance for man's foibles, especially as concerns love, keep him quite apart from the theological single-mindedness of, let us say, Calderón. The latter, even in comedy, never loses sight of the serious sense of life.[3] With Lope one is never quite sure whether he is being consciously subversive, or earnest in intent, or both at the same time. And therein rests his charm. In the pall of the Counter-Reformation offensive, the many-sided Lope prompts us to stand up and cheer. Calderón moves us to polite applause, vigorous, but never passionate. For while in Calderón we may take satisfaction in the evolution, before our eyes, of a preconceived theological truth, in Lope we savor the fullness of life, the unbridled vitality of the world in all its madness and confusion. It is an energy which at times resists containment. So much so that in *El ruiseñor de Sevilla* and *El anzuelo de Fenisa*, the dramatist seems barely able to check the high spirits and exuberant sensuality of the plays. In his passion for life Lope is open to any and all stimuli, personal and literary, which can be transported to the stage. As such, the narrative vigor of the *Decameron* is irresistible.

As the preceding chapters have shown, Lope's accommodation of these stories to the demands of the stage is neither accidental nor haphazard. The final product betrays the hand of a superb craftsman, a man of perceptive insights disciplined by the writer's skill. Lope grasped immediately the constituent

---

[3] See Bruce W. Wardropper, "Calderón's Comedy and His Serious View of Life," *Hispanic Studies in Honor of Nicholson B. Adams* (Chapel Hill: University of North Carolina Press, 1966), pp. 179–193.

elements common to both genres: a tripartite structure, lively action, and a strong forward thrust propelled by the rapid concatenation of scheme and counterscheme. The challenge to Lope's creative genius arises from those components unique to Boccaccio's tales: a tightly woven narrative content which, owing to its brevity, obviates the need to vary the pace; the presence of an omniscient narrator who controls the flow of the story; two-dimensional characters subordinated to the interests of plot; and, endings which are a logical outgrowth of the intrigue. It is the manipulation of these aspects which puts Lope's dramatic craftsmanship to the test.

Lope supplements the paucity of detail by discovering those points in the stories which may be enlarged without sacrificing the basic plot. These include elements barely alluded to in the original, hints, sensations—anything which might lend itself to theatrical expression; elements which a talent less alert than Lope's might miss in passing. The secondary intrigues evolved from these components are major points of expansion, carefully developed to serve the main plot but never overpower it. The exception to the pattern is *El anzuelo de Fenisa* where the subplot, which treats of Spanish nobles, eventually occupies center stage.

Denied recourse to a narrator, Lope is obliged to rely on the dialogue to put forth the exposition naturally and unobtrusively, to fill in background details and to reflect the emotions and attitudes of the characters throughout the play. Consequently, precision and forethought in the elaboration of dialogue are essential. Words in key passages have multilevel meanings in terms of the spectator and the rest of the play. Ideas and sentiments are expressed succinctly so as to keep the play moving at a brisk pace. Dialogue is metered, rhymed and varied according to the dignity of the speaker and the content of the conversation. The single element which approximates the function of a narrator in that it is non-dialogued commentary, is the occasional use of the *aparte*.

While Boccaccio's characters are rarely elaborated beyond the demands of the narrative, they are nonetheless memorable in their uniqueness. Readers of the *Decameron* recall easily Federico degli Alberighi, Salabaetto, the Florentine merchant and Griselda. Lope's protagonists, on the other hand, are of one mold. They are abstractions of contemporary ideals. Only where the character's identity is specified in the title of the play are we likely to recall their names. The remainder are a pleasant blur, the logical consequence of a theater at the service of an official ideology. Nevertheless, even in their quasi-anonymity, they are infused with a warm humanity which does not escape us. This is especially true of the female protagonists. In the rejection, at least on the stage, of the limitations placed on them by society, the female characters are at the center of that escape from reality with which the *comedia* is charged. Their stage reality is pure fiction, a testament to Lope's imaginative power when his creative energies are allowed to flow freely.

The endings of Boccaccio's stories evolve logically from the narrative ingredients. Lope, on the other hand, is forced to redirect the content to a conclusion prescribed for him long before he writes the play. The theater public expected to see virtue rewarded, culprits punished and the couple happily united at the end of the play even if such a resolution jarred the unity of the work. Compliance with the first two requisites was a simple matter since in each of the eight source stories goodness is rewarded and evil chastised. However, Boccaccio's appellation of good and evil was not necessarily as Lope's spectator would have it. We need but look at the sources for *El llegar en ocasión* and *La discreta enamorada* to understand the divergence. Neither tale ends in a manner acceptable to a seventeenth-century Spanish audience. In the first case, though robbed by highwaymen and left to die, Rinaldo's faith in the efficacy of prayer to Saint Julian brings him not only a night's lodging but also a mistress. The elderly wool merchant of *Decameron* III, 3 who neglects his conjugal duties to a young and beautiful wife is justly punished, in the logic of the *Decameron*, when the lady takes a lover. Lope resolves the problems by focusing on the woman in each case. He changes the "merry" widow of *Decameron* II, 2 to one sincerely interested in remarrying. In the second instance, Lope takes his cue from the expurgated *Decameron* of 1582 and casts the heroine as a young girl in search of a husband.

Lope senses a kindred spirit in Boccaccio, not only as concerns the warm humanity which flows from his work but in the vision of the motive forces against which Boccaccio's human comedy is played. They were universal questions which fascinated Lope's age as well. To Boccaccio's proposition that man has only a fifty-fifty chance to withstand the vagaries of *Fortuna*, Lope counters the notion of man's power to turn the tide of Fortune by seizing the occasion, or through the use of discretion and prudence. Lope is sensitive to those areas of Boccaccio's stance which make possible the shift to a more current interpretation, one which denies the power of Fortune and charges man, instead, with the responsibility for making right judgments. Even in those instances where man is treated harshly, the culprit is not Fate but the illwill and thoughtlessness of others, to which one can only oppose the Christian stoic precept of patience in adversity. In his opposition to Boccaccio's posture we perceive Lope's faith in the capacity of the individual to determine, through his own conduct, the course of his existence.

As for Boccaccio's view of love as youthfully natural, spontaneous and irrepressible, Lope's earnest support of those lovers who turn the tables on convention is as committed and wholehearted as any instance in the *Decameron*. The only preestablished limitation is that the love matches end in marriage. In the achievement of that goal, however, every conceivable manner of subterfuge or erratic behavior is pardonable in the name of youthful ardor. Like Boccaccio, Lope suggests the wisdom of applying less rigid criteria for the restoration of honor, since love, as an unreasoned passion, transcends all boundaries.

In Lope's approach to intelligence we perceive the same affective response evidenced by Boccaccio. Although in *El anzuelo de Fenisa* Lope is forced to subdue his personal enthusiasm for human cunning by reducing the *Decameron* material to secondary status, we cannot help but sense a mechanical compliance. The Spanish nobles (except for Dinarda) who come to occupy center stage resemble puppets in comparison to the vital portrayals of the cortesan and the Valencian merchant. Even in the delineation of Dinarda we sense Lope's admiration not so much for her virtue as for her cleverness in outwitting the Italian cortesan. It is, of course, ingenuity at the service of right deeds,—in this case, marriage—which ensures Dinarda's place in society. The spirit of the times demanded that Lope hold up for imitation those aspects of intelligence appropriate to a well-ordered universe, one in which each man plays his role according to his place in society. In the subordination of the Boccaccian material to the *caso de honor*, Lope affirms a hierarchy of values which parallels the social hierarchies.

But the *comedia* is more than a written text which subscribes to contemporary morality and social ideals. It is an art form which demands representation, and a most convincing one at that, if its message is to be conveyed successfully. No single group performed to greater acclaim during Lope's early years as a dramatist than the *Commedia dell'Arte* players. Their arrival at a time when Spanish drama was still experimental provided the technical and theatrical innovations which are at the heart of the *comedia nueva*. That Lope should absorb a number of the *Commedia dell'Arte* techniques into the elaboration of the Boccaccian plays is quite natural. The Italian comic mode bears a close resemblance to the spirit and artistry of the *Decameron*. Like Boccaccio's work, its only purpose is to entertain. Lope recognized in the rollicking good fun of the Italians and, especially in the *disfraz varonil*, an unfailing means of sustaining audience interest. Yet the dramatist's recourse to those elements is neither servile nor injudicious. The *lazzi* and comic pauses are taken up only to the degree required to give a preconceived theme added vitality; they are never an end in themselves. In keeping with the mandates of his era and of his craft, Lope took to himself the vibrancy and representational skills of the *comici* as suited his dramatic vision. He left behind the *Commedia dell'Arte's* disregard for literary tradition, its satirization of the upper classes and its gross humor and antics.

An inseparable part of the theatrical energy which flows from the Boccaccian plays is the unique compenetration of the

Erratum

p.181: The third sentence from the end is corrected to read as follows:

In these plays, the Boccaccian inheritance as well as that of the *Commedia dell'Arte* are "absorbed, assimilated and transcended;" the emphasis shifts perceptibly, and "the new total is somehow greater than the sum of its constituent parts."[4]

---

[4] R. Hastings, *Nature and Reason*, p. 104. Although these phrases were originally intended to characterize Boccaccio's transformation of a medieval legacy into a collection of tales reflecting the emerging values of the Renaissance, they are, in my opinion, singularly appropriate to Lope's refurbishings.

author and his public. Like a physician with his finger on the patient's pulse, Lope is alert to every rhythmic change; the cure ready and waiting in the wings. In this world of illusion, as much the creation of the dramatist as of the spectator for whom it is intended, Lope winks an eye and the audience responds with like gesture. They had not come to see reality, only a rose-colored version of it.

The ease with which Lope makes the transition from *novella* to drama despite extraliterary strictures attests to his consummate artistry as a dramatist. His success lay precisely in the ability to conform yet remain flexible; to entertain while upholding the moral truths of his epoch and in the capacity to create characters who, though abstractions of contemporary ideals, remain credibly human. In these plays the Boccaccian inheritance, as well as that of the *Commedia dell'Arte*, are absorbed, assimilated and transcended; the emphasis shifts perceptibly and the new total is somehow greater than the sum of its constituent parts. The finished products are Spanish plays. They speak to Spanish reality, tradition and values.

Index

Bernardo, Captain, in *La discreta ena-morada*, 41, 46–49; as the composite of Pantalone and the Capitano, 143–46. *See also* Pantalone; Capitano
Biagi, G., 18
Blanco Jiménez, José, 12
Blas de Castro, Juan, as singer of Lope's songs, 77
Blüher, K. A., 50, 57
Boccaccio, Giovanni, 12, 22, 23, 28; and *Fortuna*, 30–31, 33–34, 41, 42, 49, 50, 51, 55–56, 58; and *Amore*, 63–65, 69, 81, 82, 91–93; and *Ingeg-no*, 105–8, 149, 150–51, 174–75, 177–80; *Decameron*, Spanish manu-script translation, 11, 19; Catalan manuscript translation, 11, 19; first printed Spanish translation, 11–12; possible source for Lope's adapta-tions, 20–22; expurgated Italian edition of 1573, 15, 20, 21, 28; ex-purgated Italian edition of 1582, 15, 20, 21, 26, 28, 29; approved for cir-culation in Spain, 15; as indulgent, uncensored literature, 175; Days VI, VII and VIII, 105–6; individual *Decameron* stories:
II, 2: xi, 20, 32–33
II, 4: 13
III, 3: xi, 28, 41, 49
IV, 1: 66
IV, 5: 66
IV, 8: 64
V, 1: 12–13
V, 4: xi, 21, 69
V, 9: xi, 21, 82
VIII, 10: xi, 26, 107–8
X, 1: xi, 26, 50–51
X, 7: 94
X, 8: xi, 26, 64, 91–93
X, 10: xi, 10, 22, 55–56, 58, 61
Bocchi, Achille, 35
Boda entre dos maridos, La, xi, 26, 27, 32, 66, 67, 91–104, 131, 132, 133–34, 154, 155, 158–59
botarga, as costume in Spanish festi-vals, 130–31
Bottargo, Stefanello, 130, 131
Bourland, Caroline B., 2, 6, 14, 69; on delineation of male characters, 167

Branca, Vittore, 30, 40, 93, 107; *Boc-caccio, The Man and His Works*, 107
Bravo-Villasante, C., 137
burla, 133, 134, 140
Cabrera, Fray Alonso de, 79
Calderón de la Barca, Pedro, 176
Callistratus, 34
Camila Lucinda, 111, 112. *See also* Luján, Micaela de
Camilo, in *El halcón de Federico*, 67, 81, 82, 86, 167, 168
Camilo, in *El anzuelo de Fenisa*, 112, 113, 114
Capellanus, Andreas, 85, 90, 91
Capitano, Il, *Commedia dell'Arte* mask, 128; as symbol of Spanish *soberbia*, 128, 144; as object of ridi-cule, 128, 144; as model for Captain Bernardo of *La discreta enamorada*, 143–47
capocomico, 126, 128, 145
Castiglione, Baldassare, *Il Cortegiano*, 43; Spanish translation by Juan Boscán, 44
Castigos y dotrinas que un sabio dava á sus hijas, 12, 22
Castillo Solórzano, Alonso de, 3
Castro, Américo, y Rennert, Hugo A., *Vida de Lope de Vega*, 70, 73, 74, 77, 112, 114
Caterina, in *Decameron V, 4*: 20, 69, 78, 169
Cecchini, Pier Maria, 127
Celia, in *El halcón de Federico*, 65, 67, 81, 83, 84, 85, 86, 87, 89, 90, 91, 157, 168, 169
Celia, in *El ruiseñor de Sevilla*, 73. *See also* Trillo de Armenta, Antonia de
Cejador y Frauca, J., 34
Cervantes Saavedra, Miguel de, *Don Quijote de la Mancha*, 4; *Galatea*, 4; *Comedias y entremeses*, 9; "La gita-nilla," 42
Chew, Samuel C., 35, 37
Cioffari, Vincenzo, 30, 51
Christian Stoicism, and *El ejemplo de-casadas*, 57–59
Cocco, E., 125
comedia, 127; relationship between the sexes in, 158; courtship con-ventions in, 158–59; characteriza-

stuðia humanitatis

PUBLISHED VOLUMES

Louis Marcello La Favia, *Benvenuto Rambaldi da Imola: Dantista.* xii–188 pp. US $9.25.

John O'Connor, *Balzac's Soluble Fish.* xii–252 pp. US $14.25.

Carlos García, *La desordenada codicia*, edición crítica de Giulio Massano. xii–220 pp. US $11.50.

Everett W. Hesse, *Interpretando la Comedia.* xii–184 pp. US $10.00.

Lewis Kamm, *The Object in Zola's* Rougon-Macquart. xii–160 pp. US $9.25.

Ann Bugliani, *Women and the Feminine Principle in the Works of Paul Claudel.* xii–144 pp. US $9.25.

Charlotte Frankel Gerrard, *Montherlant and Suicide.* xvi–72 pp. US $5.00.

The Two Hesperias. Literary Studies in Honor of Joseph G. Fucilla. Edited by Americo Bugliani. xx–372 pp. US $30.00.

Jean J. Smoot, *A Comparison of Plays by John M. Synge and Federico García Lorca: The Poets and Time.* xiii–220 pp. US $13.00.

Laclos. Critical Approaches to Les Liaisons dangereuses. Ed. Lloyd R. Free. xii–300 pp. US $17.00.

Julia Conaway Bondanella, *Petrarch's Visions and their Renaissance Analogues.* xii–120 pp. US $7.00.

Vincenzo Tripodi, *Studi su Foscolo e Stern.* xii–216 pp. US $13.00.

Genaro J. Pérez, *Formalist Elements in the Novels of Juan Goytisolo*. xii–216 pp. US $12.50.

Sara Maria Adler, *Calvino: The Writer as Fablemaker*. xviii–164 pp. US $11.50.

Lope de Vega, *El amor enamorado*, critical edition of John B. Wooldridge, Jr. xvi–236 pp. US $13.00.

Nancy Dersofi, *Arcadia and the Stage: A Study of the Theater of Angelo Beolco* (called *Ruzante*). xii–180 pp. US $10.00

John A. Frey, *The Aesthetics of the* Rougon-Macquart. xvi–356 pp. US $20.00.

Chester W. Obuchowski, *Mars on Trial: War as Seen by French Writers of the Twentieth Century*. xiv–320 pp. US $20.00.

Jeremy T. Medina, *Spanish Realism: Theory and Practice of a Concept in the Nineteenth Century*. xviii–374 pp. US $17.50.

Mauda Bregoli-Russo, *Boiardo Lirico*. viii–204 pp. US $11.00.

Robert H. Miller, ed. *Sir John Harington: A Supplie or Addicion to the Catalogue of Bishops to the Yeare 1608*. xii–214 pp. US $13.50.

Nicolás E. Álvarez, *La obra literaria de Jorge Mañach*. vii–279 pp. US $13.00.

Mario Aste, *La narrativa di Luigi Pirandello: Dalle novelle al romanzo Uno, Nessuno, e Centomila*. xvi–200 pp. US $11.00.

Mechthild Cranston, *Orion Resurgent: René Char, Poet of Presence*. xxiv–376 pp. US $22.50.

Frank A. Domínguez, *The Medieval Argonautica*. viii–122 pp. US $10.50.

Everett Hesse, *New Perspectives on Comedia Criticism*. xix–174 pp. US $14.00.

Anthony A. Ciccone, *The Comedy of Language: Four Farces by Molière*. xii–144 $12.00.

Antonio Planells, *Cortázar: Metafísica y erotismo*. xvi–220 pp. US $10.00.

Mary Lee Bretz, *La evolución novelística de Pío Baroja*. viii–476 pp. US $22.50.

Romance Literary Studies: Homage to Harvey L. Johnson, ed. Marie A. Wellington and Martha O'Nan. xxxvii–185 pp. US $15.00.

George E. McSpadden, *Don Quijote and the Spanish Prologues*, volume I. vi–114 pp. US $17.00.

Studies in Honor of Gerald E. Wade, edited by Sylvia Bowman, Bruno M. Damiani, Janet W. Díaz, E. Michael Gerli, Everett Hesse, John E. Keller, Luis Leal and Russell P. Sebold. xii–244 pp. US $20.00.

LOIS ANN RUSSELL, *Robert Challe: A Utopian Voice in the Early Enlightenment*. xiii–164 pp. US $12.50.

CRAIG WALLACE BARROW, *Montage in James Joyce's* ULYSSES. xiii–218 pp. US $16.50.

MARIA ELISA CIAVARELLI, *La fuerza de la sangre en la literatura del Siglo de Oro*. xii–274 pp. US $17.00.

JUAN MARÍA COROMINAS, *Castiglione y La Araucana: Estudio de una Influencia*. viii–139 pp. US $14.00.

KENNETH BROWN, *Anastasio Pantaleón de Ribera (1600–1629) Ingenioso Miembro de la República Literaria Española*. xix–420 pp. US $18.50.

JOHN STEVEN GEARY, *Formulaic Diction in the* Poema de Fernán González *and the* Mocedades de Rodrigo. xv–180 pp. US $15.50.

HARRIET K. GREIF, *Historia de nacimientos: The Poetry of Emilio Prados*. xi–399 pp. US $18.00.

El cancionero del Bachiller Jhoan López, edición crítica de Rosalind Gabin. lvi–362 pp. US $30.00.

VICTOR STRANDBERG, *Religious Psychology in American Literature*. xi–237 pp. US $17.50.

M. AMELIA KLENKE, O.P., *Chrétien de Troyes and "Le Conte del Graal": A Study of Sources and Symbolism*.xvii–88 pp. US $11.50.

MARINA SCORDILIS BROWNLEE, *The Poetics of Literary Theory: Lope de Vega's* Novelas a Marcia Leonarda *and Their Cervantine Context*. x–182 pp. US $16.50.

NATALIE NESBITT WOODLAND, *The Satirical Edge of Truth in "The Ring and the Book."* ix–166 pp. US $17.00.

JOSEPH BARBARINO, *The Latin and Romance Intervocalic Stops: A Quantitative and Comparative Study*. xi–153 pp. US $16.50.

SANDRA FORBES GERHARD, *"Don Quixote" and the Shelton Translation: A Stylistic Analysis*. viii–166 pp. US $16.00.

EVERETT W. HESSE, *Essays on Spanish Letters of the Golden Age*. xii–208 pp. US $16.50.

VALERIE D. GREENBERG, *Literature and Sensibilities in the Weimar Era: Short Stories in the "Neue Rundschau."* Preface by Eugene H. Falk. xiii–289 pp. US $18.00.

ANDREA PERRUCCI, *Shepherds' Song (La Cantata dei Pastori)*. English version by Miriam and Nello D'Aponte. xix–80 pp. US $11.50.

MARY JO MURATORE, *The Evolution of the Cornelian Heroine*. v–153 pp. US $17.50.

FERNANDO RIELO, *Teoría del Quijote*. xix–201 pp. US $17.00.

GALEOTTO DEL CARRETTO, *Li sei contenti e La Sofonisba*, edizione e commento di Mauda Bregoli Russo. viii–256 pp. US $16.50.

BIRUTÉ CIPLIJAUSKAITÉ, *Los noventayochistas y la historia*. vii–213 pp. US $16.00.

EDITH TOEGEL, *Emily Dickinson and Annette von Droste-Hülshoff: Poets as Women*. vii–109 pp. US $11.50.

DENNIS M. KRATZ, *Mocking Epic*. xv–171 pp. US $12.50.

EVERETT W. HESSE, *Theology, Sex and the Comedia and Other Essays*. xvii–129 pp. US $14.50.

HELÍ HERNÁNDEZ, *Antecedentes italianos de la novela picaresca española: estudio lingüístico-literario*. x–155 pp. US $14.50.

ANTONY VAN BEYSTERVELDT, *Amadís, Esplanadián, Calisto: historia de un linaje adulterado*. xv–276 pp. US $24.50.

ROUBEN C. CHOLAKIAN, *The "Moi" in the Middle Distance: A Study of the Narrative Voice in Rabelais*. vii–132 pp. US $16.50.

JUAN DE MENA, *Coplas de los Siete Pecados Mortales* and First Continuation, Volume I. Edition, Study and Notes by Gladys M. Rivera. xi–212 pp. US $22.50.

JAMES DONALD FOGELQUIST, *El Amadís y el género de la historia fingida*. x–253 pp. US $21.50.

EGLA MORALES BLOUIN, *El ciervo y la fuente: mito y folklore del agua en la lírica tradicional*. x–316 pp. US $22.50.

La pícara Justina. Edición de Bruno Mario Damiani. vii–492 pp. US $33.50.

Red Flags, Black Flags: Critical Essays on the Literature of the Spanish Civil War. Ed. John Beals Romeiser. xxxiv–256 pp. US $21.50.

RAQUEL CHANG-RODRÍGUEZ, *Violencia y subversión en la prosa colonial hispanoamericana*. xv–132 pp. US $18.50.

DAVID C. LEONARD AND SARA M. PUTZELL, *Perspectives on Nineteenth-Century Heroism: Essays from the 1981 Conference of the Southeastern Studies Association*. xvi–164 pp. US $20.00.

La Discontenta and *La Pythia,* edition with introduction and notes by Nicholas A. De Mara. vii–214 pp. US $17.00.

CALDERÓN DE LA BARCA, *The Prodigal Magician,* translated and edited by Bruce W. Wardropper. vii–250 pp. US $20.00.

JOHN R. BURT, *Selected Themes and Icons from Medieval Spanish Literature: Of Beards, Shoes, Cucumbers and Leprosy.* xi–111 pp. US $16.50.

ALAN FRANK KEELE, *The Apocalyptic Vision: A Thematic Exploration of Postwar German Literature.* vii–129 pp. US $19.00.

ARIÉ SERPER, *Huon de Saint-Quentin: Poète satirique et lyrique.* Etude historique et édition de textes. v–135 pp. US $20.00.

ROBERT COOGAN, *Babylon on the Rhone: A Translation of Letters of Dante, Petrarch, and Catherine of Siena on the Avignon Papacy.* x–126 pp. US $19.50.

LAWRENCE H. KLIBBE, *Lorca's "Impresiones y paisajes": The Young Artist.* xi–165 pp. US $18.00.

NANCY D'ANTUONO, *Boccaccio's "Novelle" in the Theater of Lope de Vega..* xiv–190 pp. US $21.50.

FORTHCOMING PUBLICATIONS

HELMUT HATZFELD, *Essais sur la littérature flamboyante.*

Novelistas femeninas de la postguerra española, ed. Janet W. Díaz.

ALBERT H. LE MAY, *The Experimental Verse Theater of Valle-Inclán.*

ALONSO ORTIZ, *Diálogo sobre la educación del Príncipe Don Juan, hijo de los Reyes Católicos.* Introducción y versión de Giovanni Maria Bertini.

DARLENE J. SADLIER, *Cecília Meireles: Imagery in "Mar Absoluto."*

BEVERLY WEST, *Epic, Folk, and Christian Traditions in the "Poema de Fernán González."*

ROBERT A. DETWEILER AND SARA M. PUTZELL-KORAB, eds. *Crisis in the Humanities.*

JOAN CAMMARATA, *Mythological Themes in the Works of Garcilaso de la Vega.*

ERASMO GABRIELE GERATO, *Guido Gustavo Gozzano: A Literary Interpretation.*

MALCOLM K. READ, *The Birth and Death of Language: Spanish Literature and Linguistics: 1300–1700.*

Terry Smiley Dock, *Woman in the* Encyclopédie: *A Compendium.*

DATE DUE